VMware Workstation Player: A Beginner's Guide

Your first steps into virtualization

by Tuna Peyo

IT Courses Press

VMWARE WORKSTATION PLAYER: A BEGINNER'S GUIDE
by Tuna Peyo
First edition

Published by:
IT Courses Press
ISBN-13: 978-1977814500
ISBN-10: 1977814506

Disclaimer
This book is designed to provide information about VMware Workstation Player. Every effort has been made to make this book as complete and as accurate as possible, but no warranty is implied. The information is provided on an as is basis. Neither the authors, IT Courses Press, nor its resellers, or distributors will be held liable for any damages caused or alleged to be caused either directly or indirectly by this book. The opinions expressed in this book belong to the author and are not necessarily those of IT Courses Press.

Note that this is an unofficial book. VMware, Inc is in no way affiliated with this book or its content.

Trademarks
IT Courses is a trademark of IT Courses Press and may not be used without written permission. Some of the diagrams used in the book were created by Dia Diagram Editor (*http://dia-installer.de*).

Feedback Information
At IT Courses Press, our goal is to create in-depth technical books of the highest quality and value. Readers' feedback is a natural continuation of this process. If you have any comments about how we could improve our books and learning resources for you, you can contact us through email at *info@it-courses.org*. Please include the book title in your message. For more information about our books, visit our website at *http://it-courses.org*.

Errata information
We have taken every care to ensure the accuracy of our content found in this book. However, mistakes do happen. If you find a mistake, we would be grateful if you report it to us, since you can save other readers from frustration and help us improve the subsequent versions of this book. If you find any mistakes, report them to *info@it-courses.org*. Please include the book title in your description. Any existing errata can be viewed at *http://it-courses.org/errata*.

About the author

Tuna Peyo is a systems engineer and an independent author with more than 10 years of experience in the internetworking and systems engineering field. His certifications include CCNA Routing and Switching, CompTIA Network+, CompTIA Security+, and many others. Tuna is the founder and editor of *geek-university.com* and *it-courses.org*, free online education portals that offer courses covering various aspects of the IT system administration. Tuna can be reached at *info@it-courses.org*.

About this book

This book teaches you how to work with VMware Workstation Player, a free virtualization application from a company called VMware. The book is written for people with some experience in the world of computers and computer networking. Prior experience with virtualization technologies is not required.

What will you learn

You will first find out what virtualization is and what features VMware Workstation Player has to offer. You will learn how to install Player on Windows and Linux, how to install a guest operating system in a VM, how to start, stop, or suspend a VM. You will also learn some of the cool features that Player includes, such as the Drag-and-Drop and Copy features, transfering files between two VMs using shared folders, expanding virtual disks... We will wrap up by explaining different types of networking configuration available in Player.

This page intentionally left blank

Contents at a Glance

Table of contents

This page intentionally left blank

This page intentionally left blank

Chapter 1 - Introduction to VMware Workstation Player

IN THIS CHAPTER

Learning what VMware Workstation Player is and what it is used for

Reasons to use Player

System requirements needed to install Player

Installing Player on Windows and Linux

In this chapter you will learn what VMware Workstation Player is used for and the features it offers. We will then go through the system requirements needed to install and run Player on your computer. Finally, I will explain how you can download and install the application on both Windows and Linux.

What is VMware Workstation Player?

VMware Workstation Player is a free desktop application from a company called **VMware** that can be run on Windows and Linux. This application enables you to create, run, and configure virtual machines. A virtual machine can be defined as a software computer that, just like a physical computer, runs an operating system and executes programs. This allows you to run one operating system emulated within another operating system. For example, you can install a Linux operating system within your Windows OS and simply run it in a separate window, like in the following example:

Figure 1-1 *Linux running inside Windows*

Some of the features VMware Workstation Player offers are:

- support for countless guest operating systems, such as Windows 7, 8, 10, XP, Windows Server 2012, Red Hat, FreeBSD, CentOS, and many more.
- **virtual machine isolation** - it is possible to isolate a virtual machine from the host PC. This way, you can safely run programs from untrusted sources in a virtual machine, without worrying that a malware will hurt your host computer.
- **DHCP server** - VMware Workstation Player offers a built-in DHCP server to provide IP addresses to virtual machines.
- **adjustable memory** - virtual machine memory can be optimized for better performance.
- **drag & drop support** - you can drag files between the host operating system and the guest operating systems.
- **copy and paste features** - you can copy and paste text and files between the virtual machine and the host PC.

- support for USB 3.0.
- different types of network connection for the virtual machine: bridged, host-only, or NAT.

VMware Workstation Player is free for non-commercial, personal and home use. However, commercial organizations are required to pay for licenses in order to use the software. Buying a license gives you the following benefits:

- you can use the software commercially.
- you can run restricted virtual machines created by **VMware Fusion Pro** or **VMware Workstation**.
- you get a better support for mass deployments to thousands of users.

Note that VMware Workstation Player was formerly known as **VMware Player**, but in 2015 VMware decided to discontinue that software and replaced it with VMware Workstation Player. There is also a more advanced version of the desktop virtualization software called **VMware Workstation Pro**. This version supports features not available in VMware Workstation Player, such as creating snapshots, cloning of virtual machines, running multiple virtual machines at the same time, connecting to vSphere servers, creating encrypted virtual machines, etc.

Reasons to use VMware Workstation Player

There are many scenarios in which you would want to use Player, some of which are:

- **try other operating systems** - let's say that you've been using Windows all your life, and finally decided to give Linux a try. Instead of dual-booting or installing Linux on an older machine you don't quite use anymore, you could simply install Linux inside a virtual machine and try it out.
- **run older software incompatible with your current OS** - there are plenty of applications that were written way before Windows 7, 8, or 10 became popular. If the application that you would like to run is not compatible with your current operating system, you can install an older operating system in a VM and run the application from there.
- **deliberately execute malware** - security researchers commonly use virtual machines to execute programs known to contain malware. This is done in order to take apart the malware to see what vulnerabilities the malicious software is exploiting. Of course, virtual machines that are used for such purposes are isolated from the rest of the network and the Internet.
- **experiment with the OS** - you could install an OS inside a virtual machine and tinker with it, without fear of repercussion. For example, if you install a Windows OS, you can modify the registry, delete system files, kill processes, and do other dangerous things that could otherwise damage your system.
- **run virtual appliances** - virtual appliances are prebuilt and preconfigured virtual machine images that can be deployed on Player. A virtual appliance usually contains a complete software stack needed to run a particular service. For example, if you want to run WordPress in your virtual machine, you can simply download the prebuilt virtual appliance

that already contains the server, database, and WordPress installed and have a fully functional WordPress installation in a matter of minutes.

NOTE
Appendix A describes two of the scenarios mentioned in the list - how to use Player to try out Linux and how to run virtual appliances.

System requirements for VMware Workstation Player

Before we dive deeper into all the cool features that VMware Workstation Player provides, let's get the boring stuff out of the way - here is a list of all the requirements you need to fulfill in order to install and run Player on your computer:

Host operating system (this is the machine you will install Player on):

CPU

- at minimum 64-bit x86 CPU with 1.3 GHz core speed.

For 64-bit guest operating systems (the operating systems installed in a virtual machine), the host system must have one of the following processors:

- AMD CPUs need to have segment-limit support in long mode.
- Intel CPUs that has VT-x support.

The good news is that most newer processor support the requirements listed above. Check out the website of your CPU's manufacturer to determine if these features are supported. The **Appendix C** describes how to enable VT-x support for Intel processors.

Memory

- 1GB minimum, 2GB and above is recommended.
- in order to use Windows 7 Aero graphics in a virtual machine, 3GB of host system memory is required.

It's important that the host on which you plan to run virtual machines has enough RAM to operate smoothly. If the host runs out of the physical RAM, it starts swapping to disk, which drastically reduces the system performance. To make sure the swapping never happens, the total amount of RAM in your computer should be more than the total amount of RAM that your virtual machines will use, with an addition of (at least) 2 GB for the host operating system.

Hard disk

- IDE, SATA, and SCSI hard drives are supported.
- a minimum of 1GB free disk space is required for guest operating systems.

Optical CD-ROM and DVD

- IDE, SCSI, and SATA optical drives are supported.
- CD-ROM and DVD drives are supported.

- ISO disk image files are supported.

Network

- any Ethernet controller that the host operating system supports.

Host operating systems

You can install Player on a variety of Windows and Linux operating systems. Note that Player requires a 64-bit host operating system. The supported operating systems are:

- Windows 10
- Windows 8
- Windows 7
- Windows Server 2012
- Windows Server 2008
- Ubuntu 8.04 and above
- Red Hat Enterprise Linux 5 and above
- CentOS 5.0 and above
- Oracle Linux 5.0 and above
- openSUSE 10.2 and above
- SUSE Linux 10 and above

Guest operating system

A guest operating system is the operating system you will install in a virtual machine. Both 32-bit and 64-bit operating system versions are supported. Some of the most popular guest operating systems are:

- Windows 10
- Windows 8
- Windows 7
- Windows Vista
- Windows XP
- Windows Server 2016
- Windows Server 2012 R2
- Windows Server 2003 R2
- Ubuntu
- RedHat
- SUSE
- Oracle Linux
- Debian
- Fedora
- openSUSE
- Mint
- CentOS
- Solaris
- FreeBSD

Download VMware Workstation Player

VMware Workstation Player is free for personal non-commercial use, so you can download your own version of this software. You don't even have to register an account. Here are the steps:

First, go to *https://my.vmware.com/web/vmware/downloads*. You will be shown a list of VMware products. Find **VMware Workstation Player** (under the **Desktop & End-User Computing** menu) and click on the **Download Product** link on the right:

Desktop & End-User Computing

VMware Horizon	Download Product I Drivers & Tools I Download Trial I Get Training
VMware Horizon (with View)	Download Product I Drivers & Tools I Get Training
VMware Horizon Air	Download Product I Drivers & Tools I Get Training
VMware Horizon Air Hybrid-Mode (with Virtualization)	Download Product I Drivers & Tools
VMware Horizon Apps	Download Product I Drivers & Tools
VMware Horizon Cloud Service	Download Product I Drivers & Tools
VMware Horizon DaaS	Download Product I Drivers & Tools I Get Training
VMware Horizon Flex	Download Product I Drivers & Tools I Download Trial I Get Training
VMware Horizon Clients	Download Product I Drivers & Tools I Get Training
VMware User Environment Manager	Download Product I Drivers & Tools I Download Trial I Get Training
VMware App Volumes	Download Product I Drivers & Tools I Download Trial I Get Training
VMware Identity Manager	Download Product I Drivers & Tools I Download Trial
VMware Workspace	Download Product I Drivers & Tools I Get Training
VMware Mirage	Download Product I Drivers & Tools I Download Trial I Get Training
VMware vRealize Operations for Horizon and Published Applications	Download Product I Drivers & Tools I Download Trial
VMware ThinApp	Download Product I Drivers & Tools I Get Training
VMware Workstation Pro	Download Product I Drivers & Tools I Download Trial
VMware Workstation Player	Download Product
VMware Fusion	Download Product I Drivers & Tools I Download Trial
VMware TrustPoint	Download Product I Drivers & Tools

Figure 1-2 *Download VMware Workstation Player*

VMware Workstation Player is available for both Windows and Linux operating systems. Select the version you would like to download and click the **Download** button next to it:

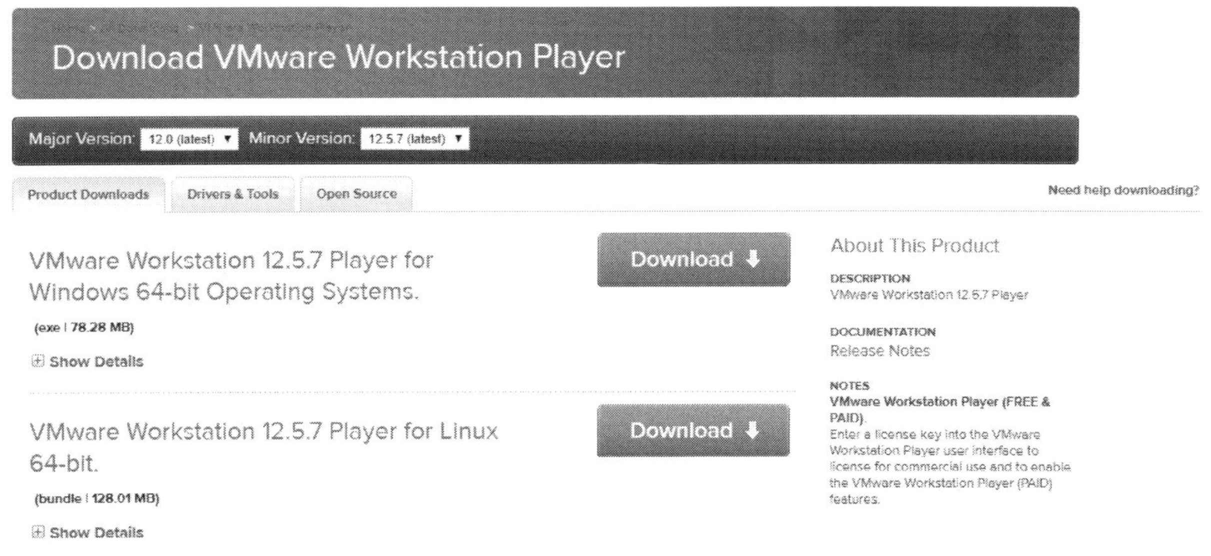

Figure 1-3 *Choose the Player version*

NOTE
You can install the software only on a 64-bit operating system.

After the download finishes, you can proceed with the Player installation.

Install VMware Workstation Player on Windows

To start the installation, double-click the installer file you've downloaded in the previous step:

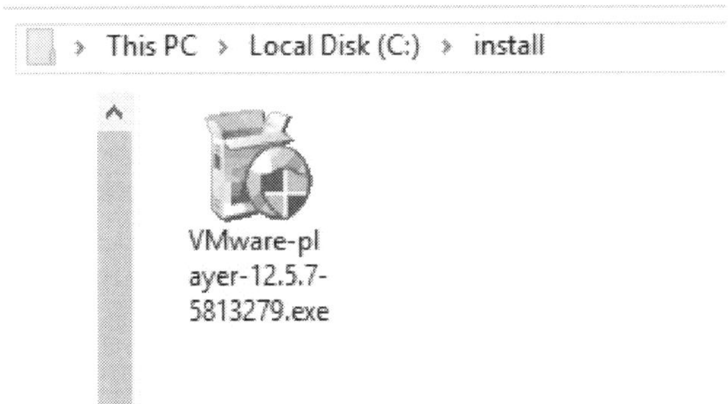

Figure 1-4 *Start the Player installation*

The VMware Workstation Player setup should start. On the Welcome screen, click Next to continue:

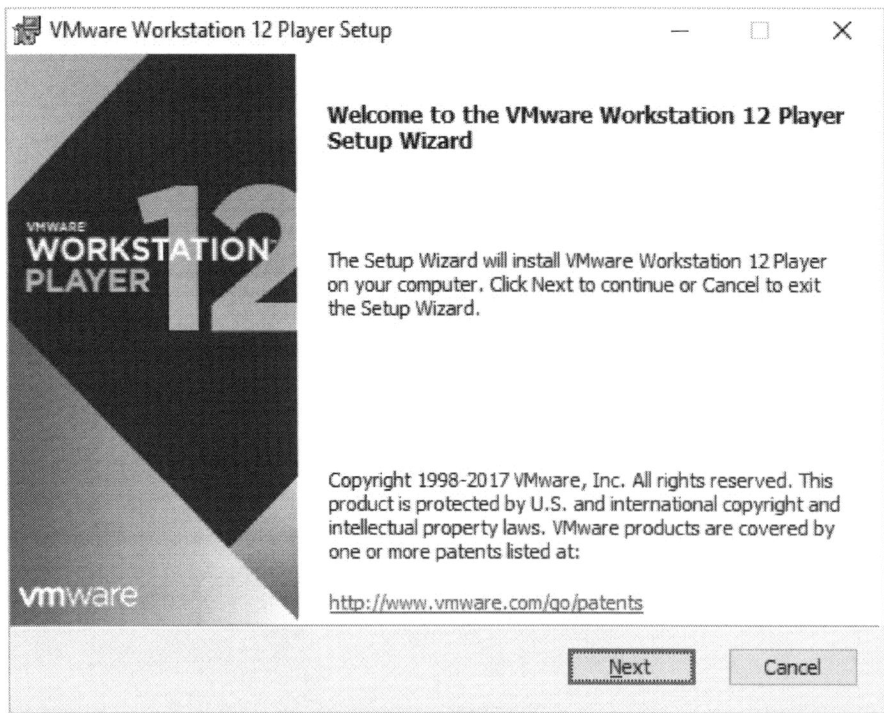

Figure 1-5 *Installation Welcome screen*

Accept the license terms and click Next:

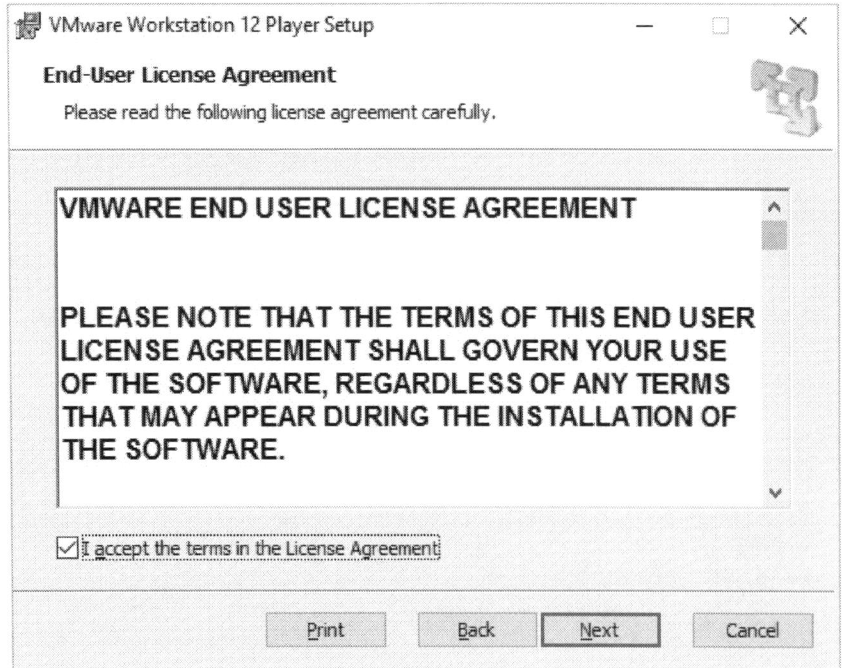

Figure 1-6 *Accept the license terms*

Select the installation location and whether to install the **Enhanced Keyboard Driver**, which provides better handling of international keyboards and keyboards that have extra keys:

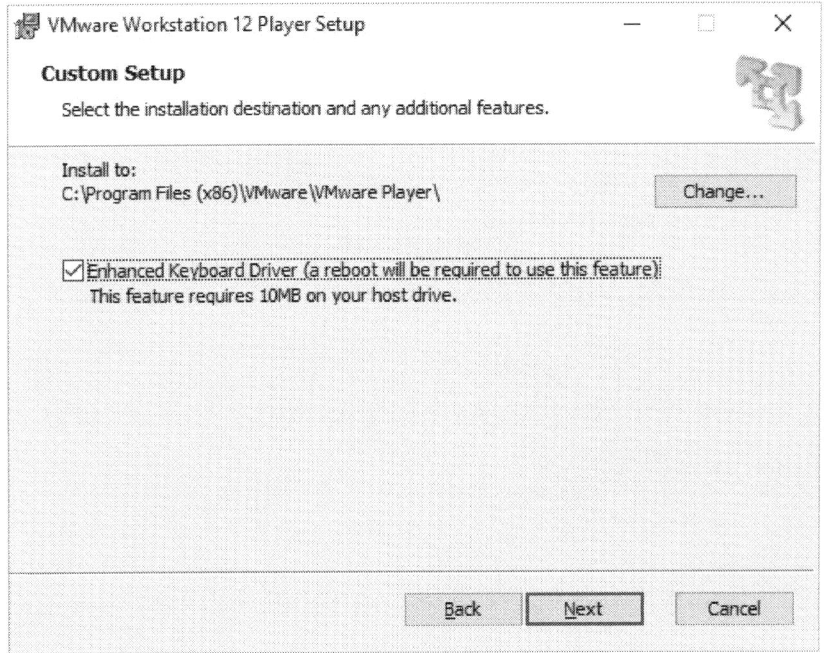

Figure 1-7 *Choose the installation location and whether to install Enhanced Keyboard Driver*

Select whether you would like to check for product updates when Player starts and whether you would like to send anonymous data and system usage to VMware:

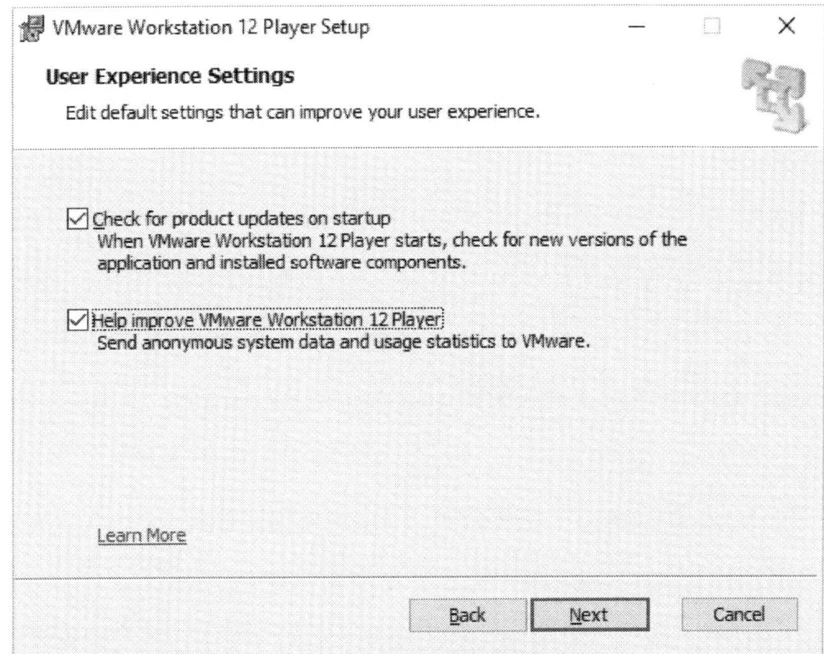

Figure 1-8 *Configure user experience settings*

Select the shortcuts you wish to create and click Next:

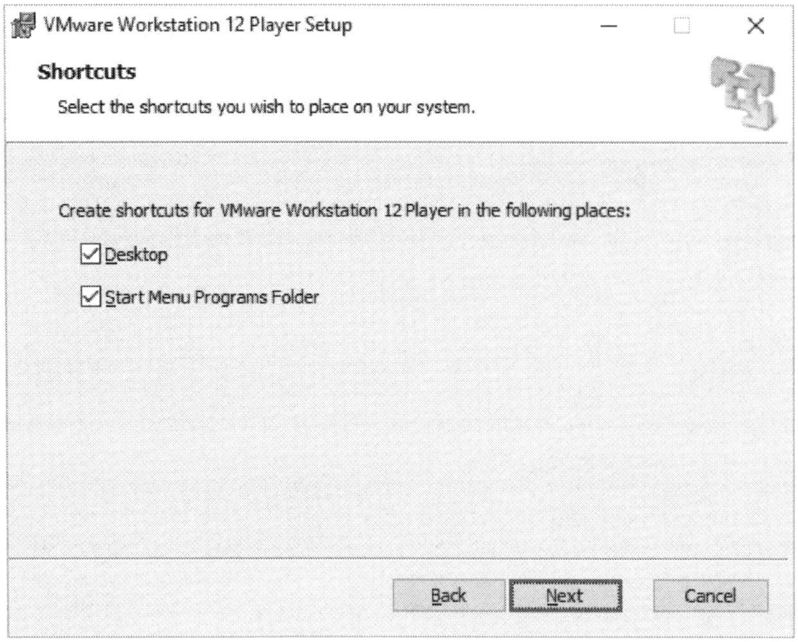

VMware Workstation 12 Player Setup

Shortcuts

Select the shortcuts you wish to place on your system.

Create shortcuts for VMware Workstation 12 Player in the following places:

☑ Desktop

☑ Start Menu Programs Folder

Back Next Cancel

Figure 1-9 *Create shortcuts*

Finally, click Install to start the installation:

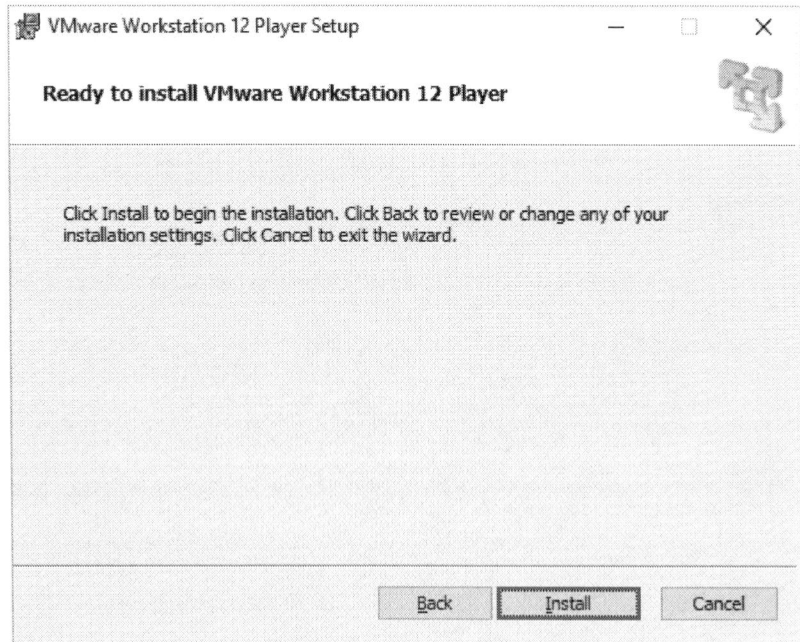

Figure 1-10 *Start the installation process*

After a minute or two the installation process should be finished:

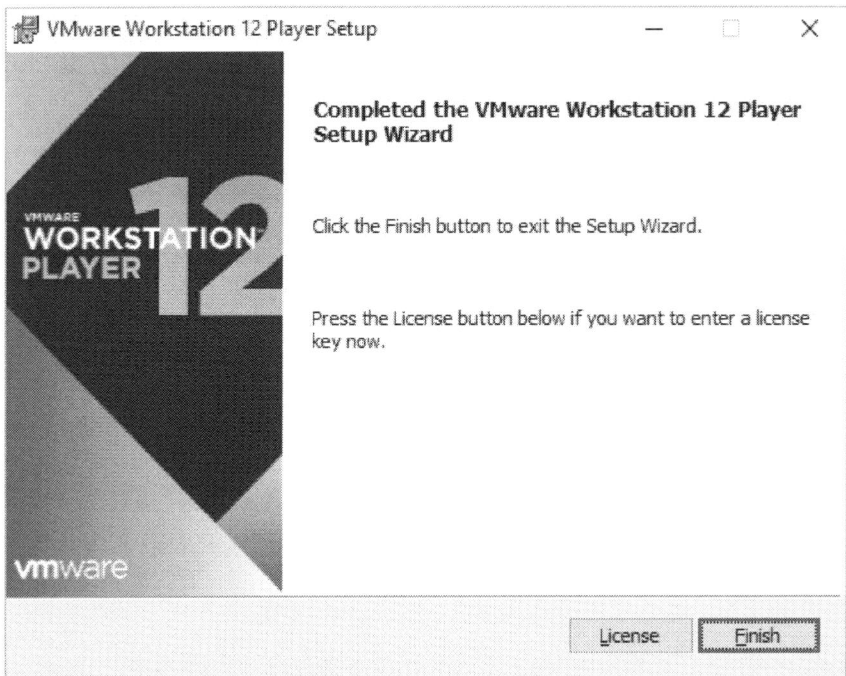

Figure 1-11 *Finish installation*

To complete the installation process, you will need to restart your computer:

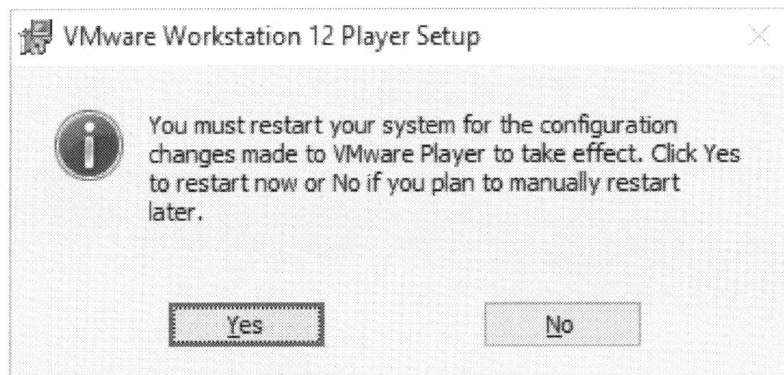

Figure 1-12 *Restart your computer*

Install VMware Workstation Player on Linux

NOTE
If you are using Windows as your operating system and are not interested in running Player on Linux, feel free to skip this lesson. This lesson explains how to install Player on Linux, not how to install a Linux distribution in a virtual machine.

VMware Workstation Player can also be installed on a Linux host. Supported Linux distributions are:

- Ubuntu 8.04 and above
- Red Hat Enterprise Linux 5 and above
- CentOS 5.0 and above
- Oracle Linux 5.0 and above
- openSUSE 10.2 and above
- SUSE Linux 10 and above

On most Linux distributions, the Linux bundle installer is installed using the GUI. However, on some Linux distributions, the bundle installer starts a command-line wizard instead of a GUI wizard. You can also manually start the command-line wizard using the *--console* option, if you want to use the shell for installation.

I will show you how to install Player on an **openSUSE** host. First, you will need to download the Linux bundle installer, available on the following link:

https://my.vmware.com/web/vmware/free#desktop_end_user_computing/vmware_workstation_player/12_0

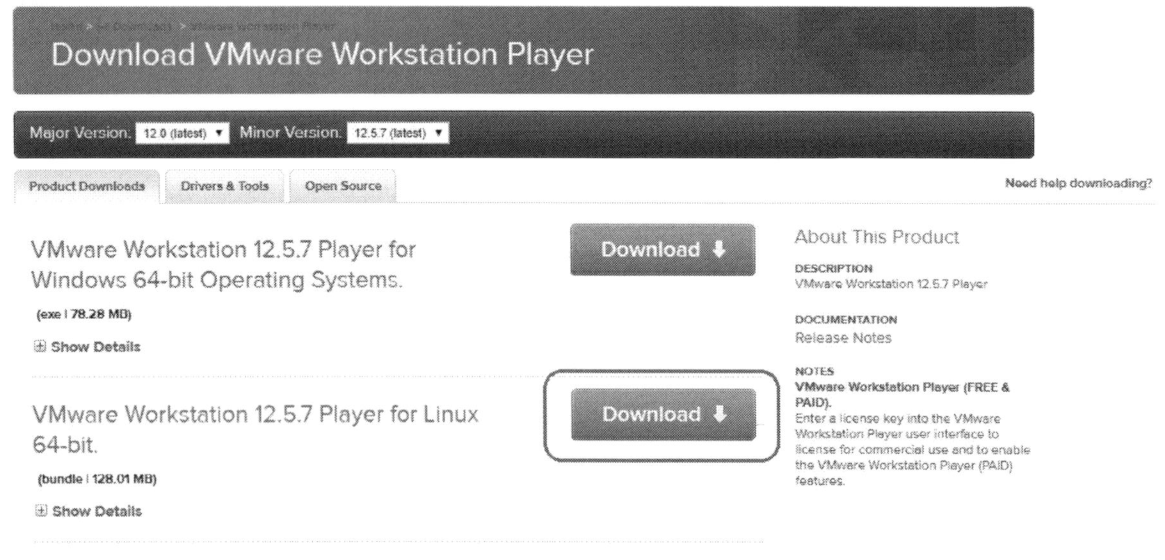

Figure 1-13 *Download Player for Linux*

Next, become **root**. On most Linux distributions, this is accomplished using the *su* - command:

```
bob@linux-bv3p:~> su -
Password:
linux-bv3p:~ #
```

Navigate to the directory in which you've stored the installer file:

```
linux-bv3p:/ # cd /tmp/player
linux-bv3p:/tmp/player # ls
VMware-Player-12.5.7-5813279.x86_64.bundle
```

Make the bundle script executable by entering the following command:

```
linux-bv3p:/tmp/player # chmod +x VMware-Player-12.5.7-5813279.x86_64.bundle
```

Run the script in order to start the installation:

```
linux-bv3p:/tmp/player # ./VMware-Player-12.5.7-5813279.x86_64.bundle
```

The installer should start. Accept the license agreement and click Next:

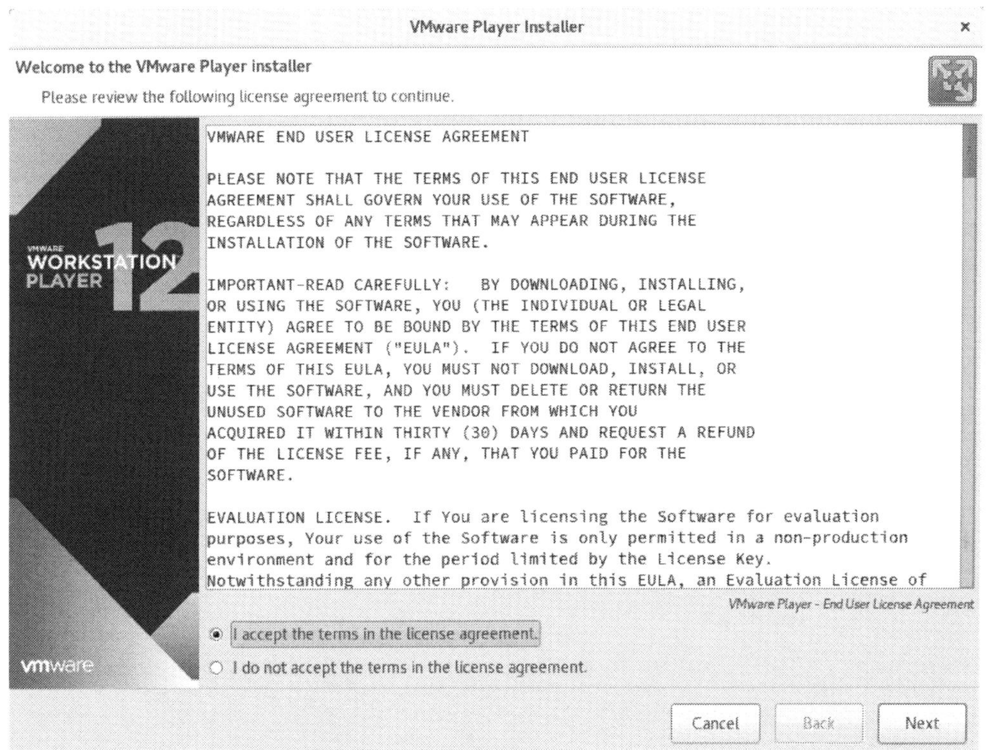

Figure 1-14 *Accept the license agreement*

Select whether you would like to check for Player updates on startup:

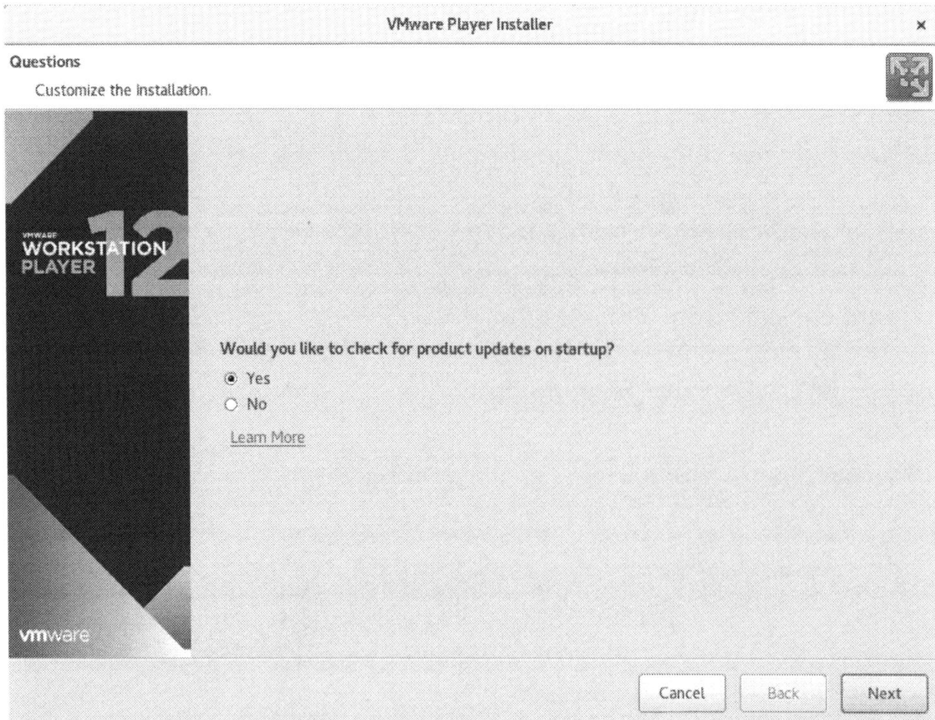

Figure 1-15 *Select whether to check for updates*

Select whether you would like to send anonymous data and system usage to VMware:

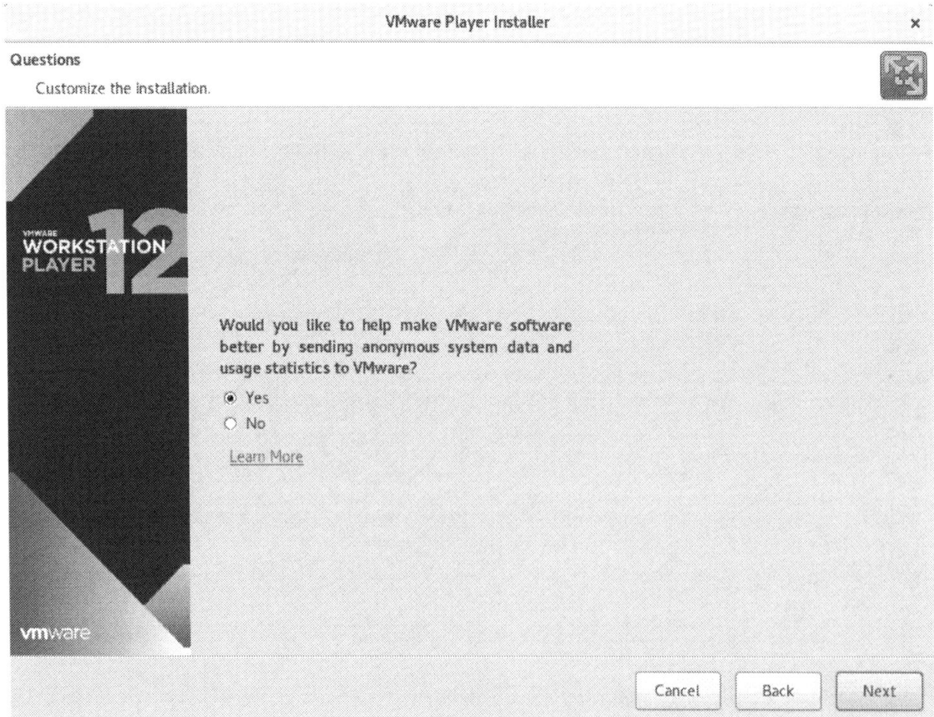

Figure 1-16 *Select whether to send data to VMware*

In the License key window, click Next unless you got a license key for VMware Player Pro:

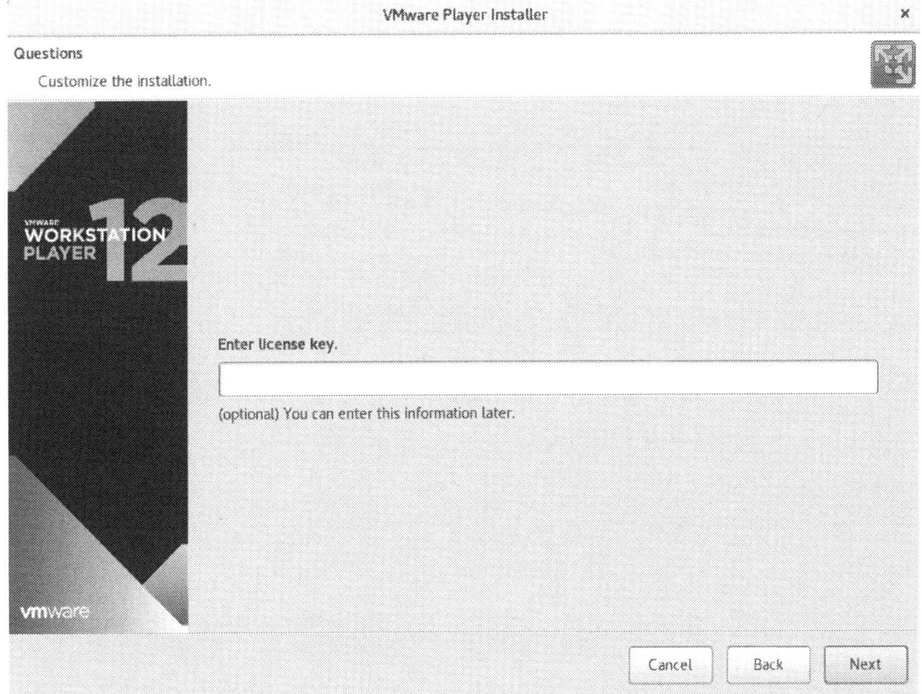

Figure 1-17 *Enter the license key*

Click Install to start the installation process:

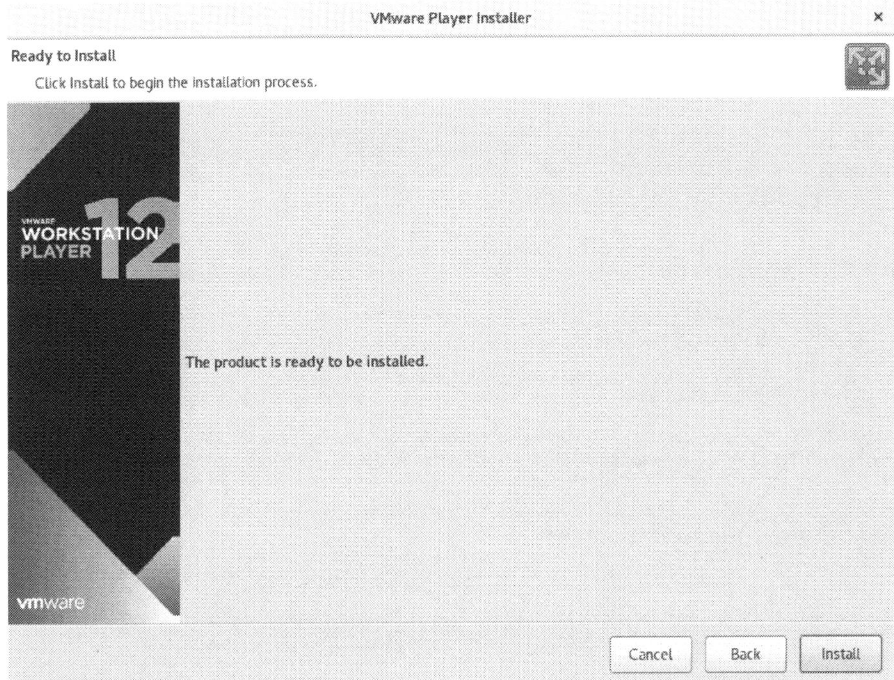

Figure 1-18 *Start the installation*

After the installation is finished, you can log out of the root account. You do not need to be root to run Player.

To start Player, simply run the *vmplayer* command in the shell.

VMware Workstation Player home screen

When you start VMware Workstation Player, you are presented with the home screen:

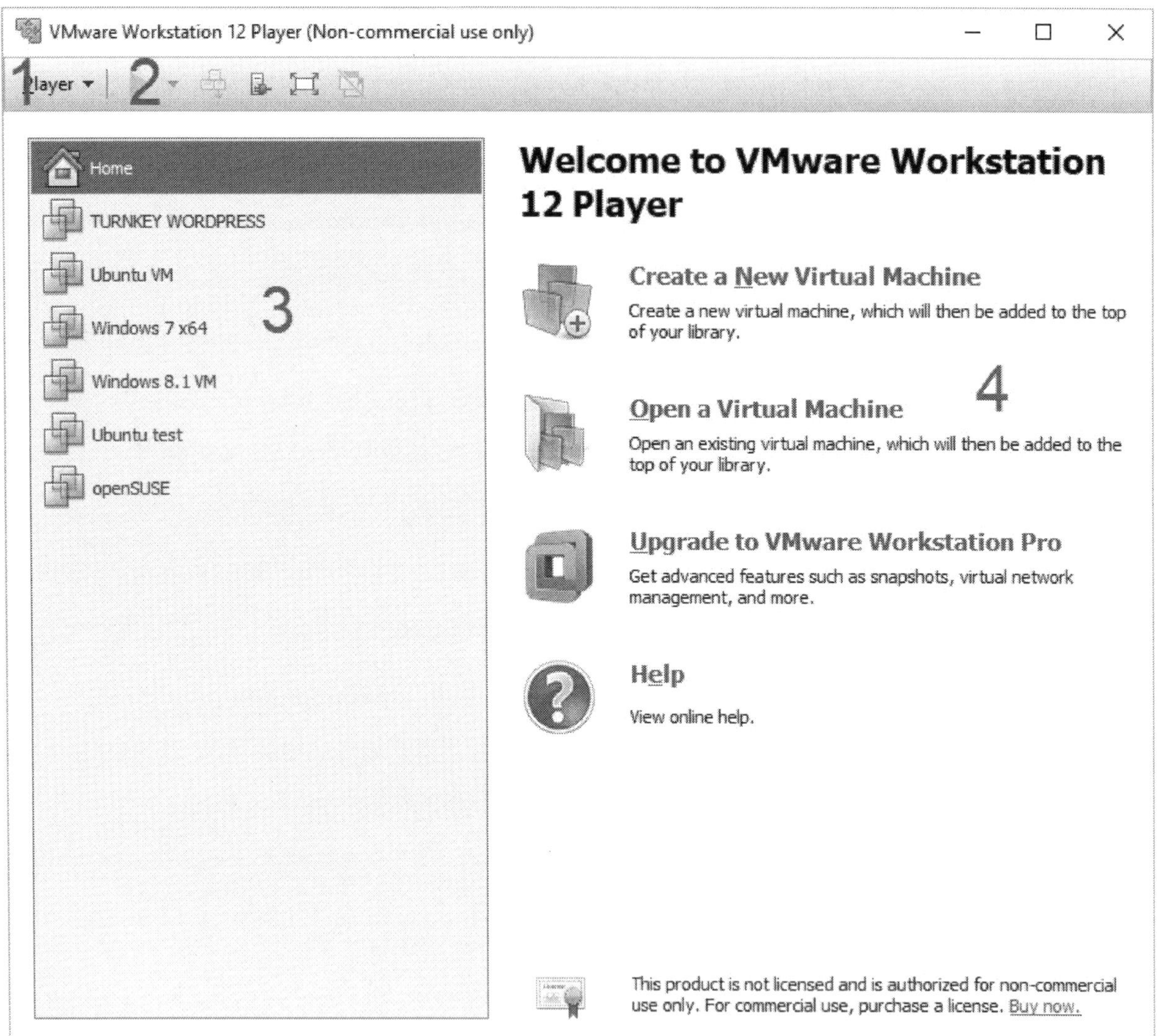

Figure 1-19 *VMware Workstation Player home screen*

The home screen consists of the following components:

1. Player menu - contains some common menus and options, such as the File menu to create or open a virtual machine, options to power off or restart the VM, run the VM in full screen, and other actions used to manage a virtual machine.

2. Action icons - the green power icon allows you to power on, restart, suspend or power off the virtual machine. The second icon on the left sends Ctrl+Alt+Del to the selected VM. The following icon enables you to connect to VMware Horizon FLEX Server (Horizon FLEX Server allows users to run locally a locked-down virtual machine). The forth icon activates the full screen mode, and the last icon enables Unity Mode, which displays applications from virtual machines directly on the host system desktop.

3. Library - contains the list of virtual machines created or opened in Player. The list will be empty if you haven't created any virtual machine.

4. Working window - when the Home icon above the Library is selected, links for some common actions in Player are displayed. When a VM listed in the Library is selected, its information are displayed, along with the option to start or edit the VM:

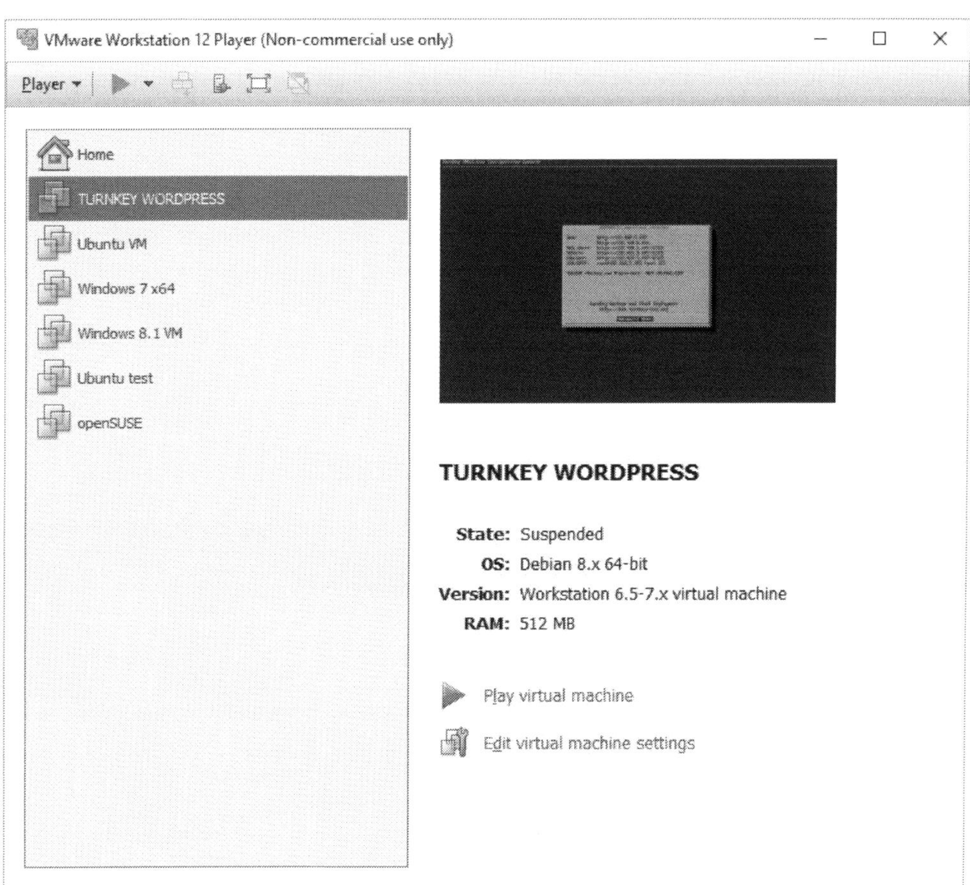

Figure 1-20 *Virtual machine information*

Summary

In this chapter you've learned what VMware Workstation Player is and what it is used for. You've learned about the minimum and recommended system requirements for Player installation. We went through the process of downloading and installing Player on Windows and Linux and even started the application for the first time.

In the next chapter you will learn how to create your first virtual machine and install an operating system in it.

This page intentionally left blank

This page intentionally left blank

Chapter 2 - Creating virtual machines

IN THIS CHAPTER

Creating virtual machines in Player

Installing a guest operating system

Using Easy Install feature

VMware Tools overview and installation

In this chapter you will create your first virtual machine. I will show you how you can use operating system images to install a guest operating system, either manually or using the Player's Easy Install feature. We will finish this chapter by learning what VMware Tools is and how to install this free set of drivers to enhance the performance of the virtual machine's guest operating systems.

What is a virtual machine?

A **virtual machine** can be defined as a software computer that, just like a physical computer, runs an operating system and executes programs. A virtual machine contains its own virtual hardware, such as the virtual CPU, memory, hard disk, and network interface cards, which provide the same functionality as the physical hardware to the operating systems and applications.

A virtual machine uses the physical resources of the physical host on which it runs. It interacts with installed hardware through a software component called the **hypervisor**. The hypervisor provides the physical hardware resources dynamically as needed and allows virtual machines to operate with a degree of independence from the underlying physical hardware. Two types of hypervisors exist:

- **type 1** - runs directly on the host's hardware to control the hardware and manage guest operating systems.
- **type 2** - runs on a conventional operating system, just like any other computer program.

VMware Workstation Player is an example of a **type 2 hypervisor**, which means that it is installed inside an existing operating system (such as Microsoft Windows or one of the numerous Linux distributions).

Consider the following example:

Figure 2-1 *Linux running inside Windows*

In the picture you can see that I have installed Player on Windows and I am running a Linux distribution (openSUSE) as a guest operating system in Player. Since VMware Workstation Player is a type 2 hypervisor, it needs to be installed inside an operating system - Windows 10 in my case.

What is a guest operating system?

A virtual machine has an operating system (called the **guest operating system**) that you install and manage in much the same way like you would do with an operating system on a physical machine. The guest operating system installation is carried out using a CD-ROM, DVD, or an ISO image that contains the operating system installation files.

NOTE
A guest operating system can be different from the host operating system (for example, you can run a Linux distribution such as openSUSE in Player installed on a Windows 10 machine, as shown in the previous example).

Many guest operating systems are supported by Player, such as Windows XP, Windows 7, Windows 8, Windows 10, Windows Server 2008, Windows Server 2012, Solaris, Debian, CentOS, SUSE, FreeBSD, Red Hat, etc. For the most recent list of the supported guest operating systems, check out the **VMware Compatibility Guide** on the following link:

https://www.vmware.com/resources/compatibility/search.php?deviceCategory=software

Workstation Player is not listed, but the information for Workstation Pro is applicable to Workstation Player:

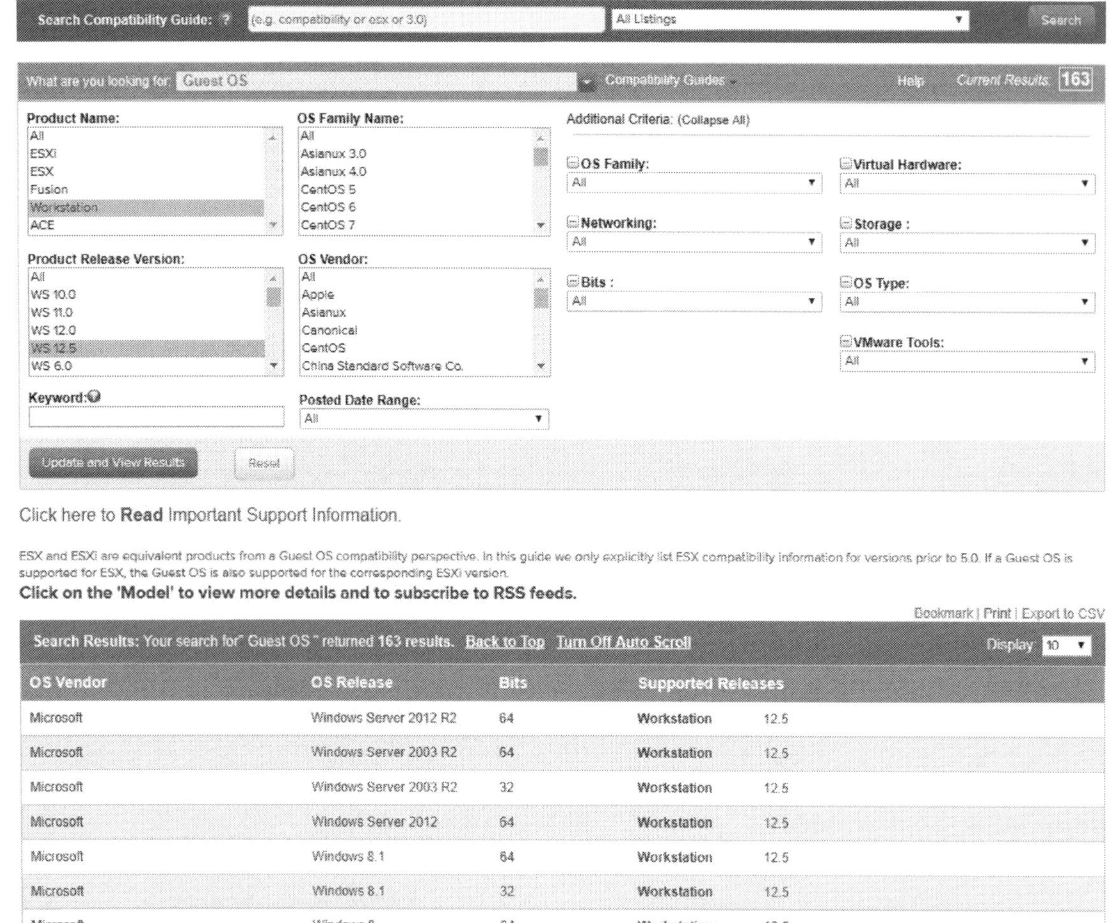

Figure 2-2 *Supported guest operating systems*

Just like with the operating system installation on a physical computer, you need to have an installer disc or an ISO image file of the operating system you would like to install. An **ISO file** (also called an ISO image) is a single file that replicates the contents of an optical disc. ISO files are used to distribute large programs over the Internet, including operating systems such as Microsoft Windows and Linux. For example, on the link below you can download an ISO version of **Damn Small Linux** and use it to install this Linux distribution in Player:

ftp://distro.ibiblio.org/pub/linux/distributions/damnsmall/current/

Create a virtual machine

Let's create our first virtual machine. To do this, we need to use the New Virtual Machine wizard. To start the wizard, select **Player > File > New Virtual Machine**:

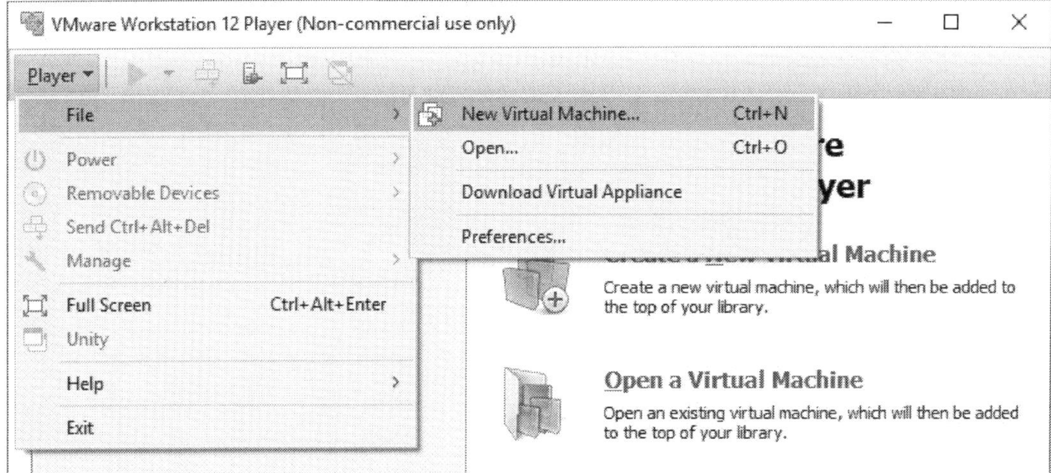

Figure 2-3 *Start New Virtual Machine Wizard*

Next, select the source from which the guest operating system will be installed. Three options are available:

- **Installer disc** - install the guest OS from an optical drive.
- **Installer disc image file (iso)** - use an ISO image file for the guest OS installation.
- **I will install the operating system later** - this option creates a new virtual machine with a blank hard disk. You will need to install the guest operating system manually after the virtual machine creation. I will select this option and install the OS later:

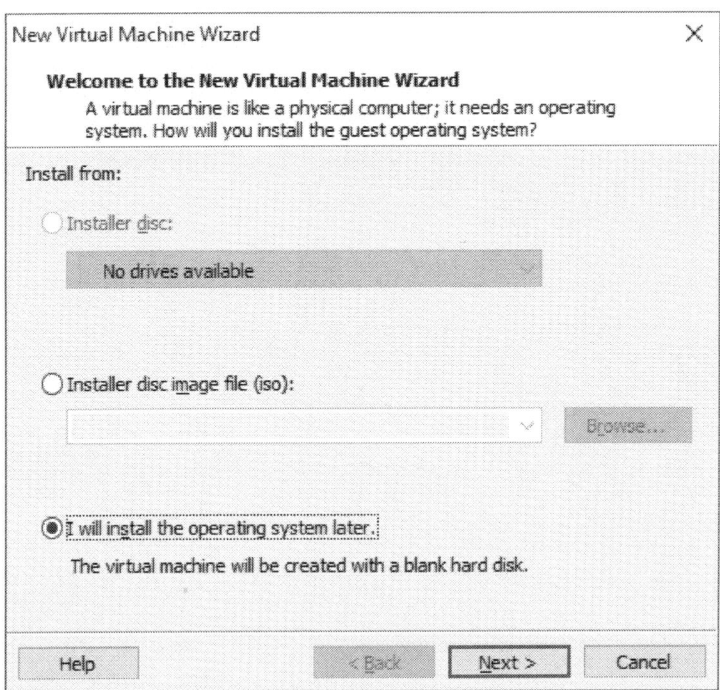

Figure 2-4 *Choose the third option to install the guest OS later*

Next, select the guest operating system that your VM will be running. If the operating system is not listed, choose the **Other** option. Since I will be installing a Linux distribution, I will select Linux under **Guest operating system**:

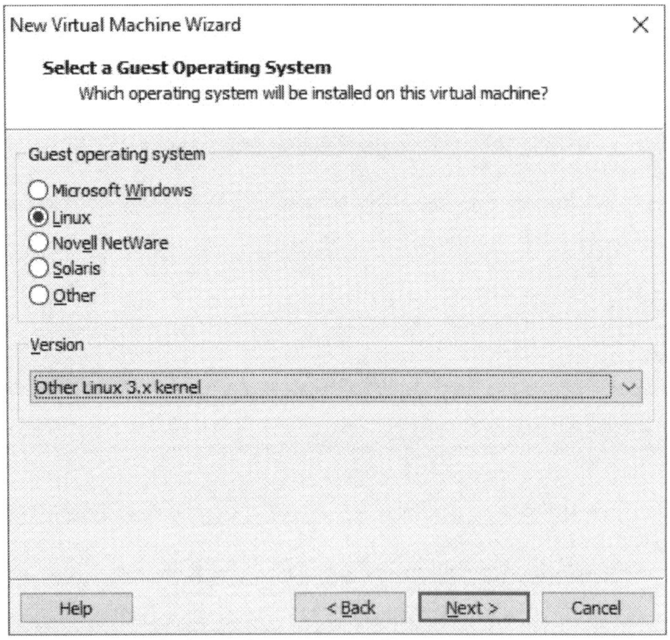

Figure 2-5 *Select the guest OS*

Type the name of the virtual machine and choose the folder on the host system where the virtual machine files will be stored. This is simply a folder on your (physical) computer - in my case the location is *C:\VMs*:

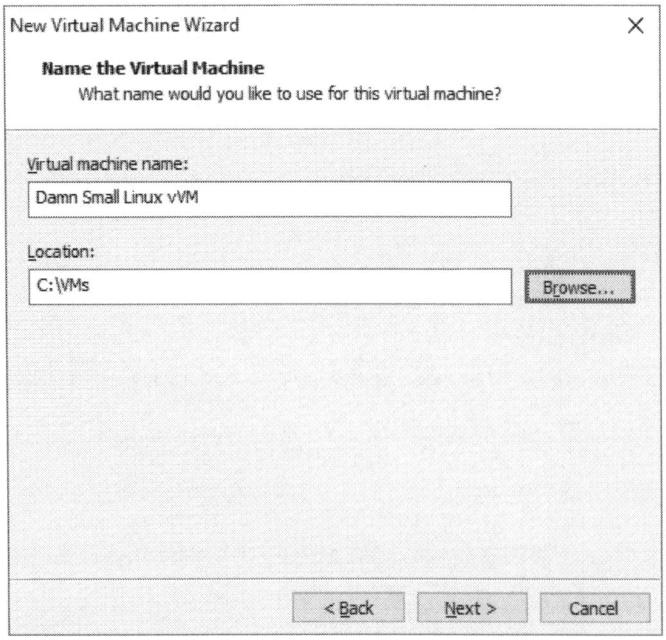

Figure 2-6 *Choose the VM name and location*

Next, select the virtual disk size. You can choose to split the virtual disk into multiple files, which makes it easier to move the virtual machine to another computer. Note that the disk space is not preallocated for the disk and the actual files that the virtual disk uses start small and expand to their maximum size as needed:

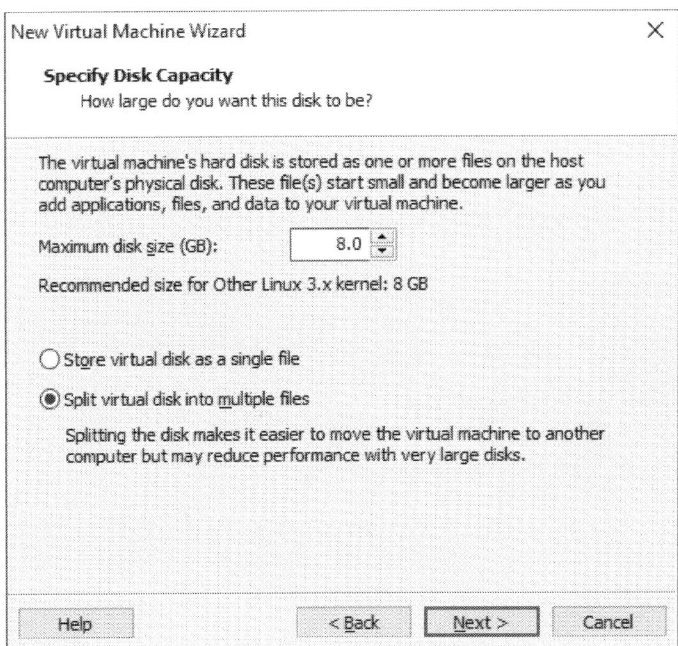

Figure 2-7 *Choose the virtual disk size*

Click Finish to create the virtual machine:

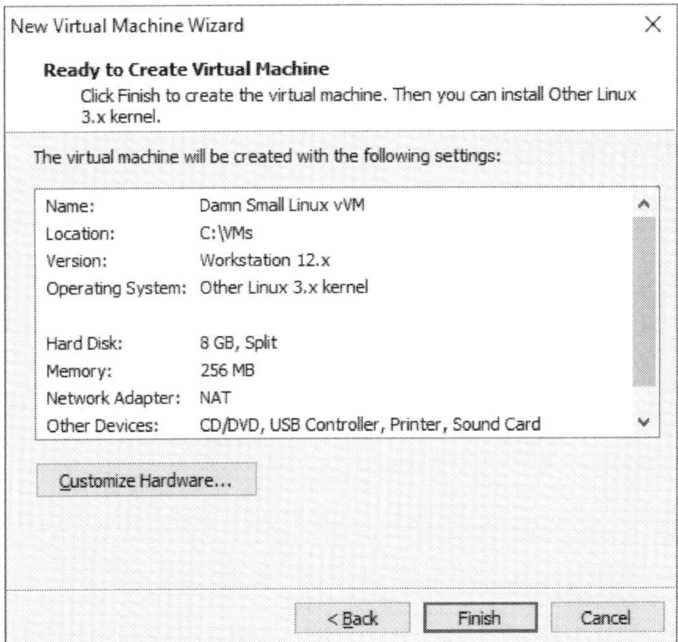

Figure 2-8 *Create the VM*

Since we've chosen an option to install the operating system later, the VM has a blank hard disk and we need install an operating system on it. So let's do than now.

Manually install a guest operating system

Since we didn't use the New Virtual Machine wizard to install the guest operating system in a virtual machine, we need to do it manually. The guest OS installation in a virtual machine is similar to installing an operating system on a physical machine. It can be done in three ways:

- install the guest OS from an installer disk.
- install the guest OS from an ISO image.
- use a PXE server to install the guest OS over the network.

In this section I will describe how you can install the guest operating system using an ISO file. I will use the ISO file containing the image of **Damn Small Linux** operating system. If you would like to follow along, you can get the ISO file here (download the **dsl-VERSION-initrd.iso** file): *ftp://distro.ibiblio.org/pub/linux/distributions/damnsmall/current/*

1. Select the virtual machine in Player and go to Player > Manage > Virtual Machine Settings:

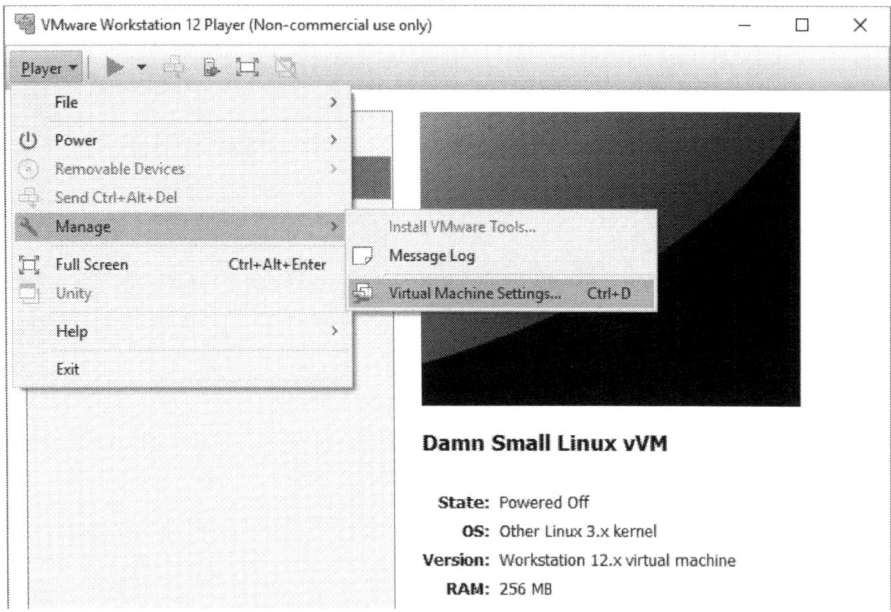

Figure 2-9 *Open Virtual Machine Settings*

2. Under the Hardware tab, select CD/DVD drive. Check the **Connect at power on** checkbox. Select **Use ISO image file** and browse to the location of the ISO file:

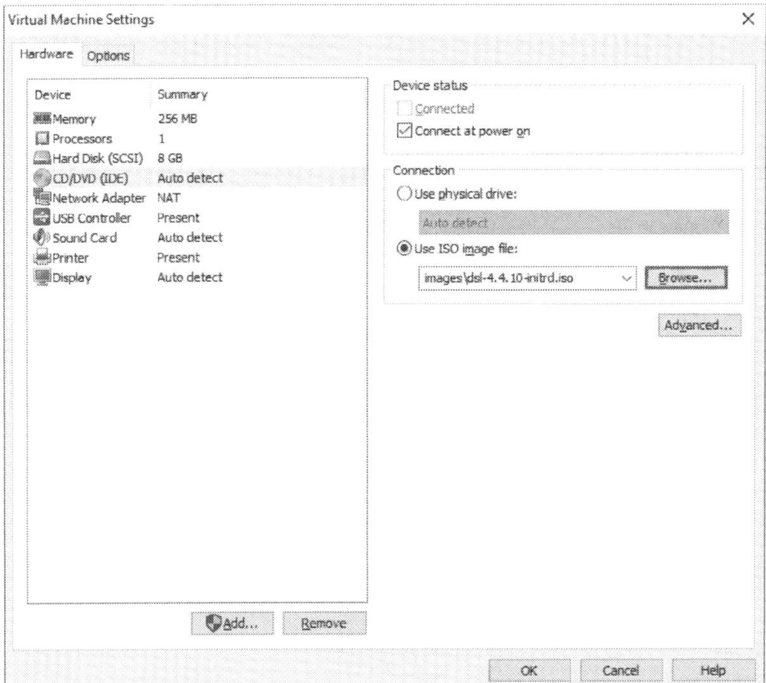

Figure 2-10 *Select the .iso file for installation*

3. Next, power on the virtual machine:

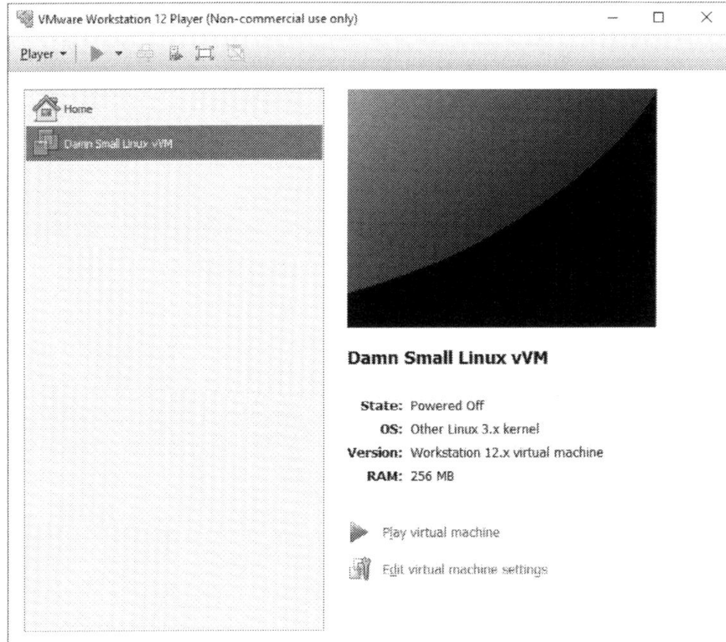

Figure 2-11 *Power on the VM*

4. The virtual machine boots from the ISO image, which contains the installation for your guest operating system. You can now install the guest OS just like you would do it on a physical machine:

Figure 2-12 *Damn Small Linux setup screen*

Easy Install feature in VMware Workstation Player

Workstation Player includes a feature called **Easy Install** for automating the guest operating system installation. When the New Virtual Machine wizard detects an operating system that supports this feature, it prompts you for information about the guest operating system, such as the product key, username, and password. After the virtual machine is created, the guest operating system installation will be automated and should finish without your intervention.

NOTE
After the guest OS is installed, Easy Install will also install VMware Tools.

Here is how you can install the guest OS using Easy Install:

1. Create a new virtual machine in Player by using the New Virtual Machine wizard. To start the wizard, go to Player > File > New Virtual Machine.

2. Select the **Installer disc image file (iso)** option and browse to the location of the ISO file. Note that VMware Workstation Player has recognized the OS version (Windows 8.1, 64-bit version) and that Easy Install will be used for the guest OS installation:

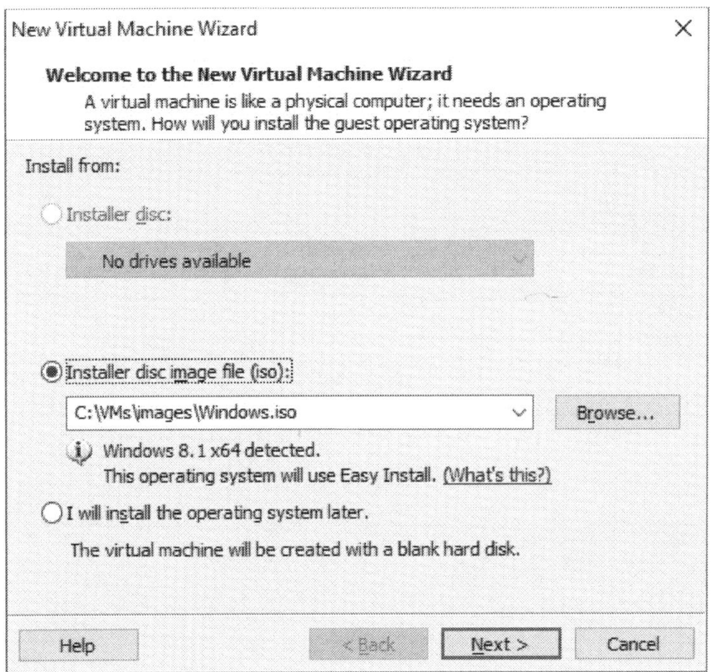

Figure 2-13 *Choose the VMware Tools .iso file*

NOTE
ISO files containing Windows 8.1 installation can be downloaded here: *https://www.microsoft.com/en-us/software-download/windows8*. You will need to provide a valid Windows product key .

3. Provide the Easy Install information for the guest operating system (you can enter the Windows product key later):

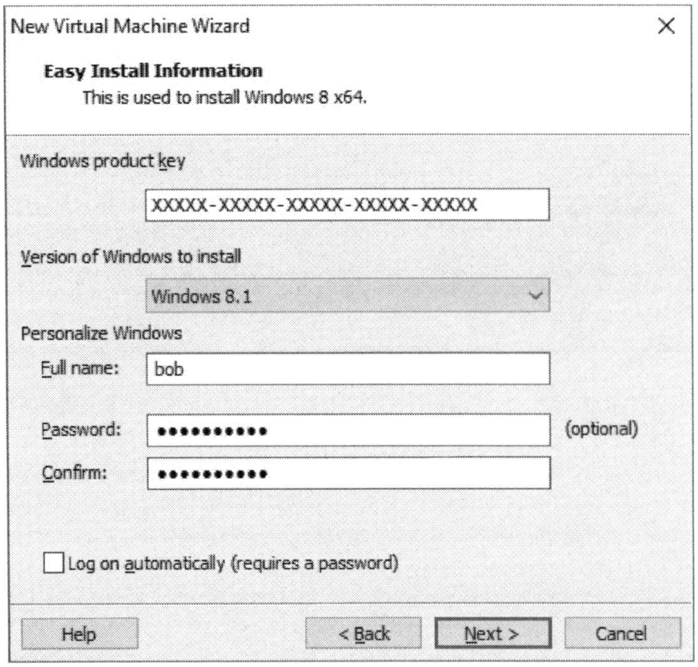

Figure 2-14 *Provide Easy Install information*

4. Type the virtual machine name and choose the the folder on the host system where the VM will be stored:

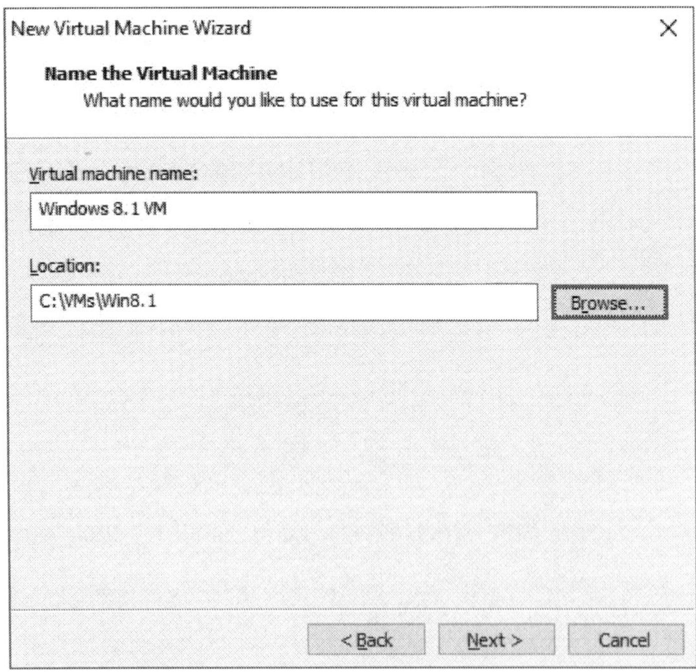

Figure 2-15 *Choose the VM name and location*

5. Select the virtual disk size. You can split the virtual disk into multiple files, which makes it easier to move the virtual machine to another computer:

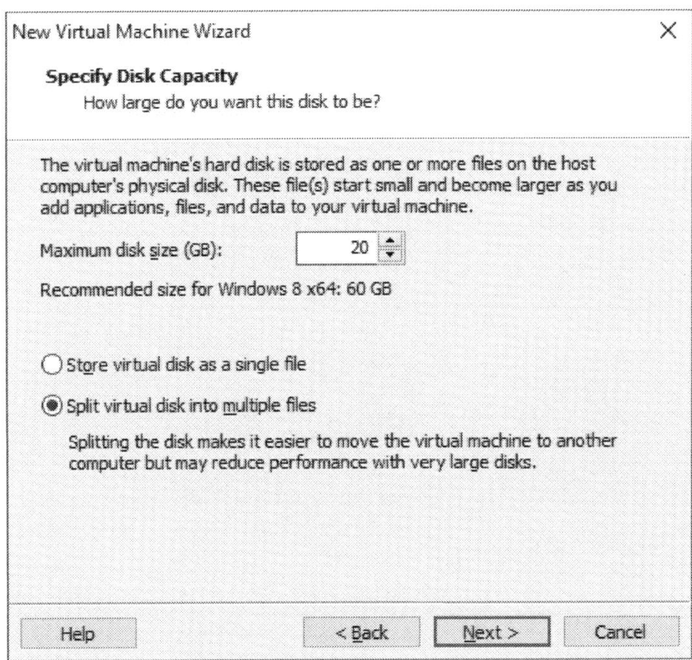

Figure 2-16 *Choose the disk size and whether to split the disk into multiple files*

6. Click Finish to create the VM:

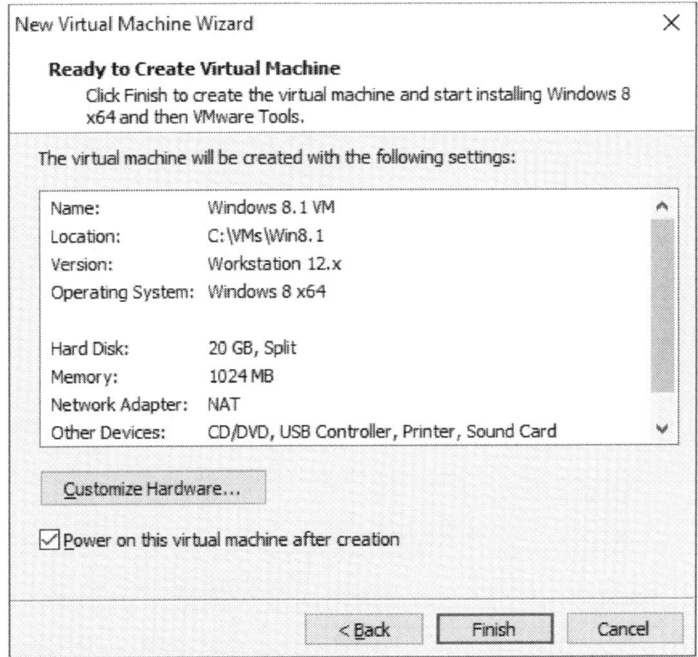

Figure 2-17 *Create the VM*

7. The guest operating system installation should begin when the virtual machine is powered on. The installation is automated and should finish without your intervention. Easy Install will also install VMware Tools:

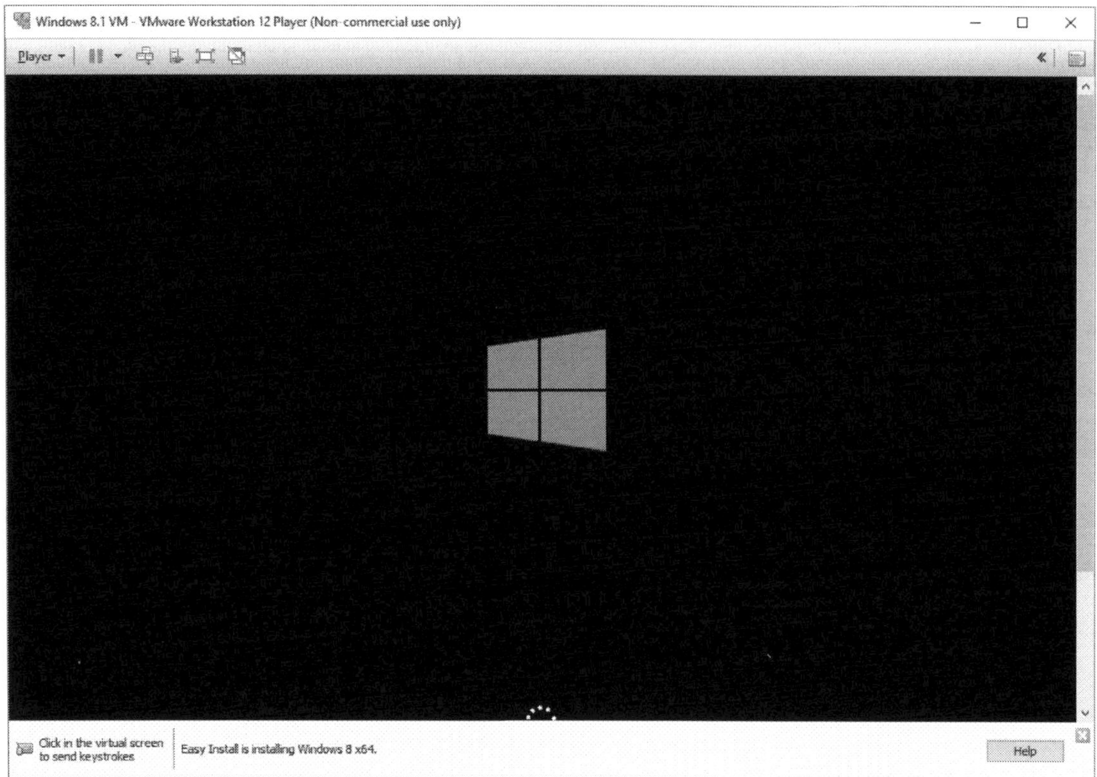

Figure 2-18 *Easy Install installing Windows*

VMware Tools overview

VMware Tools is a free set of drivers and utilities that enhances the performance of the virtual machine's guest operating systems and improves management of virtual machines in VMware Workstation Player. Although VMware Tools is not installed by default and is not required for the guest OS to run, VMware strongly recommends installing it in all of your virtual machines because of the following benefits:

- enhanced and faster graphics.
- improved mouse performance.
- time synchronization with the host operating system.
- the ability to shut down or restart a virtual machine.
- the ability to copy and paste between the guest OS and the host OS.

VMware Tools is available for a number of guest operating systems, such as Windows, Linux, Solaris, FreeBSD, and NetWare. The installers for VMware Tools are ISO files. The most recent versions of the ISO image files are stored on the VMware official website. When you start a VMware Tools installation, Player downloads the file and the installation is started. The virtual machine's first virtual CD-ROM drive temporarily connects to the VMware Tools ISO file for the guest OS.

NOTE
The Windows or Linux **Easy Install** feature will install VMware Tools as soon as the operating system is finished installing and the virtual machine is powered on.

Install VMware Tools in Windows

VMware strongly recommends installing VMware Tools in a virtual machine running Windows OS. If you didn't use the Easy Install option for Windows installation, you can install VMware Tools manually. Here are the steps:

1. If the virtual machine is turned off, power it on. The guest OS must be running in order to install VMware Tools.

2. Configure the virtual CD/DVD drive to autodetect a physical drive. This enables the virtual machine's first virtual CD/DVD drive to detect and connect to the VMware Tools ISO file. To do this, go to Player > Manage > Virtual Machine Settings.

Under Hardware, go to CD/DVD and select the **Use physical drive** option on the right. Make sure that the **Auto detect** option is selected:

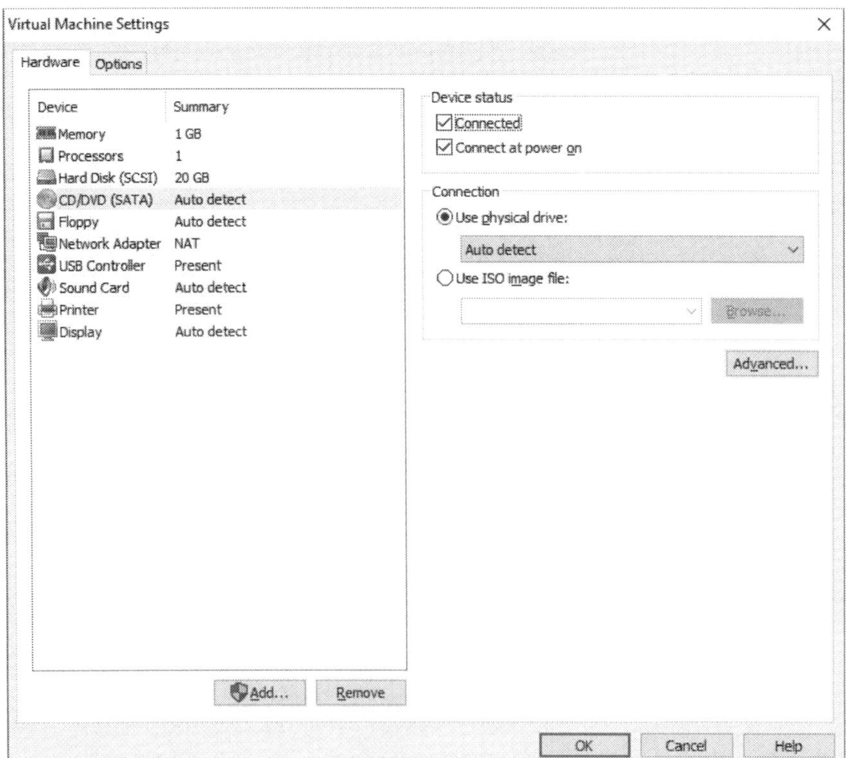

Figure 2-19 *Configure the virtual CD/DVD drive to autodetect a physical drive*

3. Log in to the guest OS as the administrator.

4. From the Player menu bar, select Player > Manage > Install VMware Tools to start the VMware Tools installation:

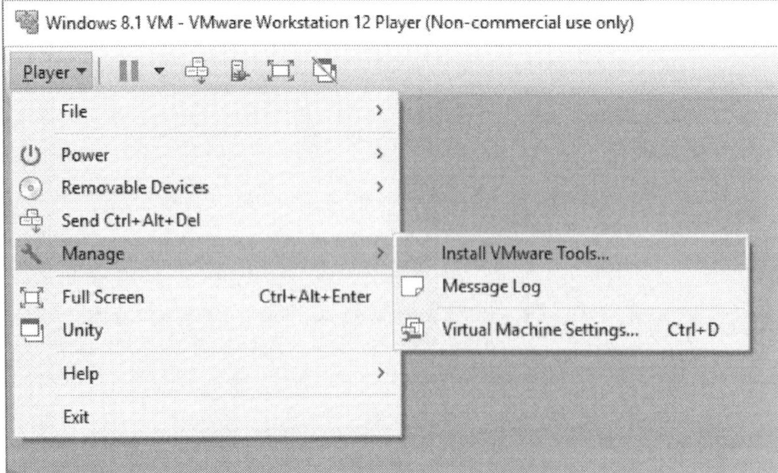

Figure 2-20 *Start VMware Tools installation*

5. Click **Download and Install** in the Software Updates window that opens:

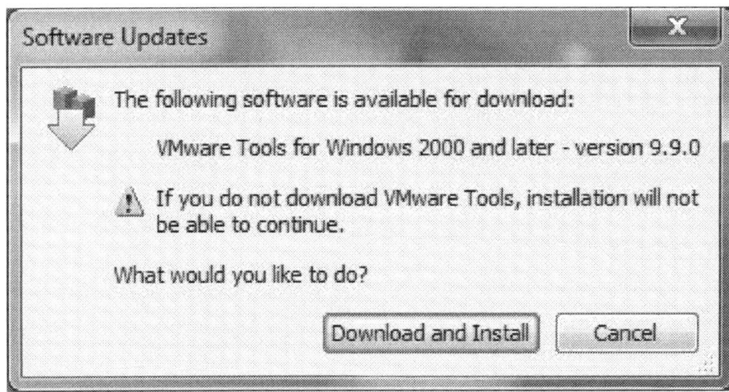

Figure 2-21 *Download VMware Tools*

6. After the download finishes, the AutoPlay window should open. Click on **Run setup64.exe** to start the VMware Tools installation. If you didn't get the AutoPlay window, go to **D:\setup.exe**, where D: is the virtual CD-ROM drive, and run the setup from there.

7. Click Next in the Welcome to the installation wizard window:

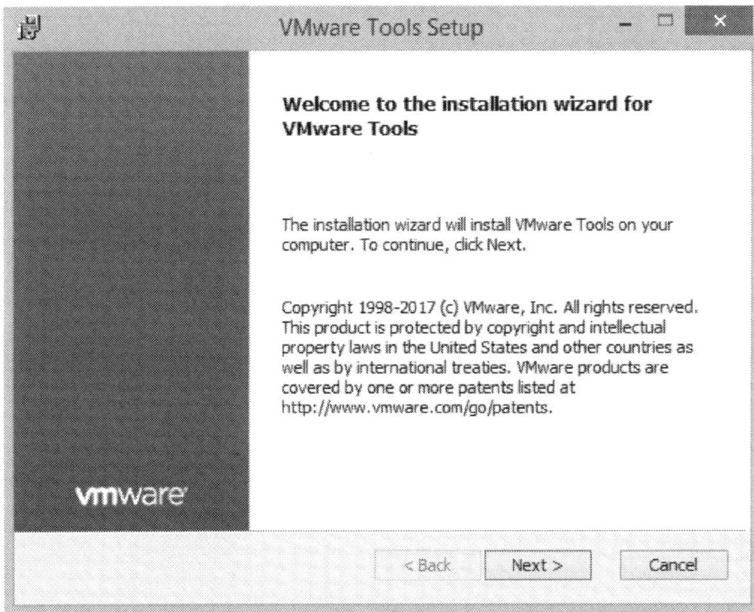

Figure 2-22 *VMware Tools installation Welcome screen*

8. Select the installation type and click Next. The **Typical** installation option will suffice for most situations. The **Complete** installation option installs all VMware Tools features, while the **Custom** installation option lets you decide which features to install:

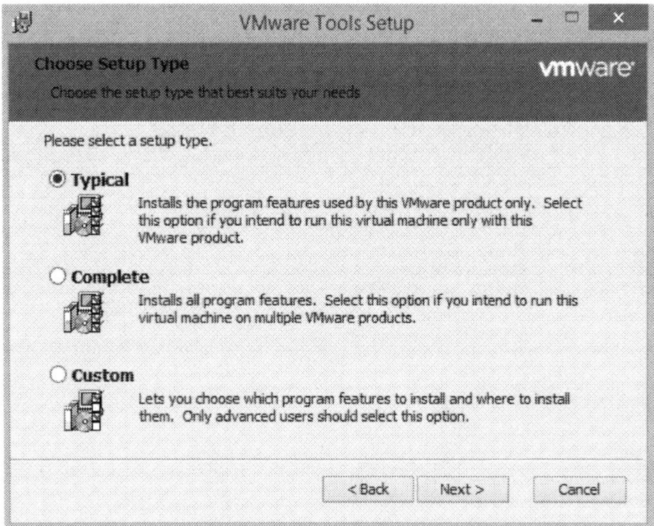

Figure 2-23 *Select the setup type*

9. Click Install to start the installation process:

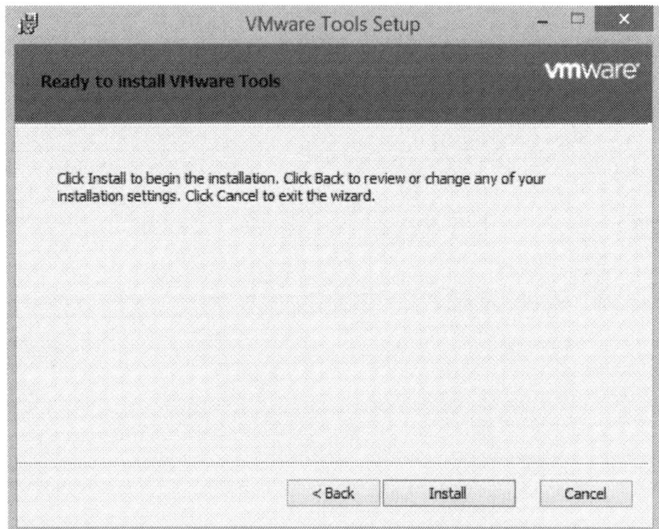

Figure 2-24 *Start VMware Tools installation*

10. When prompted, restart the VM's guest OS:

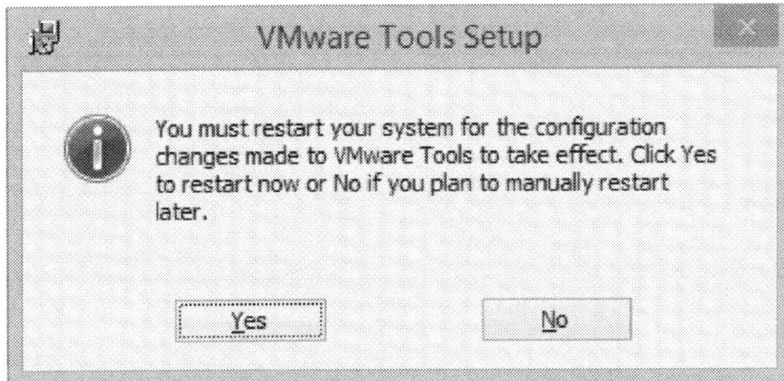

Figure 2-25 *Restart the computer to apply changes*

Install VMware Tools in Linux

VMware Tools is automatically installed when the Easy Install option is used for Linux installation, but if you didn't use this option, you will need to install VMware Tools manually. Installation of VMware Tools in Linux is done through the shell.

Here are the steps for installing VMware Tools in Ubuntu, a popular Linux distribution:

1. If the virtual machine is turned off, power it on. The guest operating system must be running in order to install VMware Tools.

2. Configure the virtual CD/DVD drive to autodetect a physical drive:

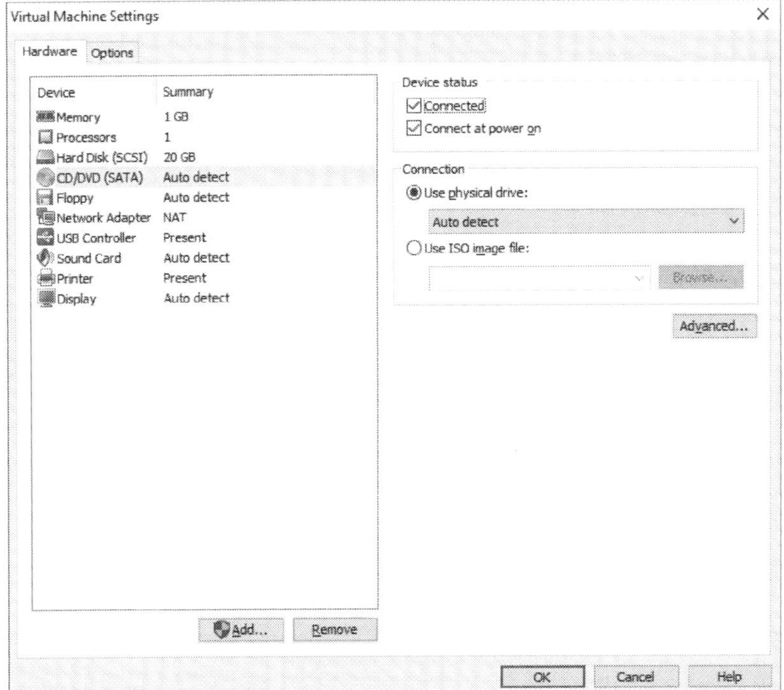

Figure 2-26 *Configure the virtual CD/DVD*

3. Log in into the guest OS as the user that has **root** privileges and open up the shell.

4. The VMware Tools installer is written in Perl, so Perl has to be installed in the guest operating system. Verify that Perl is indeed installed by entering the *perl -v* command, which should return the Perl version:

```
bob@ubuntu:~$ perl -v

This is perl 5, version 22, subversion 1 (v5.22.1) built for x86_64-linux-gnu-thread-multi
(with 58 registered patches, see perl -V for more detail)

Copyright 1987-2015, Larry Wall

Perl may be copied only under the terms of either the Artistic License or the
GNU General Public License, which may be found in the Perl 5 source kit.

Complete documentation for Perl, including FAQ lists, should be found on
this system using "man perl" or "perldoc perl".  If you have access to the
Internet, point your browser at http://www.perl.org/, the Perl Home Page.
```

If Perl is not installed, install it using the packet manager of your Linux distribution. In Ubuntu, this can be done by using the following command:

```
bob@ubuntu:~$ sudo apt-get install perl
```

5. From the Player menu bar, select Player > Manage > Install VMware Tools to start the VMware Tools installation.

6. Click Download and Install in the Software Updates window:

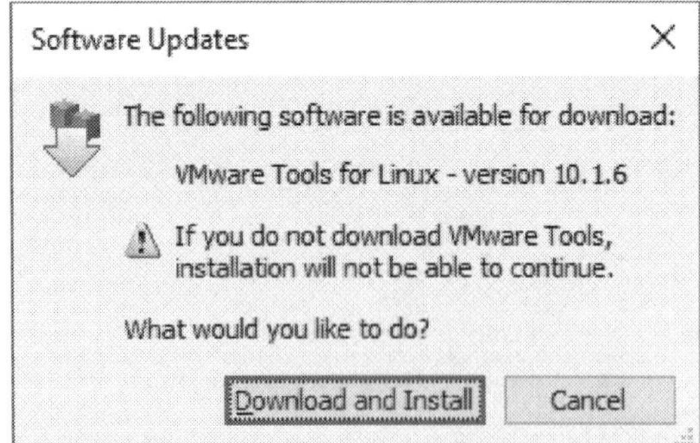

Figure 2-27 *Download VMware Tools*

7. The VMware Tools virtual CD-ROM image should be mounted after the download finishes.

8. Find out the *mount* directory location by running the *mount* command:

```
bob@ubuntu:~$ mount
sysfs on /sys type sysfs (rw,nosuid,nodev,noexec,relatime)
proc on /proc type proc (rw,nosuid,nodev,noexec,relatime)
...
output shortened for clarity
...
fusectl on /sys/fs/fuse/connections type fusectl (rw,relatime)
/dev/sr0 on /media/bob/VMware Tools type iso9660
(ro,nosuid,nodev,relatime,uid=1000,gid=1000,iocharset=utf8,mode=0400,dmode=0500,uhelper=udisks2)
```

In my case, the directory has been mounted at */media/bob/VMware Tools*.

List the content of the mount directory using the *ls -l* command:

```
bob@ubuntu:~$ ls -l /media/bob/VMware\ Tools/
total 56377
-r-xr-xr-x 1 bob bob     1975 Mar 17 07:10 manifest.txt
-r-xr-xr-x 1 bob bob     2287 Mar 17 07:07 run_upgrader.sh
-r--r--r-- 1 bob bob 56072885 Mar 17 07:11 VMwareTools-10.1.6-5214329.tar.gz
-r-xr-xr-x 1 bob bob   802620 Mar 17 07:08 vmware-tools-upgrader-32
-r-xr-xr-x 1 bob bob   848816 Mar 17 07:08 vmware-tools-upgrader-64
```

9. Create the *tmp* directory and enter it:

```
bob@ubuntu:~$ mkdir /tmp/vmtools
bob@ubuntu:~$
bob@ubuntu:~$ cd /tmp/vmtools
```

10. Uncompress the installer using the following command:

```
tar zxpf /PATH/VMWARE_TOOLS_VERSION
```

In my case, the command looks like this:

```
bob@ubuntu:/tmp/vmtools$ sudo tar zxpf /media/bob/VMware\ Tools/VMwareTools-10.1.6-5214329.tar.gz
[sudo] password for bob:
```

11. Enter the *vmware-tools-distrib* directory and run the Perl installer:

```
bob@ubuntu:/tmp/vmtools/vmware-tools-distrib$ sudo ./vmware-install.pl
```

12. The installer will ask you a series of questions. In most cases, it is recommended to keep the default values by simply pressing Enter.

13. Once the installation finish, reboot the virtual machine in order for the installation of VMware Tools to take full effect.

Summary

In this chapter you've learned how to create your own virtual machine and install a guest operating system in it. I've showed you how to use the Easy Install feature to automatically install a guest OS. We've then discussed VMware Tools and how to install this set of drivers to a VM running Windows or Linux.

In the next chapter we will various features Player offers - Suspend, Drag-and-Drop, Copy and Paste, and Shared Folders, I will also explain how to use Unity Mode to display applications from virtual machines directly on the host system desktop.

This page intentionally left blank

This page intentionally left blank

Chapter 3 - Using virtual machines

IN THIS CHAPTER

- **Starting and stopping virtual machines**
- **Working with the Drag-and-Drop and Copy/Paste features**
- **Transferring files using shared folders**
- **Using Unity mode**
- **Connecting USB devices to a VM**

This is the chapter in which we are going to do some real work with our virtual machines. I will show you a couple of cool features that Player has to offer, such as copying files between your host system and a virtual machine using drag-and-drop, using shared folders to share files between virtual machines and the host system, and how to use Unity Mode to display applications from virtual machines directly on the host system desktop.

Start a virtual machine

The library on the left site of the VMware Workstation Player window is populated with virtual machines you've created. To start a virtual machine, simply select a virtual machine from the library and click **Play virtual machine**:

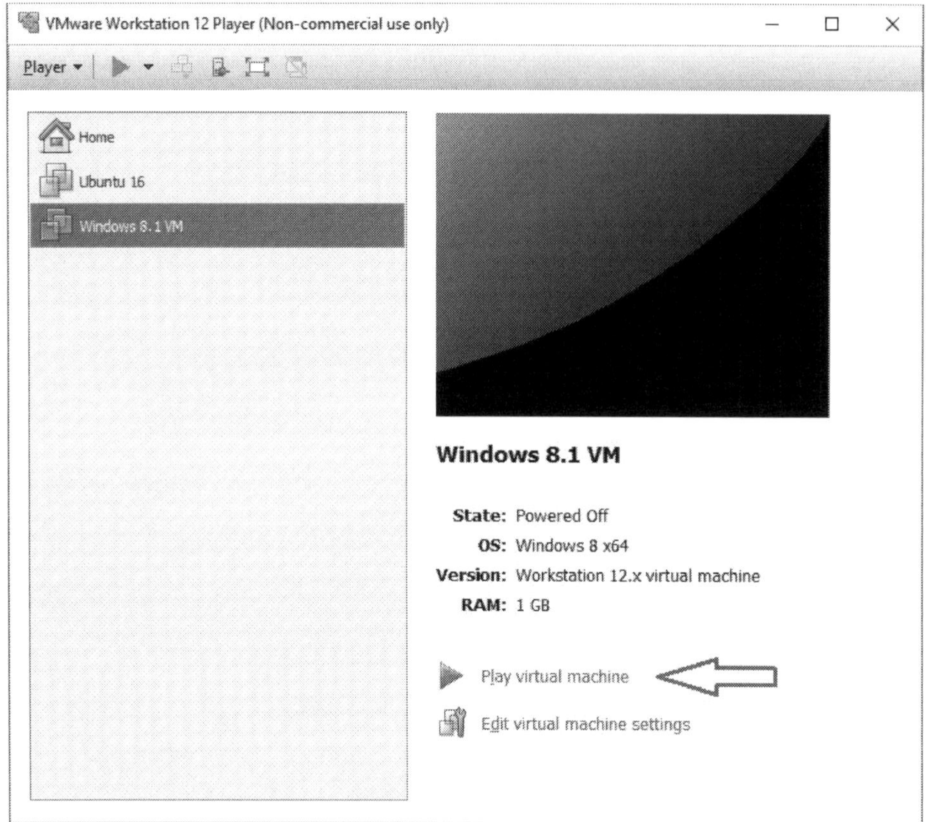

Figure 3-1 *Play virtual machine*

If the virtual machine you've created is not listed in the library, select Player > File > Open. Browse to the virtual machine configuration (.vmx) file, and click Open:
Once you start a VM, click inside the virtual machine console to give the virtual machine control of the mouse and keyboard of the host system. To release the input from the virtual machine and return the control to the host system, use the *Ctrl+Alt* hotkey. To send the *Ctrl-Alt-Delete* keystroke combination to a virtual machine, select **Player > Send Ctrl+Alt+Del**:

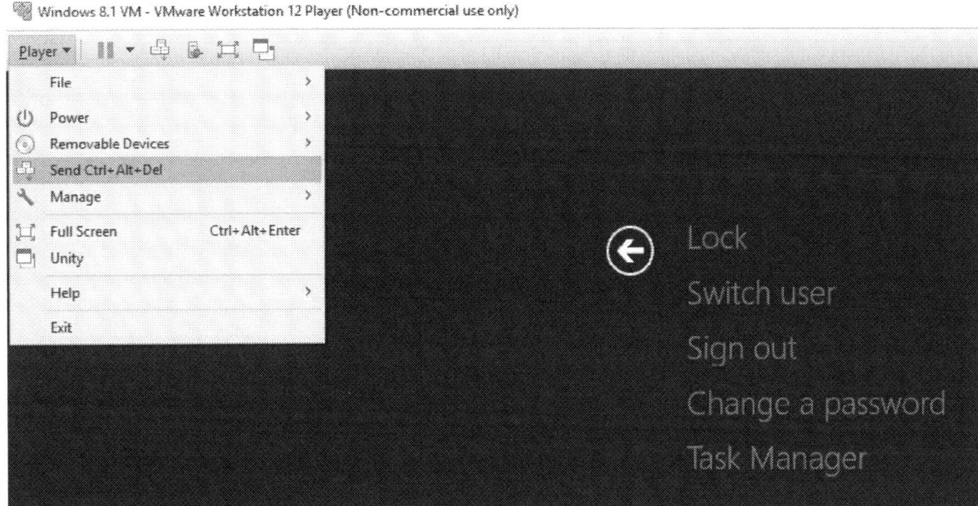

Figure 3-3 *Send Ctrl+Alt+Del to the VM*

Suspend a virtual machine

You can save the current state of a virtual machine by suspending it. The suspend feature is useful when you want to save the current state of the virtual machine, and resume your work later from the same state. All documents and applications you were working on will be in the same state as they were at the time you suspended the virtual machine.

To suspend a virtual machine, choose Player > Power > Suspend Guest:

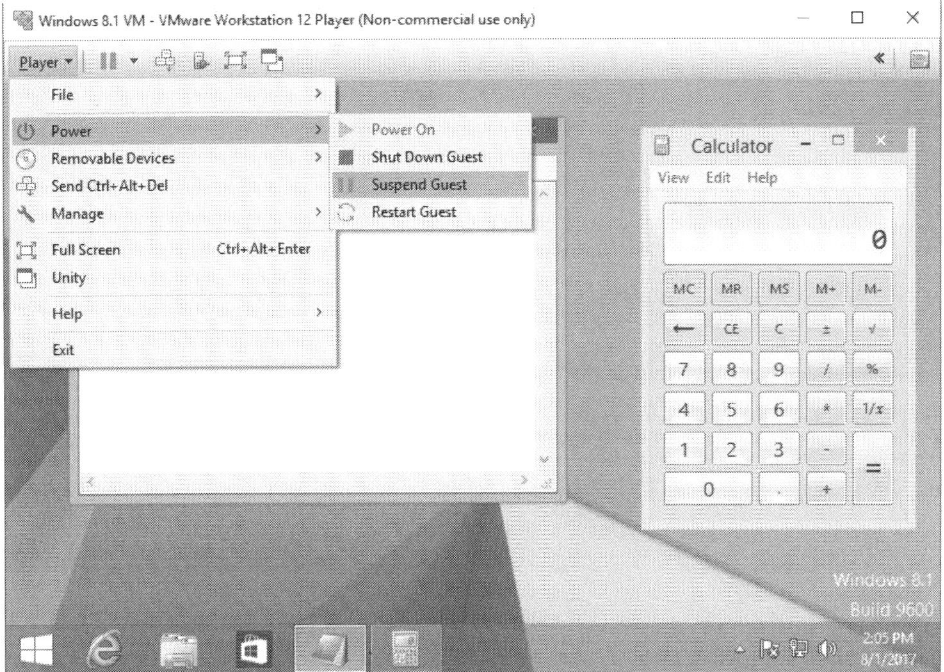

Figure 3-4 *Suspending a VM*

In the warning window that opens, choose Yes:

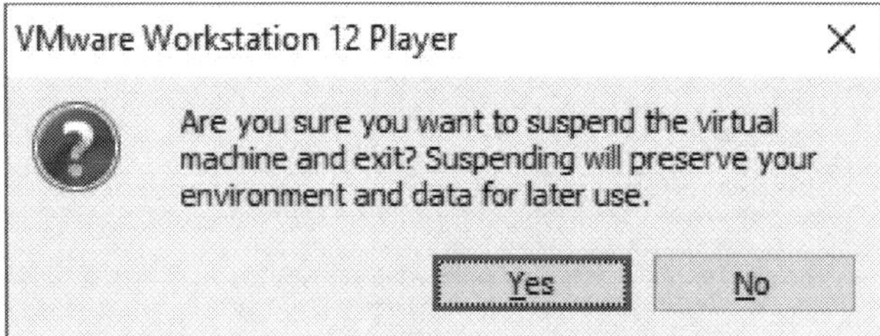

Figure 3-5 *Confirm VM suspension*

You can now exit Player and even turn off your computer. The state of a suspended virtual machine is stored in a file with a *.vmss* extension. When the virtual machine is resumed, its state is restored from this file.

To resume a suspended virtual machine, select the suspended virtual machine from the library and click Play virtual machine:

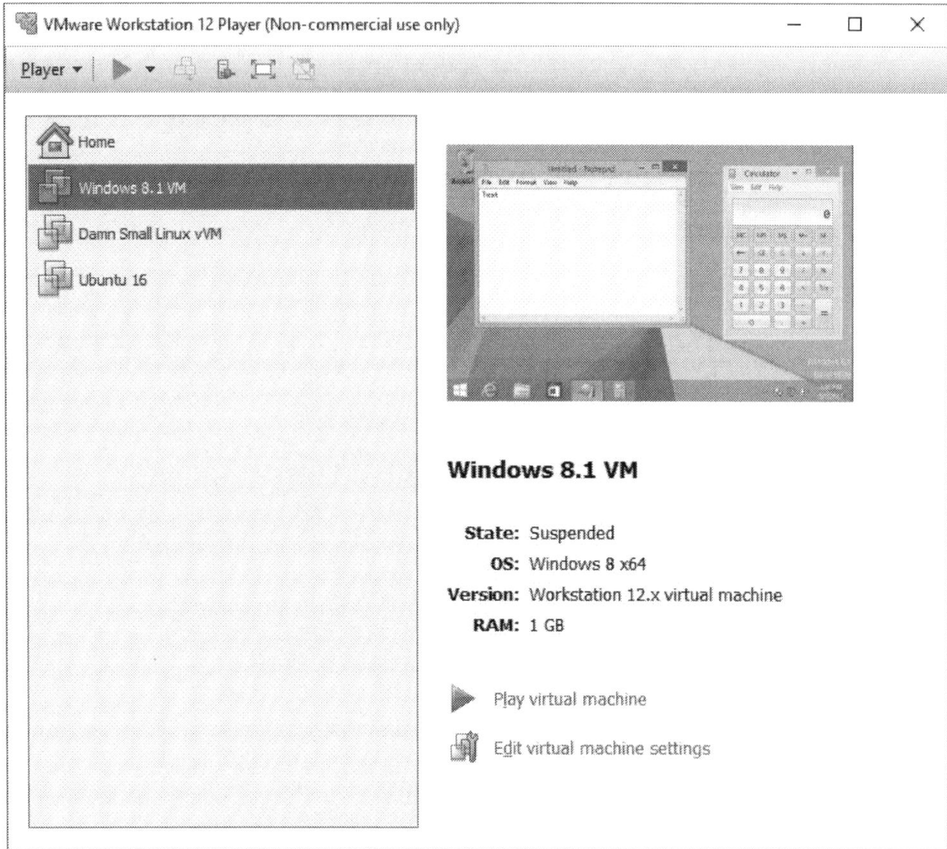

Figure 3-6 *Resume a suspended VM*

The resumed VM will be in the same state as before the suspend operation:

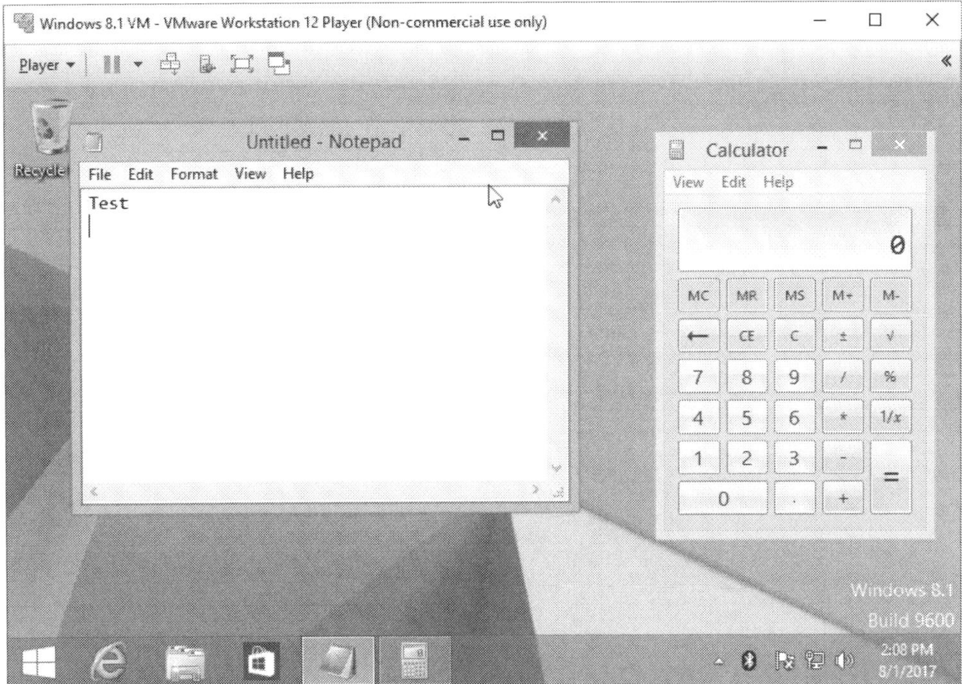

Figure 3-7 *Resumed VM*

NOTE
The speed of the suspend and resume operations depends on how much data changed after you started the virtual machine. The first suspend operation usually takes a bit longer than the subsequent suspend operations do.

Drag-and-Drop feature

The **Drag-and-Drop** feature in VMware Workstation Player enables you to easily move files between the host system and virtual machines. You can move files, directories, email attachments, plain or formatted text, and images using a simple drag-and-drop operation.

The Drag-and-drop feature has the following requirements:

- VMware Tools must be installed.
- Linux hosts and guests must run X-Windows. Solaris 10 guests must run run an Xorg server and JDS/Gnome.
- images can be dragged only between applications on Windows hosts and applications on Windows guests. Linux hosts or guests don't support image dragging.
- you can only drag email attachments smaller than 4MB.
- you can only drag text smaller than 4MB.
- you can drag Unicode text only.

When you drag a file between the host and a virtual machine, VMware Workstation Player copies the file to the location where you drop it. In the example below I've dragged a text file called *important.txt* to from Windows 10 (the host system) to a virtual machine running Windows 8.1 (the guest OS):

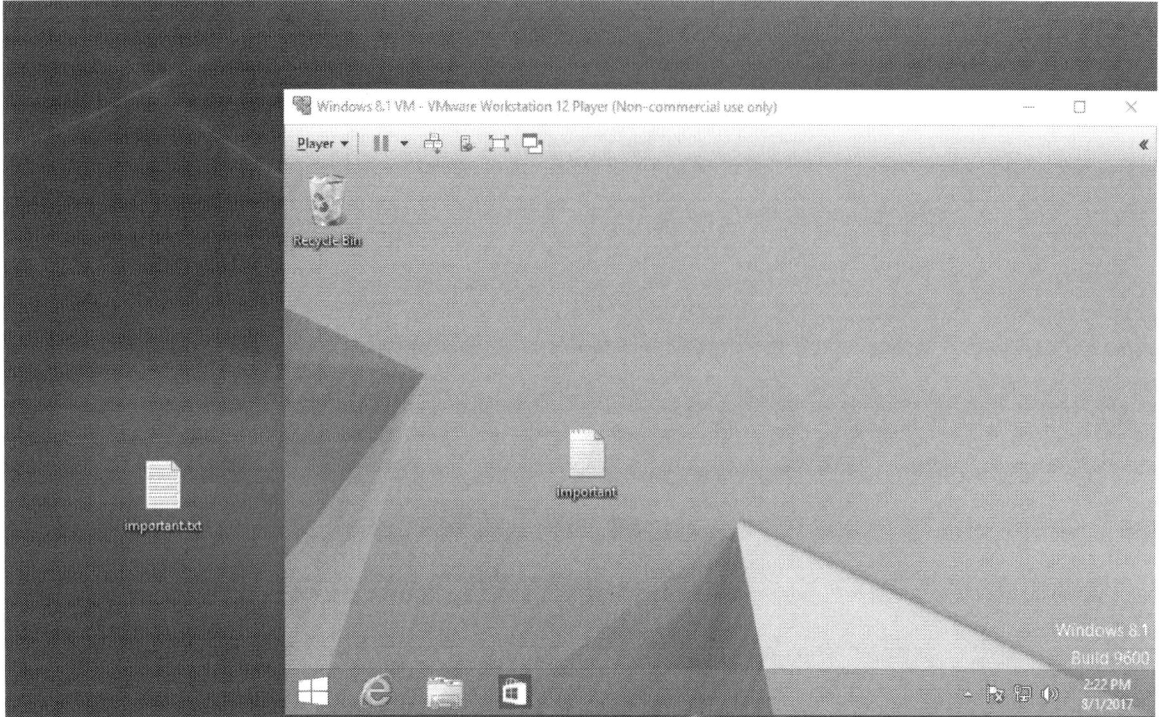

Figure 3-8 *Dragging a file in Player*

NOTE
The file that was dragged will not be deleted from the original location. Any changes made to the copied file will not be reflected to the original file.

Copy and Paste feature

You can cut, copy, and paste text, images, email attachments and other types of files between applications running on the host system and applications running in a virtual machine.

The Copy and Paste feature has the following requirements:

- VMware Tools must be installed in a virtual machine.
- this feature works only with Linux and Windows host systems and Linux, Windows, and Solaris 10 guests.
- Linux hosts and guests must run X-Windows. Solaris 10 guests must run run an Xorg server and JDS/Gnome.
- you can only copy email attachments smaller than 4MB.

- you can only copy Unicode text smaller than 4MB.

You can use the usual hot keys or menu choices to cut, copy and paste. For example, here is how I can copy a file from the host system and paste it into the guest OS:

1. First, I will copy a file from the desktop of the host operating system:

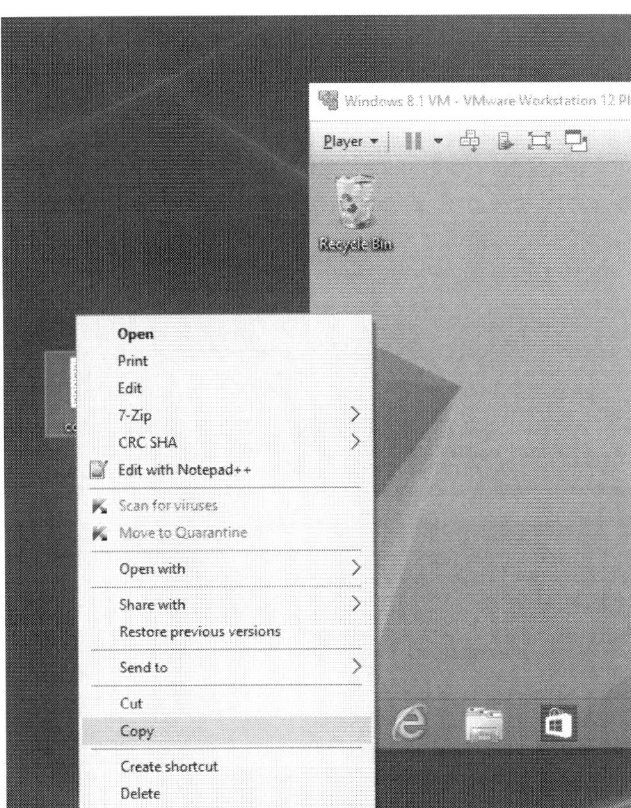

Figure 3-9 *Copying a file on the host OS*

2. Next, I can paste this file on the desktop of the guest operating system:

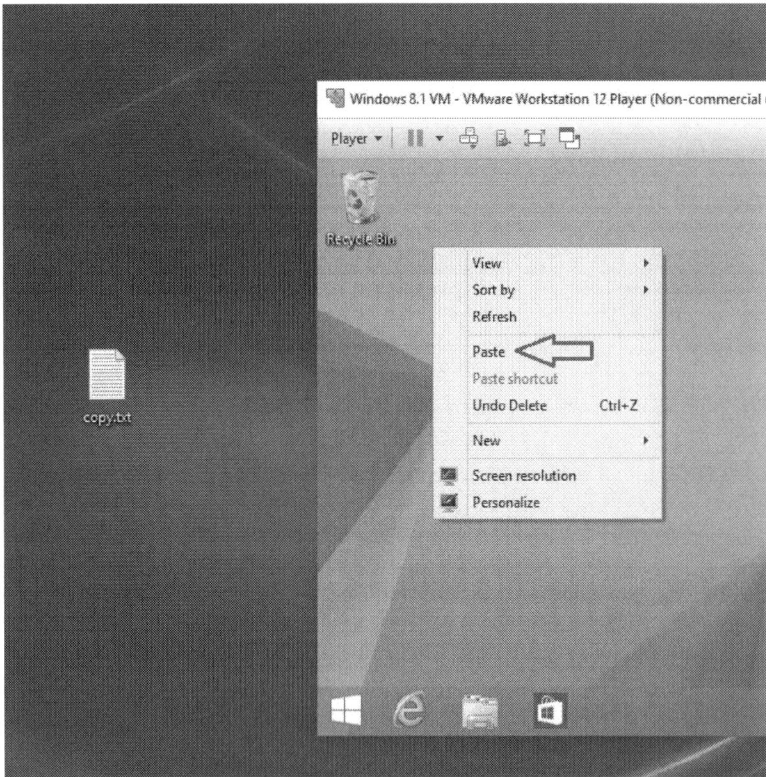

Figure 3-10 *Pasting a file into a VM*

3. The file has been copied to the guest OS:

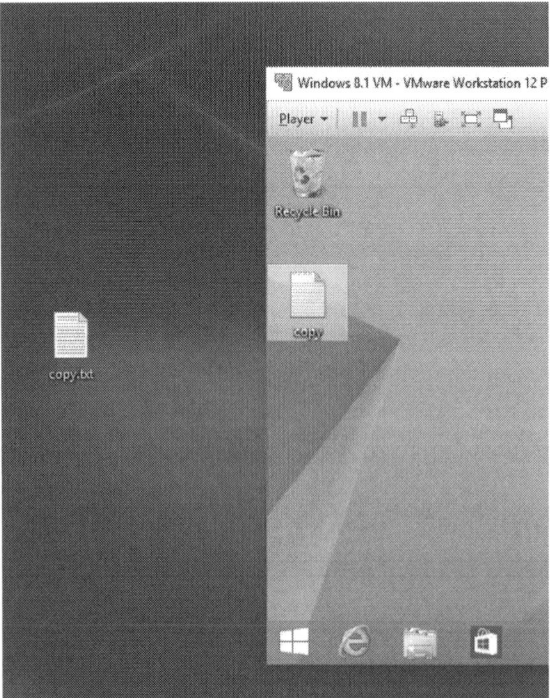

Figure 3-11 *The file has been copied*

NOTE
The same procedure can be used to copy text from the host OS to the guest OS and vice versa - simply copy the text from application in one operating system and paste it into the appropriate application running in the other.

Shared folders overview

Using **shared folders**, you can share files between virtual machines and the host system. The shared directories can be on the host system, or they can be network directories that are accessible from the host computer. Shared folders can save you a lot of time, especially when you are installing software that would otherwise take a long time to download - you can download the software only once on the host system, and then use shared folders to distribute the software to all the VMs in your environment.

To use shared folders, you must install VMware Tools in the guest operating system, specify which directories are to be shared, and use one of the following supported guest operating systems:

- Windows Server 2003 R2
- Windows Server 2008 R2
- Windows Server 2012 R2
- Windows Vista
- Windows 7, Windows 8, Windows 10
- Linux with a kernel version of 2.6 or later
- Solaris x86 10

Enable a shared folder for a virtual machine

You can enable shared folders for a specific virtual machine. Here are the steps:

1. Choose the virtual machine and select Player > Manage > Virtual Machine Settings.

2. Go to the Options tab and select the **Shared Folders** option:

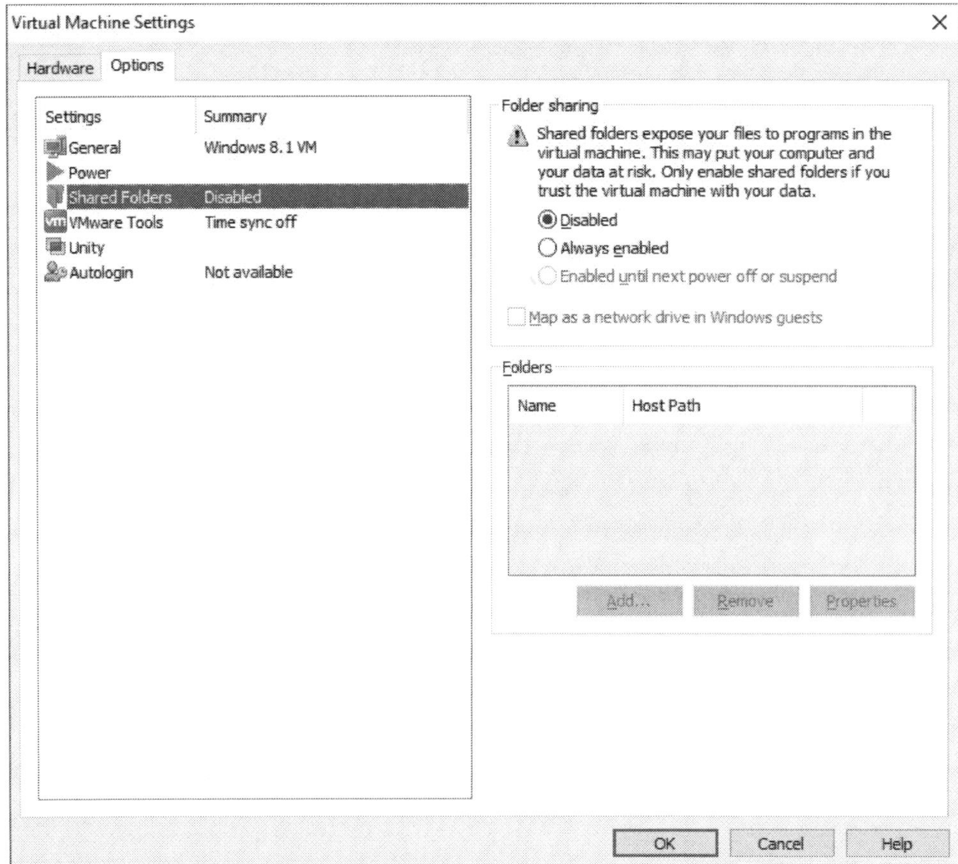

Figure 3-12 *Folder sharing options*

3. Under Folder sharing, choose a sharing option. Besides the **Disabled** option, two other options are available:

- **Always enabled** - keeps folder sharing enabled, even when the virtual machine is shut down, suspended, or powered off. Use this option if you want the files on the shared folder to be always accessible.
- **Enabled until next power off or suspend** - enables folder sharing temporarily, until the virtual machine is shut down, suspended, or powered off. Note that if the guest operating system is restarted, shared folders will remain enabled. This option is grayed out in the picture above because the VM is currently not running.

4. (Optional) You can also map the drive to the Shared Folders directory that contains all shared folders. To do that, select the **Map as a network drive in Windows guests** option. This option is described in more detail in the next section.

5. Click Add to add a share folder:

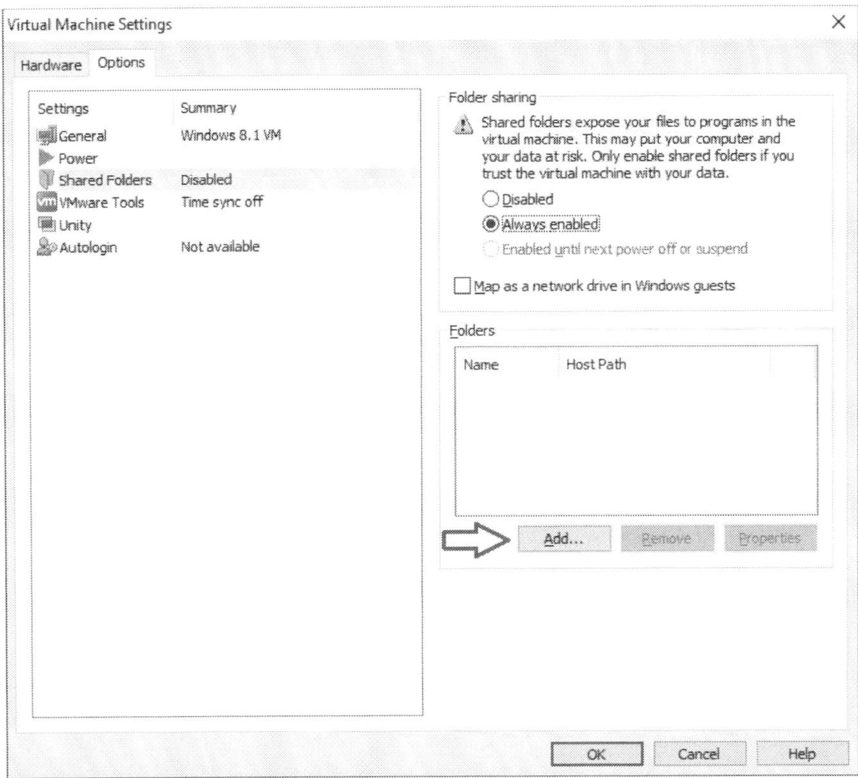

Figure 3-13 *Add shared folder*

6. The Add Shared Folder Wizard opens. Click Next to Continue:

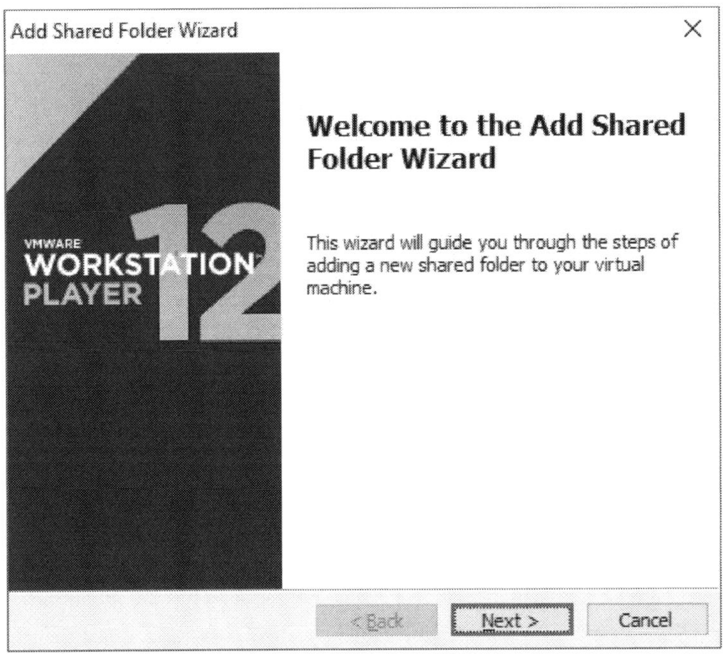

Figure 3-14 *Shared folder wizard Welcome screen*

7. Type the path on the host system to the directory you want to share and specify the name under which the folder will appear inside the virtual machine:

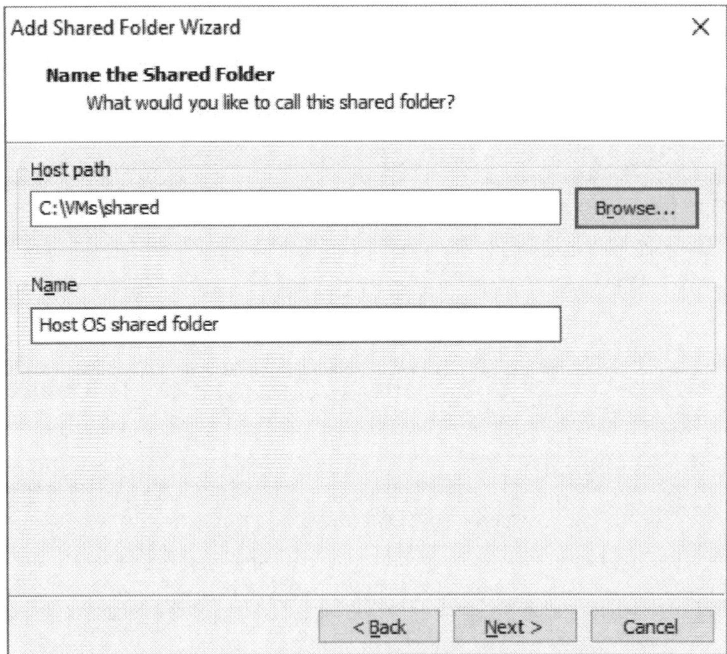

Figure 3-15 *Type the shared folder path and name*

8. Select the shared folder options:

- **Enable this share** - enables the shared folder. Deselect this option when you want to disable the shared folder without deleting it from the virtual machine configuration.
- **Read-only** - makes the shared folder read-only. The virtual machine users can view and copy files from the shared folder, but they cannot add, change, or remove files.

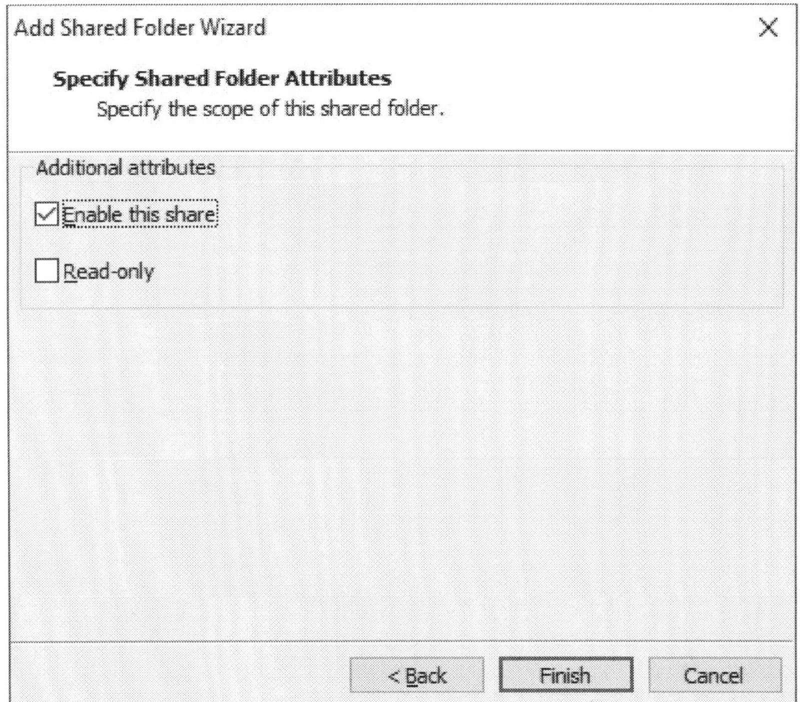

Figure 3-16 *Choose shared folder options*

9. Click Finish to finish adding the shared folder.

Access a shared folder

The way in which a shared folder can be accessed from the VM depending on the guest operating system type and version. To view a shared folder in a Windows guest OS, go to File Explorer > Network. You should see a list of computer available on the network, including a computer called **vmware-host**:

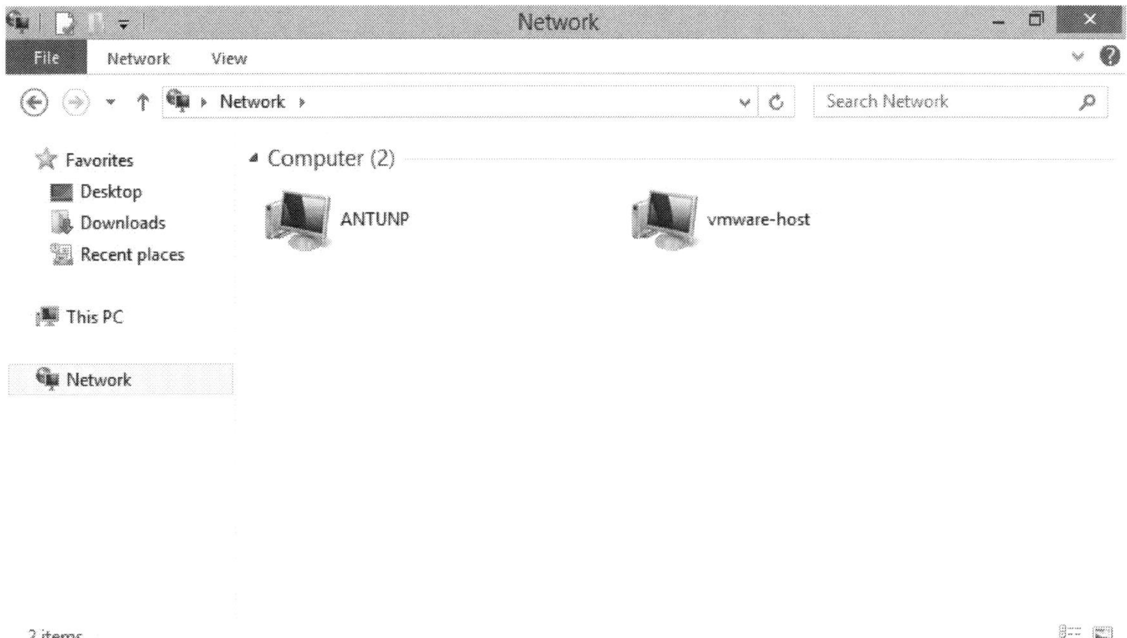

Figure 3-17 *List of computers in my network*

Double click **vmware-host** and browse to the shared folder:

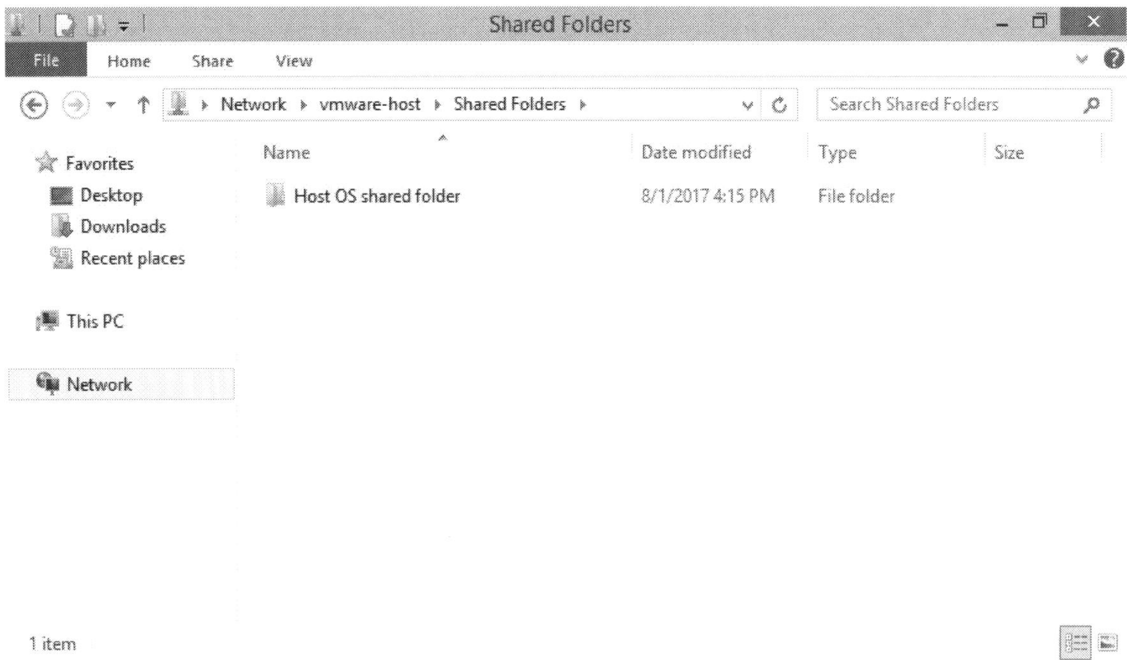

Figure 3-18 *View shared folder*

You can also go directly to the shared folder by using its UNC path:

Figure 3-19 *Accessing shared folder using its UNC path*

In a Linux virtual machine, shared folders usually appear under the */mnt/hgfs* directory:

```
bob@ubuntu:~$ cd /mnt/hgfs/
bob@ubuntu:/mnt/hgfs$ ls
Host OS shared folder
```

NOTE
Do not open a file stored in a shared folder in more than one application at once! For example, do not open the same file in an application on the host operating system and in another application in the guest operating system. If either of the applications writes to the file, data might become corrupted.

Map the shared folder as a network drive

In the last lesson, when we enabled shared folders, there was an option **Map as a network drive in Windows guests** under the Shared Folders menu. When enabled, this option allows you to display the shared folder in File Explorer in Windows, so you don't have to look for it or type its network address each time.

You can enable this option by going to Virtual Machine Settings > Options > Shared Folders tab:

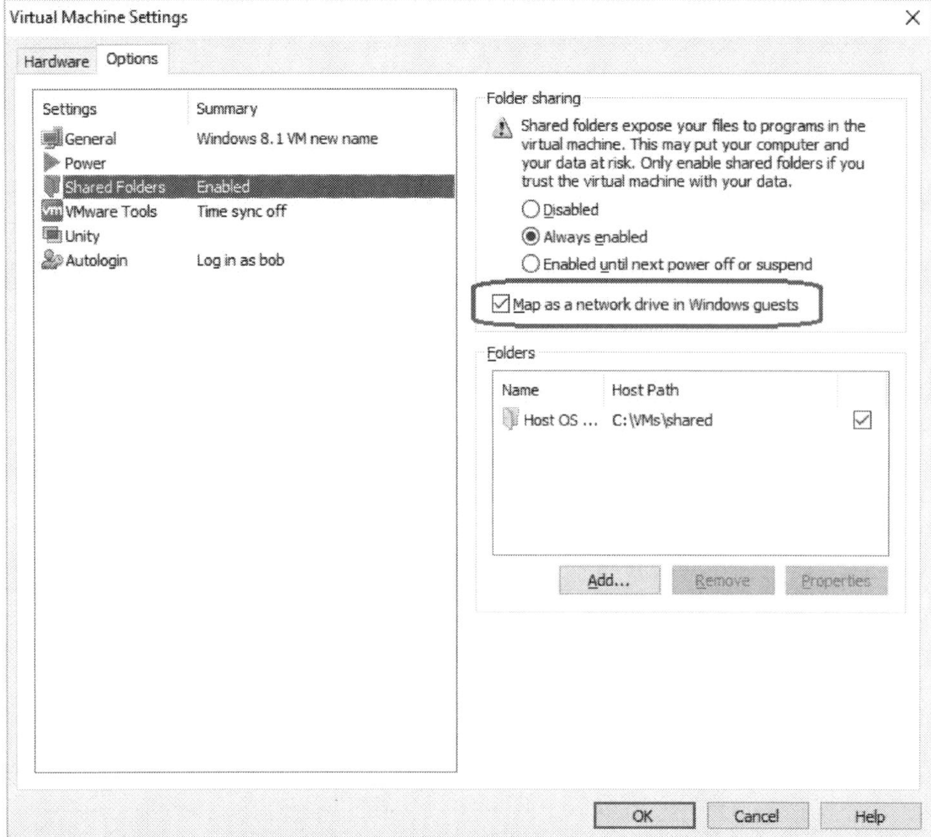

Figure 3-20 *Mapping the shared folder as a network drive*

Once this option is enabled, you should see the shared folder mapped to a drive letter in your Windows guest operating system:

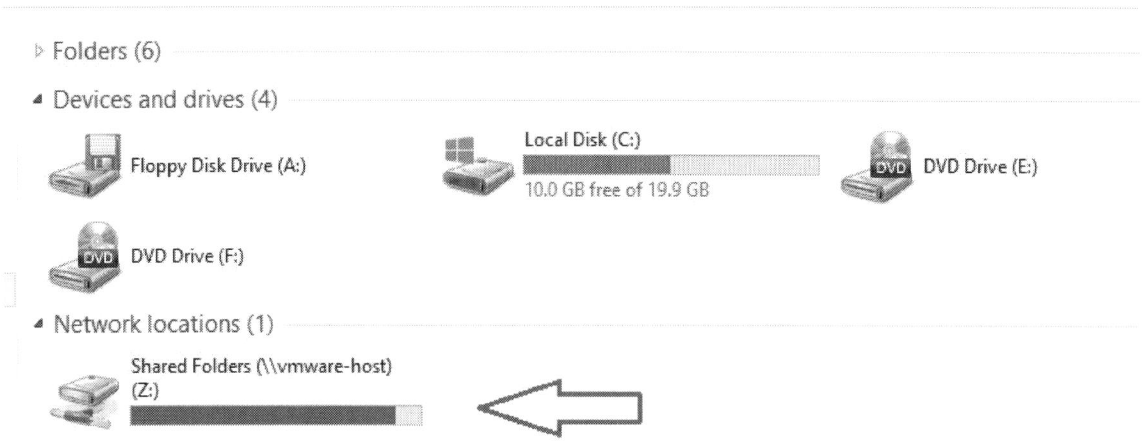

Figure 3-21 *Shared folder mapped as a network drive*

Connect or disconnect a USB device to a virtual machine

You've probably noticed that you can connect and disconnect USB devices to a virtual machine in Player. If you plug an USB device into the host system while a virtual machine is running and its window is the active window, the device should connect to the virtual machine instead of the host system.

When an USB device connected to the host system does not connect to a virtual machine at power on, you can manually connect it to the VM. Here are the steps:

1. Make sure that the virtual machine is powered on.

2. Select Player > Removable Devices. You should get a list of removable devices. Select the removable device and click **Connect (Disconnect from host)**:

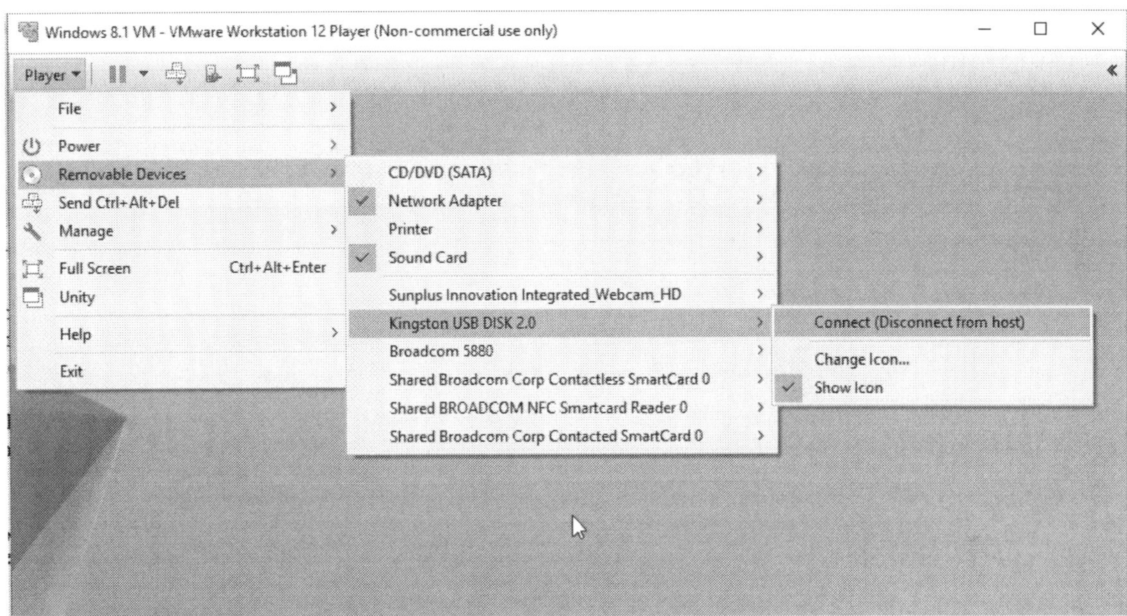

Figure 3-22 *Connecting USB device to VM*

3. The USB device should now appear in a guest OS:

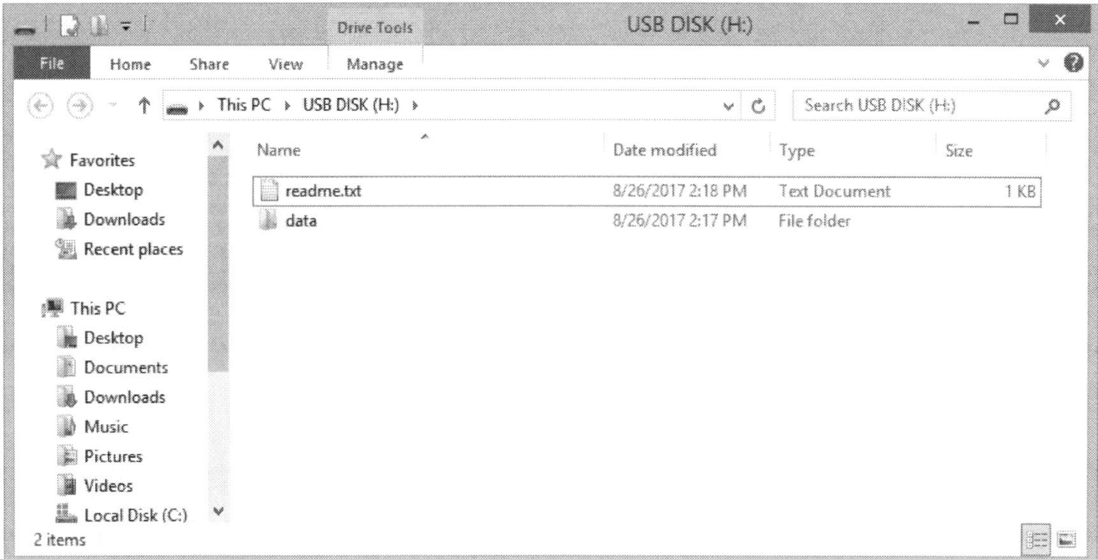

Figure 3-23 *USB drive in a VM*

4. To disconnect a removable device from the VM and connect it back to the host system, repeat the process, but this time, select the **Disconnect (Connect to host)** option:

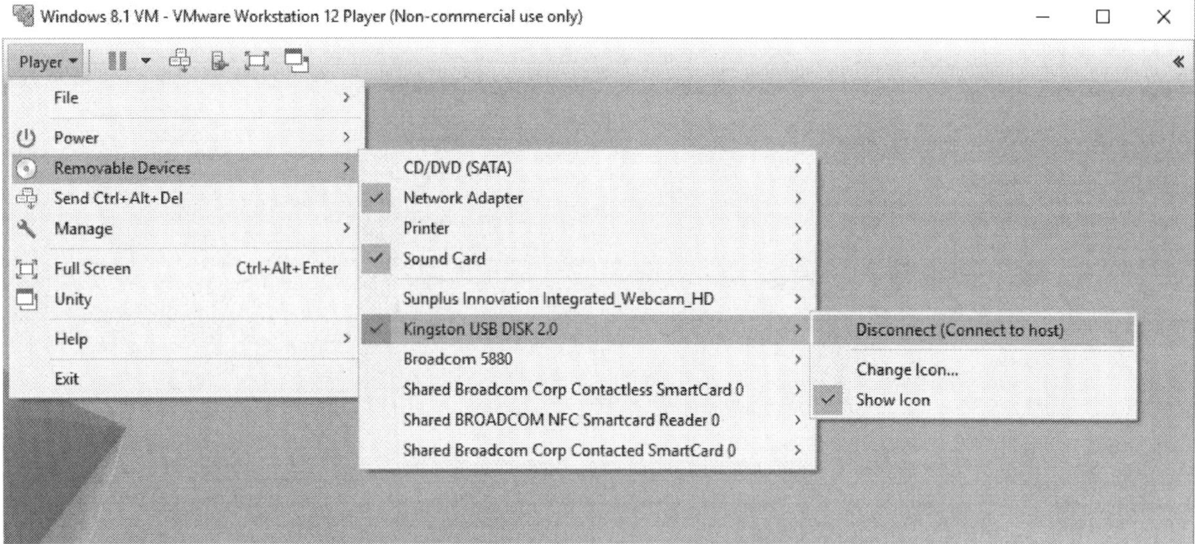

Figure 3-24 *Disconnect USB device from VM*

You can also connect or disconnect the device by right-clicking the device icon on the virtual machine taskbar:

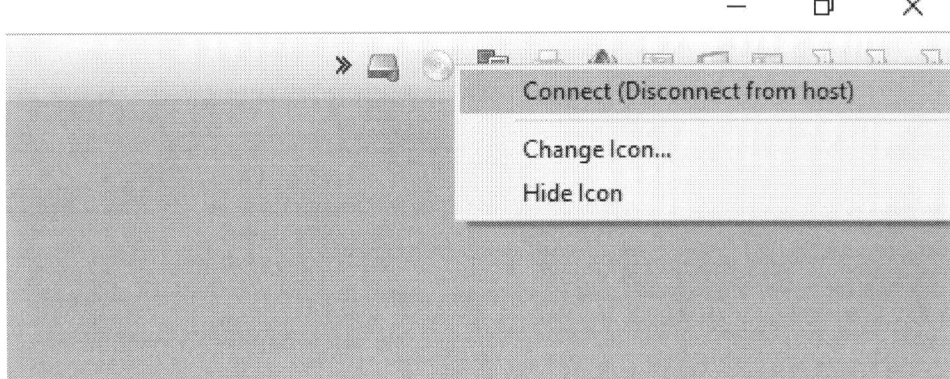

Figure 3-25 *Connect or disconnect USB devices using taskbar icons*

Choose what happens when you connect USB devices

By default, when you plug a new USB device into your host system and the VM has focus, the USB device will automatically connect to the VM, and not to the host system. If you don't want this to happen and want to keep control of the USB device in your host system, you can disable this autoconnect feature. Note that this is a per-VM feature, so you have to change it for each VM individually.

Here are the steps:

1. Make sure that the virtual machine is powered off.

2. Select the virtual machine from the library in Player and select Player > Manage > Virtual Machine Settings.

3. Select USB Controller under the Hardware tab and clear the checkbox next to **Automatically connect new USB devices**:

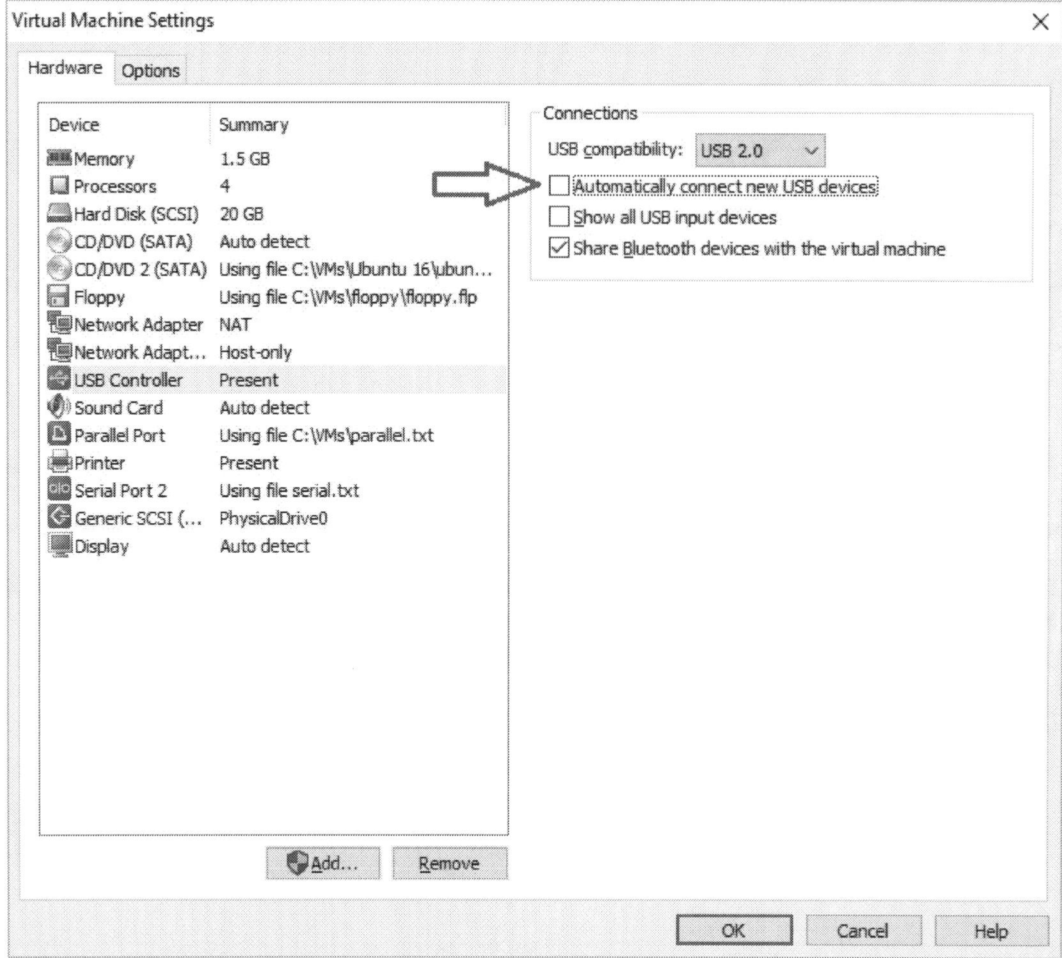

Figure 3-26 *Disabling the autoconnect feature*

Connect USB HIDs to a virtual machine

By default, USB HIDs (human interface devices), such as USB keyboards, mice, or game controllers, do not appear in the Removable Devices menu in a virtual machine, even though they are connected to the USB ports on the host system. To connect these devices exclusively to a virtual machine, you must configure the virtual machine to show all USB devices in the Removable Devices menu.

Here are the steps:

1. Make sure that the virtual machine is powered off.

2. Select the virtual machine from the library in Player and select Player > Manage > Virtual Machine Settings.

3. On the Hardware tab, select USB Controller and check the **Show all USB input devices** checkbox on the right:

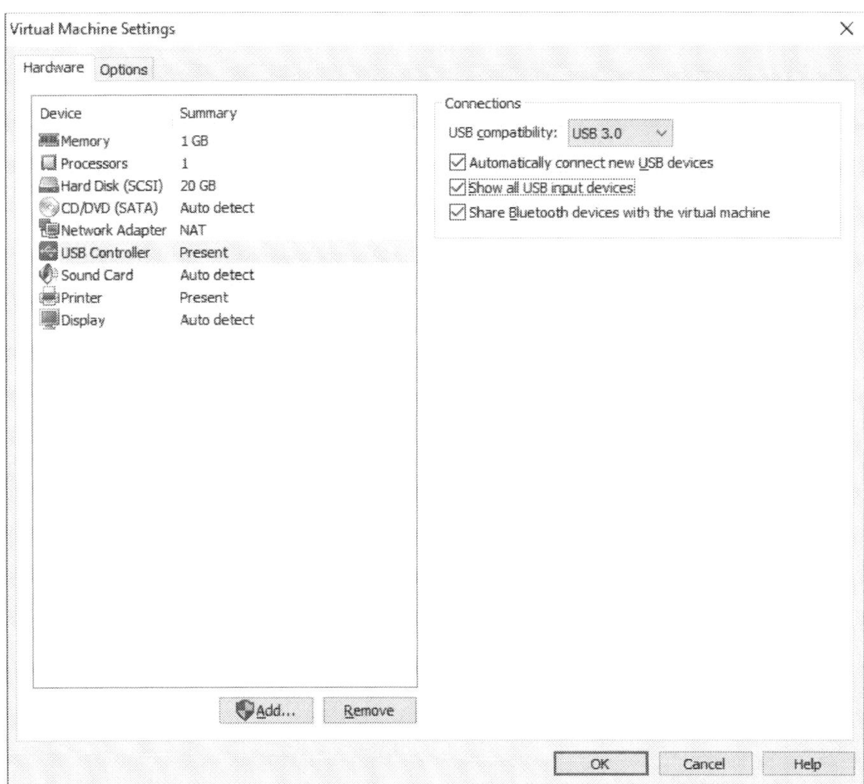

Figure 3-27 *Show USB HIDs*

4. USB human interface devices should appear in the Removable Devices menu after you power on the virtual machine:

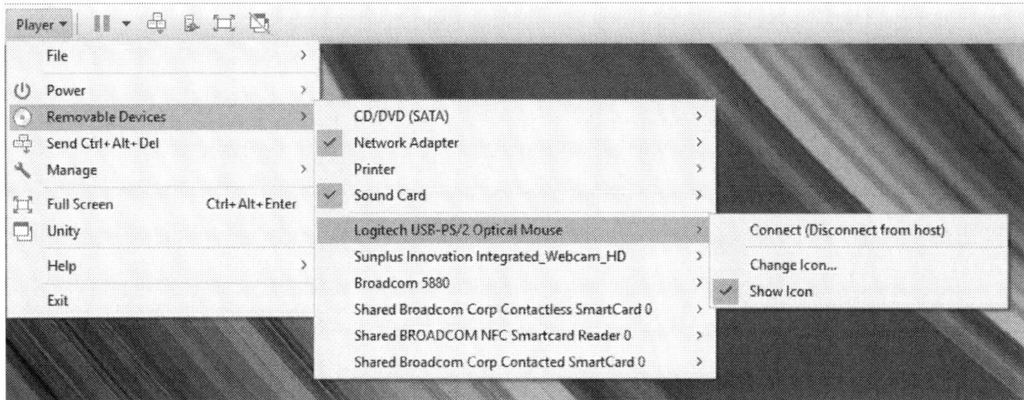

Figure 3-28 *USB HIDs now appear in under Removable Devices*

NOTE
An USB human interface device that is connected to a virtual machine is not available to the host system.

Unity Mode

Unity Mode enables you to display applications from a virtual machine directly on the host system desktop. You can access the VM's Start and Applications menus from the host system while the virtual machine console view is hidden. Items for open virtual machine applications are displayed on the host system taskbar in the same way as open host applications.

Unity Mode has the following requirements:

- virtual machine must be powered on.
- virtual machine must be a Player 3.x or later virtual machine.
- VMware Tools must be installed.
- the guest OS must be Linux or Windows 2000 or later.
- Linux guests and hosts must have a recent version of Metacity or KDE installed.

NOTE
When you save or open a file from an application in Unity Mode, the file system you see is the file system inside the virtual machine. You cannot open or save a file from the host operating system. You can, however, copy and paste files between the host and the guest operating system.

Enabling Unity Mode

Here is how you can enable Unity Mode in VMware Workstation Player:

1. Make sure that the virtual machine is powered on.

2. Select Player > Unity:

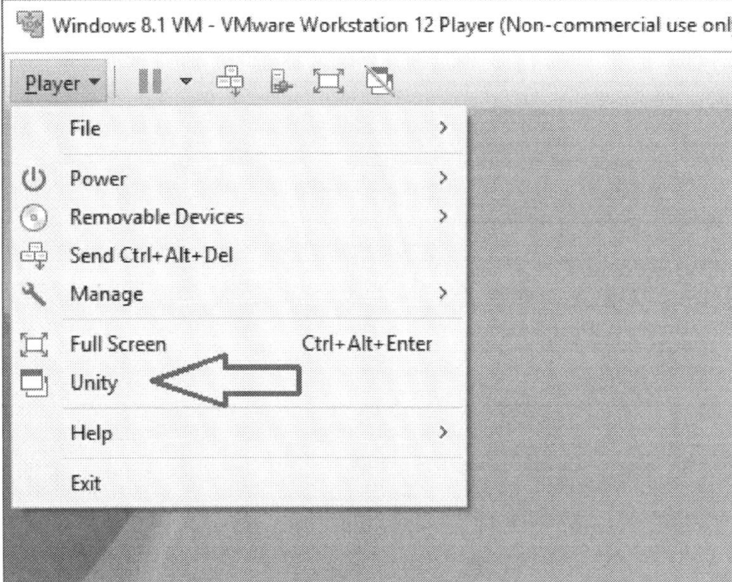

Figure 3-29 *Start Unity Mode*

3. The Player window should be hidden and applications opened in a VM should appear on the host system taskbar.

4. You can display the virtual machine Start menu on the host system by pointing to the Start menu:

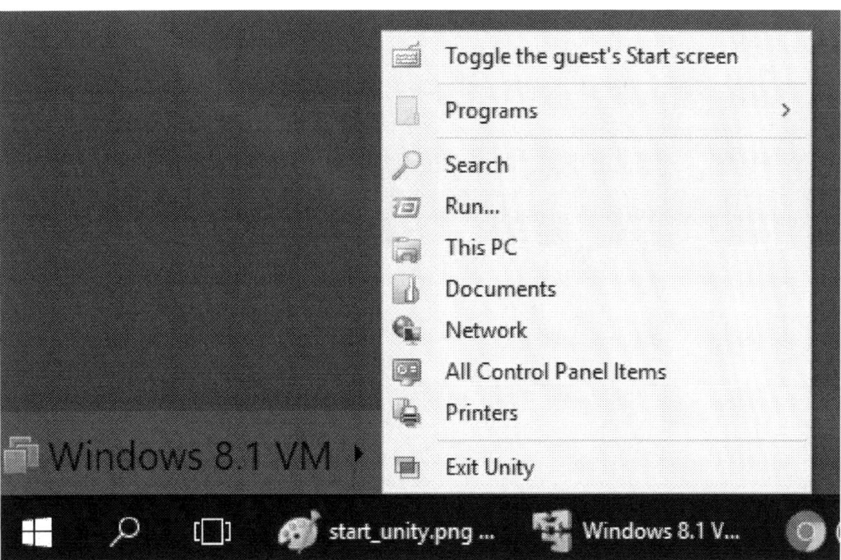

Figure 3-30 *VM's Start menu, accessed from the host system*

5. If you run an application from the virtual machine Start menu on the host system, the application will be displayed on the host system desktop:

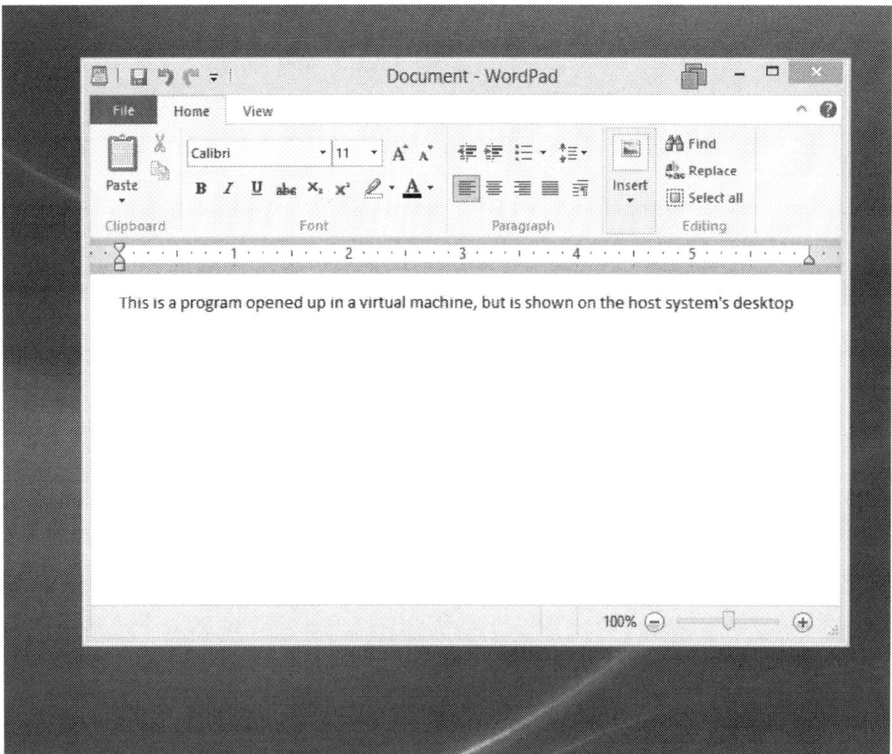

Figure 3-31 *Application in VM running in the host OS*

As you can see from the picture, I've run WordPad from the virtual machine Start menu on the host system. You can see that the WordPad window appears on the host system desktop, just like any other application.

NOTE

You can't open a file from the host operating system in the application in Unity Mode. Also, you can't save from an application in Unity mode to the host operating system - you can only save it on the guest OS filesystem.

6. To exit Unity Mode, display the Player window and click Exit Unity:

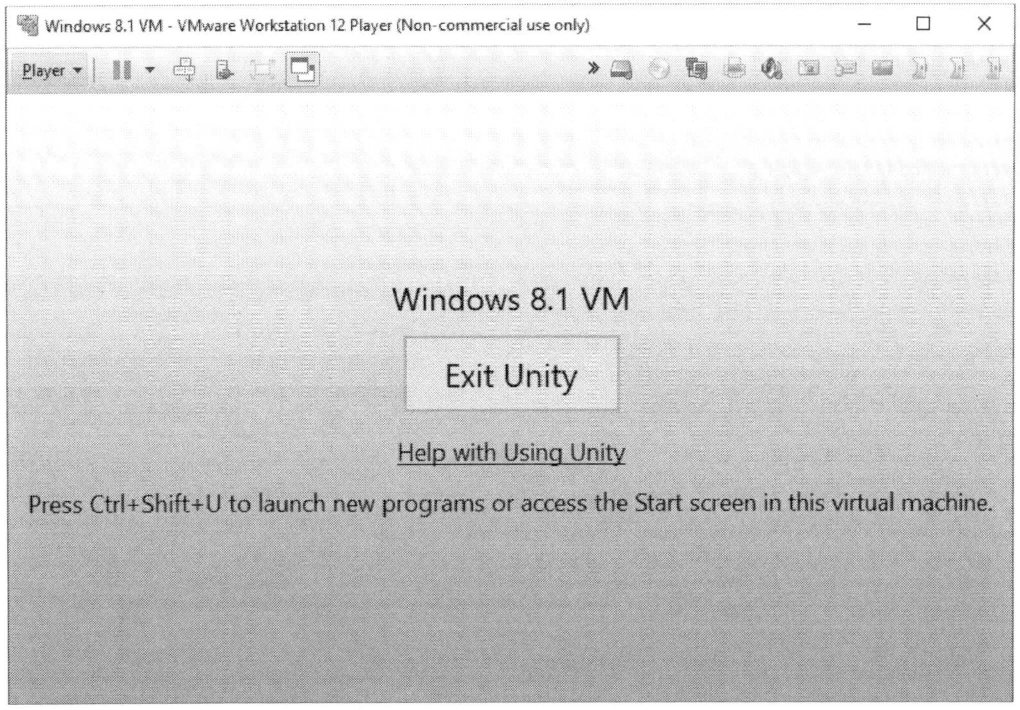

Figure 3-32 *Exit Unity Mode*

Summary

In this chapter we've gone through some of the features Player offers - Suspend, Drag-and-Drop, and Copy and Paste. You've learned how to transfer files between the host and guest operating systems using shared folders. I've then explained how you can use Unity Mode to display applications from virtual machines directly on the host system desktop.

In the next chapter you will learn how to change some basic properties of your VM, such as its name, working directory, and the guest OS version. We will also go through the process of allocating more RAM to a VM.

This page intentionally left blank

This page intentionally left blank

Chapter 4 - Managing virtual machines

IN THIS CHAPTER

Modifying VM properties

Adding more memory to a VM

Moving and deleting VMs

Viewing logs

In this chapter you will learn how to modify various properties of a virtual machine, such as its name, the working directory, and memory allocated to it. I will explain how you can move and run a virtual machine on another host system and how you can use log files to get more information about what is going on with your virtual machines.

Change the virtual machine name

You can change the name under which the virtual machine appear in Player. Here are the steps:

1. Select Player > Manage > Virtual Machine Settings.

2. Go to the Options tab and select General. On the right side of you screen you should see the **Virtual machine name** field. Enter the new virtual machine name and click OK:

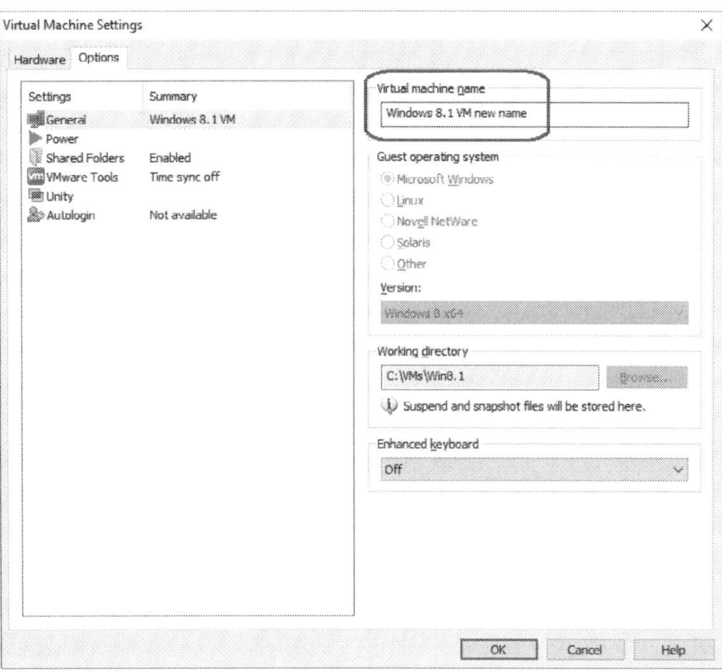

Figure 4-1 *Changing the VM name*

3. The VM should appear under the new name in the library:

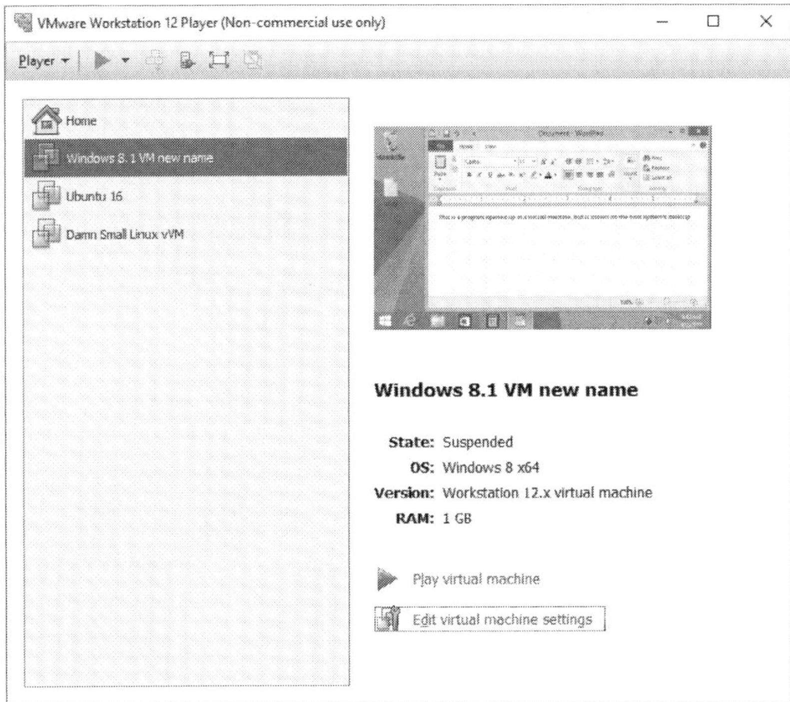

Figure 4-2 *VM appears under the new name in the library*

Note that changing the name of a virtual machine **does not** change the name of the virtual machine directory or the names of the virtual machine files on the host system. VM files retain the original name of the virtual machine:

This PC › OS (C:) › VMs › Win8.1 ›

Quick access, Downloads, Desktop, Documents, Pictures, OneDrive, This PC, Desktop, Documents, Downloads, Music, Pictures, Videos, OS (C:)

Name	Date modified
caches	2.8.2017. 9:28
Windows 8.1 VM.vmx.lck	2.8.2017. 10:15
vmware.log	2.8.2017. 9:43
vmware-0.log	2.8.2017. 9:19
vmware-1.log	1.8.2017. 17:07
vmware-2.log	1.8.2017. 17:01
Windows 8.1 VM.nvram	2.8.2017. 9:43
Windows 8.1 VM.vmdk	2.8.2017. 9:20
Windows 8.1 VM.vmsd	31.7.2017. 15:18
Windows 8.1 VM.vmx	2.8.2017. 10:17
Windows 8.1 VM.vmxf	31.7.2017. 16:27
Windows 8.1 VM-3a6473b5.vmem	1.8.2017. 17:03
Windows 8.1 VM-3a6473b5.vmss	2.8.2017. 9:43
Windows 8.1 VM-s001.vmdk	2.8.2017. 9:42
Windows 8.1 VM-s002.vmdk	2.8.2017. 9:42
Windows 8.1 VM-s003.vmdk	2.8.2017. 9:42

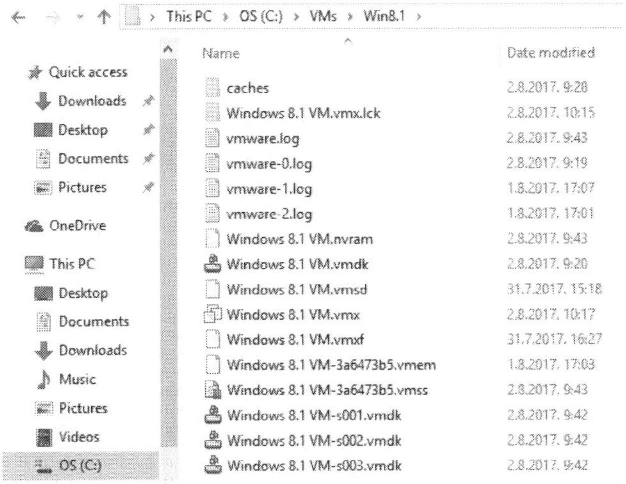

Figure 4-3 *Changing VM name doesn't change the names of the VM files*

Change the guest operating system version

The operating system version is specified when you create the virtual machine. If you've specified the wrong operating system version or you plan to upgrade the already installed guest operating system, you should change the guest operating system version.

Here are the steps:

1. Power off the virtual machine.

2. Select the virtual machine from the library and select Player > Manage > Virtual Machine Settings.

3. Go to the Options tab and select General. On the right side of you screen you should see the **Guest operating system** and **Version** menus. Select the new operating system or version and click OK:

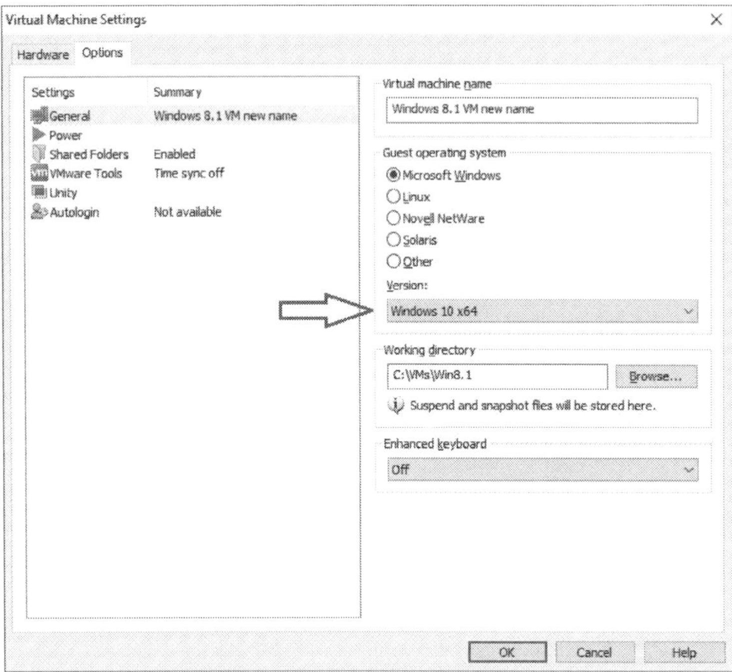

Figure 4-4 *Selecting the new OS version*

NOTE
When you change the operating system version, the virtual machine configuration file (.vmx) changes. Of course, the guest operating system itself does not change. To change the guest operating system, you need to install the new operating system in the virtual machine.

Change the working directory of a virtual machine

The VM's working directory is where Player stores the suspended state (*.vmss*), snapshot (*.vmsn*), virtual machine paging (*.vmem*), and redo log files for a virtual machine. By default, this directory is the same as where the virtual machine files are stored.

The working directory can be changed in order to improve system performance. For example, you can create a paging file on a fast disk that has a lot of disk space but leave the virtual disk and configuration file on a different disk.

Here are the steps to change the working directory of a virtual machine:

1. Power off the virtual machine.

2. Select the VM from the library and go to Player > Manage > Virtual Machine Settings.

3. Go to the Options tab and select General. Find the **Working directory** field:

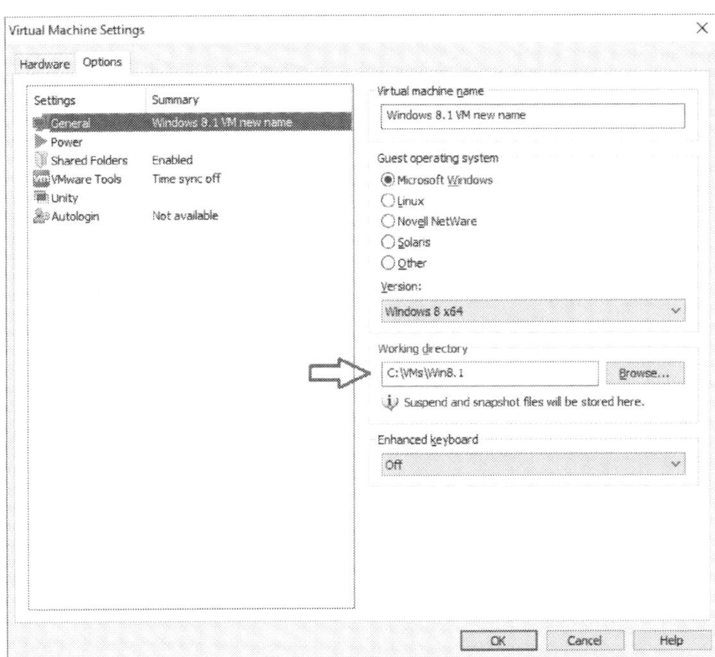

Figure 4-5 *Changing VM working directory*

4. Click Browse and choose the new working directory for your VM.

NOTE
Changing the working directory does not change the directory where the virtual machine configuration file (.vmx) or the log files are stored.

Change the memory allocation

You can adjust the amount of memory that is allocated to a virtual machine in Player. The guest operating system memory size should not be set lower than the minimum recommendations of the operating system provider. For example, because Windows 10 64-bit require at least 2 GB of RAM, you will need to allocate at least that amount of RAM to a virtual machine if you plan on running that operating system.

Let's say that my Windows 8.1 virtual machine is slow and I want to enhance its performance by adding more memory to it. Right now my VM has only 1 GB of RAM, so I need to add more memory to it:

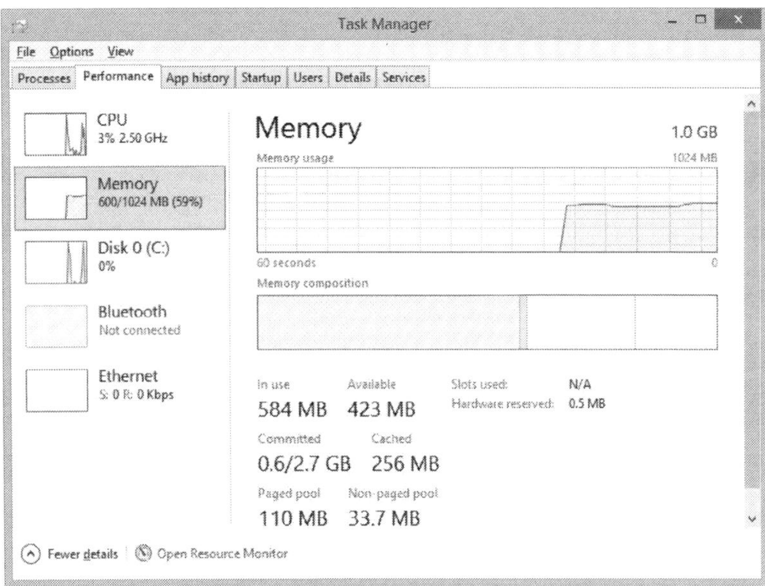

Figure 4-6 *Guest OS with low memory*

Here are the steps to adjust the amount of RAM a VM has:

1. Power off the VM.

2. Select the VM from the library and select Player > Manage > Virtual Machine Settings.

3. On the Hardware tab, select Memory. On the right side of the screen you will see the Memory panel with information that can help you select the appropriate amount of memory for the virtual machine. The size must be a multiple of 4:

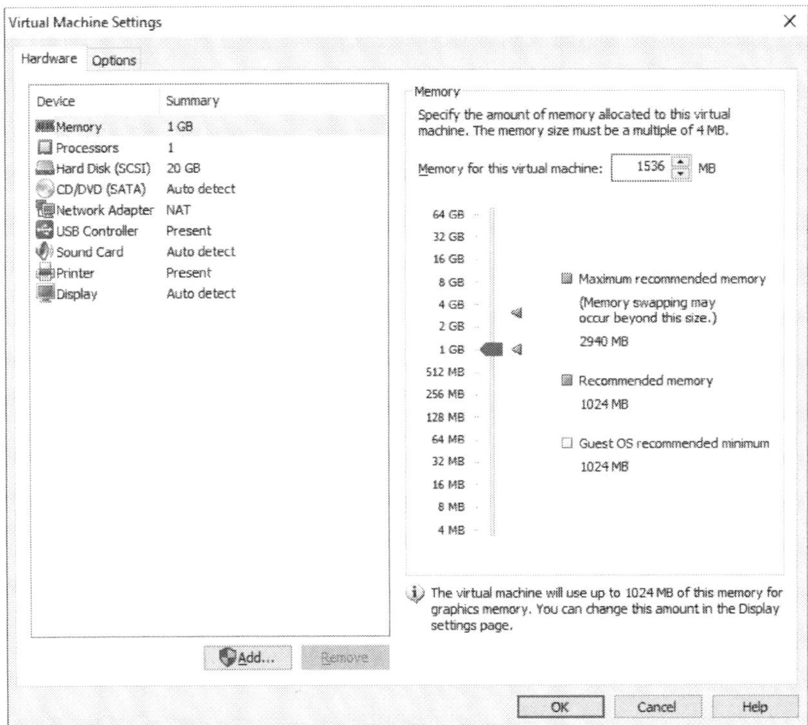

Figure 4-7 *Adjusting the memory for a VM*

4. Power on the VM in order for the changes to take effect. My VM now shows 1.5 GB of RAM:

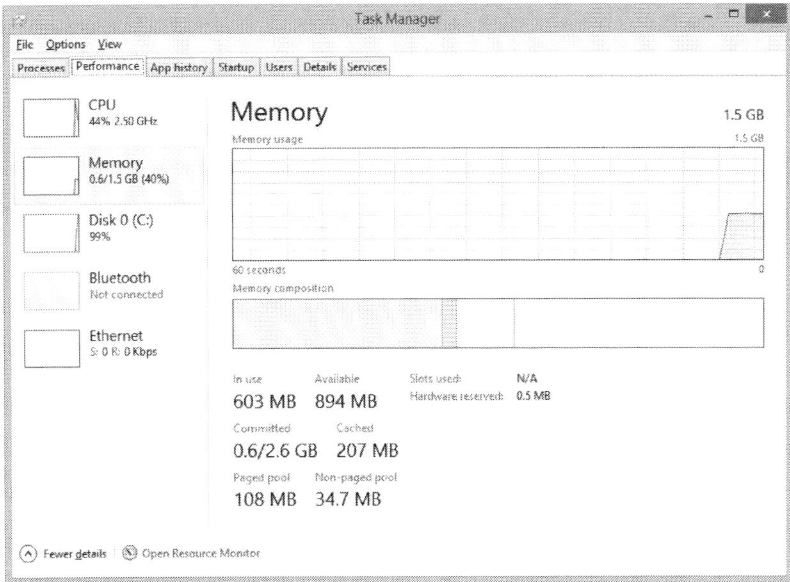

Figure 4-8 *Guest OS with additional memory allocated*

NOTE
On 64-bit host systems, the maximum amount of memory for each VM is 64GB. On 32-bit hosts, the maximum amount of memory for each VM is 8GB. There is no limit in VMware Workstation Player on the total amount of memory that you can assign to all virtual machines running on a single host system.

Move a virtual machine

You can move a virtual machine to a different location on the same host system or even to a different host system. Usually all files needed to run a virtual machine are stored into a single folder and can be moved quickly to another location. It is even possible to move a virtual machine to the host system that is running a different operating system.

There are certain things you need to be aware of before moving a virtual machine to a different host system:

- the virtual machine might not work correctly on the new host if the new host has significantly different hardware.
- you can move a virtual machine from a 32-bit host to a 64-bit host, but cannot move a virtual machine from a 64-bit host to a 32-bit host unless the 32-bit host has a supported 64-bit processor.
- when you move a virtual machine, Player generates a new MAC address for the virtual network adapter(s).

Here are the steps to move a virtual machine created in Player to a different host system:

1. Verify that all virtual machine files are stored in the same virtual machine directory, since some files might reside outside of the virtual machine directory. For example, if you configured the working directory to reside in a different location, you will need to move files from the working directory into the virtual machine directory and change the VM's working directory to this location.

2. Power off the virtual machine that you would like to move.

3. Copy the virtual machine files to the new location. In my example I will copy the virtual machine files from the *C:\VMs\Ubuntu 16* directory on the host system and move them to the *E:\VMs\Ubuntu 16* directory on another host system.

4. Open the virtual machine in VMware Workstation Player installed on the computer that the virtual machine has been moved to by selecting File > Open and browsing to the *<VM-name>.vmx* file in its new location:

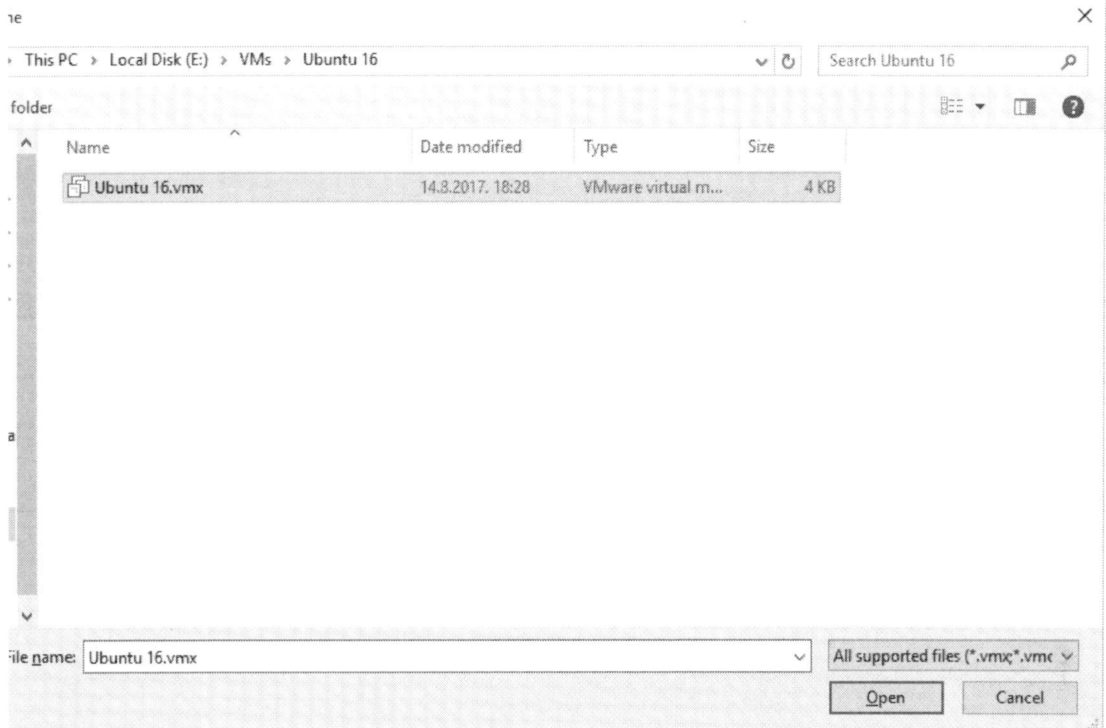

Figure 4-9 *Open VM in a new location*

5. Power on the virtual machine on the new host to make sure it is working correctly.

Configure a virtual machine for compatibility

Sometimes, you might want to create a virtual machine with the intention of distributing it to other users. It is recommended to configure the virtual machine for maximum compatibility with all expected host machines and systems.

Here is a list of recommendations that can help you configure virtual machines for maximum compatibility:

- install VMware Tools in the virtual machine.
- determine which virtual devices are actually required. Do not include virtual devices that are not needed for the software you are distributing with the virtual machine.
- if you want to connect a physical device to a virtual device, always use the **Auto detect** option when configuring the virtual machine. This option allows the virtual machine to adapt to the user's system, whether the host operating system is Windows or Linux.
- if you want to connect a CD-ROM to an image file that you ship with the virtual machine, make sure the image file is in the same directory as the virtual machine and make sure that

a relative path to access the image file is being used (e.g. use *images\windows8.iso* instead of *C:\images\windows8.iso*).

- choose a reasonable amount of memory to allocate to the virtual machine. If the user's host machine doesn't have enough physical memory to support the memory allocation, the user might not be able to power on the virtual machine.
- choose a reasonable screen resolution for the guest operating system.

Universal Unique Identifier (UUID)

Each virtual machine is automatically assigned a **universal unique identifier (UUID)**. The UUID is generated when you initially power on the virtual machine and ensures that the VM is properly identified. It is stored in the SMBIOS system information descriptor and can be accessed using standard the SMBIOS scanning software, such as SiSoftware Sandra, smbios2, or FirmwareTablesView.

The UUID will remain constant as long as the virtual machine is not moved or copied to another location. If you move or copy the virtual machine to another location, you will be prompted to specify whether you moved or copied the virtual machine the first time you power it on. If you specify that the virtual machine was copied, the virtual machine will receive a new UUID.

NOTE
Appendix D describes the process of finding the VM's UUID.

Configure a virtual machine to keep the same UUID

A virtual machine can be configured to always keep the same UUID, even when it is moved or copied. When you configure a virtual machine to keep the same UUID, you will not be prompted to specify whether you moved or copied the virtual machine the first time you power it on. Here are the steps to do it:

1. Power off the virtual machine.

2. Open the virtual machine configuration file (*<VM-NAME>.vmx*) in a text editor of your choice and add the following property at the end of the file: *uuid.action = "keep"*

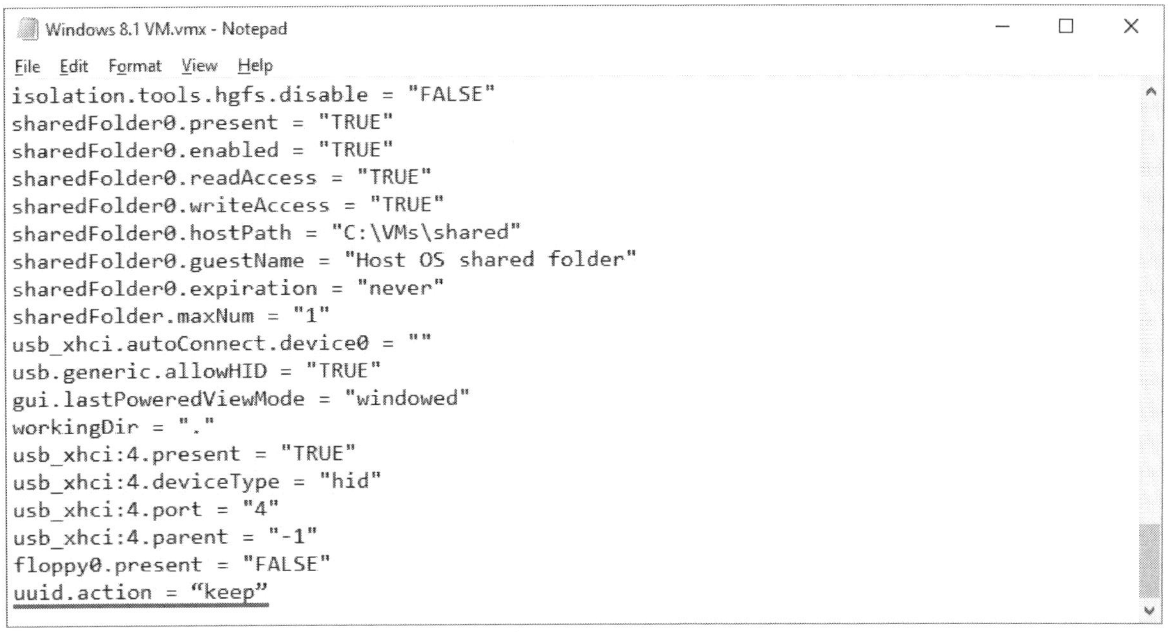

Windows 8.1 VM.vmx - Notepad

File Edit Format View Help

```
isolation.tools.hgfs.disable = "FALSE"
sharedFolder0.present = "TRUE"
sharedFolder0.enabled = "TRUE"
sharedFolder0.readAccess = "TRUE"
sharedFolder0.writeAccess = "TRUE"
sharedFolder0.hostPath = "C:\VMs\shared"
sharedFolder0.guestName = "Host OS shared folder"
sharedFolder0.expiration = "never"
sharedFolder.maxNum = "1"
usb_xhci.autoConnect.device0 = ""
usb.generic.allowHID = "TRUE"
gui.lastPoweredViewMode = "windowed"
workingDir = "."
usb_xhci:4.present = "TRUE"
usb_xhci:4.deviceType = "hid"
usb_xhci:4.port = "4"
usb_xhci:4.parent = "-1"
floppy0.present = "FALSE"
uuid.action = "keep"
```

Figure 4-10 *Specifying the VM to keep the same UUID*

Delete a virtual machine

You can delete a virtual machine and its files from the host file system. You do not need to manipulate files in the host file system in order to delete a virtual machine; the whole process can be done through the VMware Workstation Player interface. Note that this action is irreversible.

Here are the steps:

1. Power off the virtual machine.

2. Right-click the virtual machine in the library and select the **Delete from Disk** option:

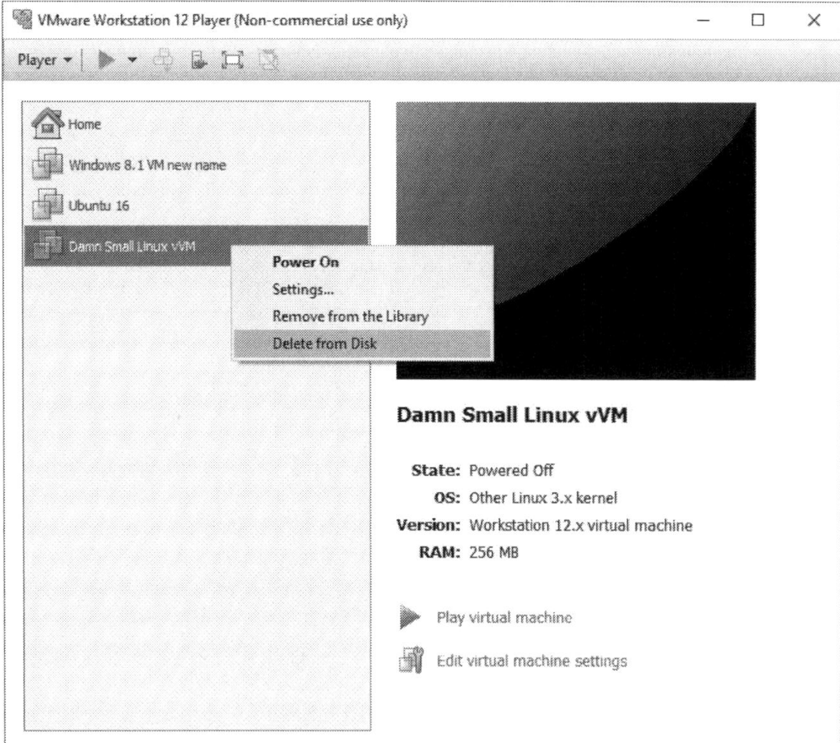

Figure 4-11 *Delete VM from disk*

3. Click Yes when prompted for the confirmation:

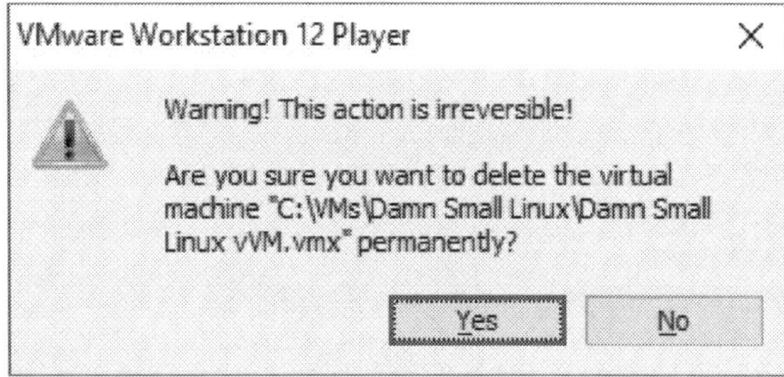

Figure 4-12 *Confirm VM deletition*

4. The virtual machine and all of its files should be deleted from the host file system.

NOTE
To simply remove a VM from the library, right click the VM and select **Remove From the Library**. This option will not delete any of the VM's files and you can add the VM back later.

Log files

You can view the **Message Log** of a virtual machine in VMware Workstation Player. This log contains various warning information, such as driver and display errors. Here are the steps:

1. Power on the virtual machine.

2. Go to Player > Manage > Message Log:

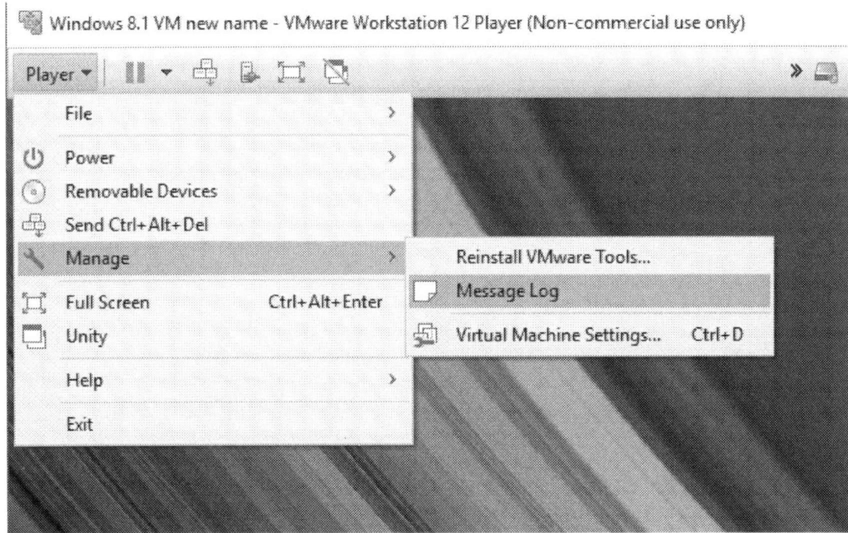

Figure 4-13 *Open Message Log*

3. The Message Log window opens:

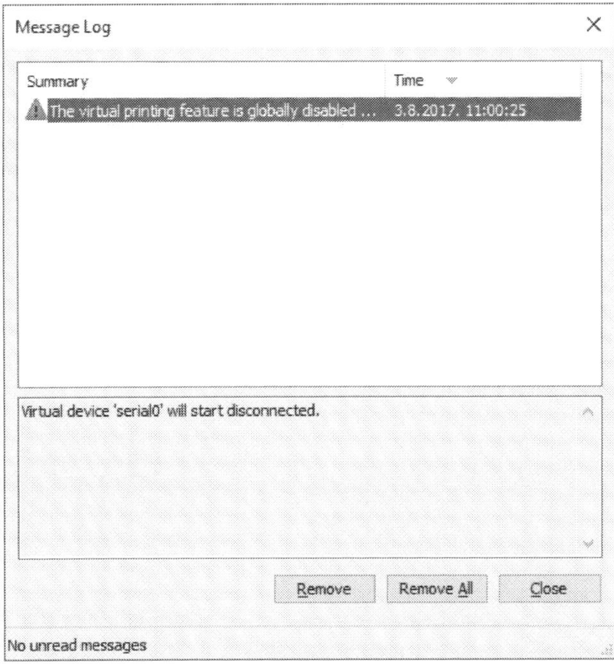

Figure 4-14 *The Message Log window*

The Message Log displays only warning information about the virtual machine. To view more information about the virtual machine, browse to the directory on the host system where the virtual machine files are stored. You should see a file called *vmware.log*:

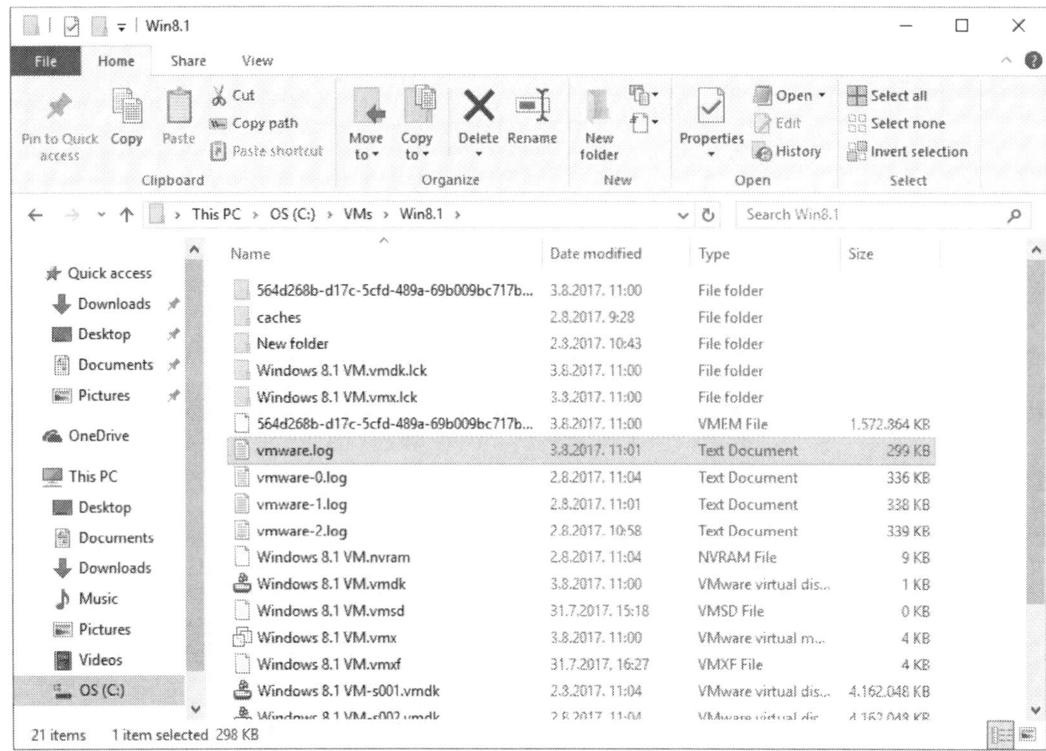

Figure 4-15 *Accessing vmware.log*

This file contains information specific to a running instance of the virtual machine, such as startup configuration, operations, and shutdown of the virtual machine. You can open this file in a text editor of your choice to review it:

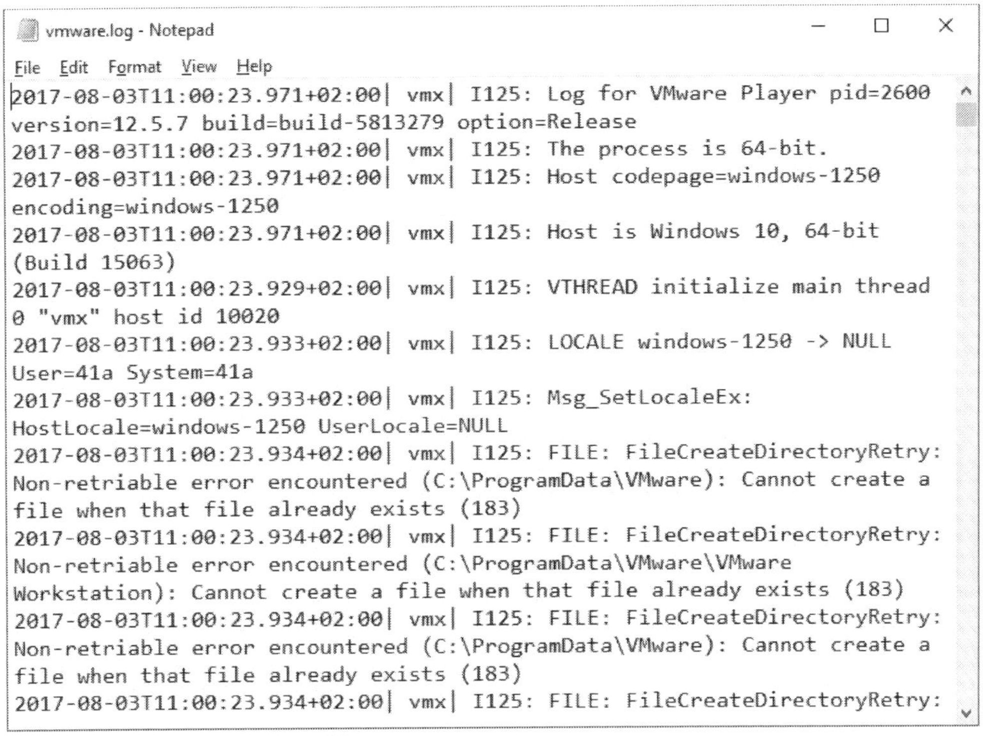

```
vmware.log - Notepad
File Edit Format View Help
2017-08-03T11:00:23.971+02:00| vmx| I125: Log for VMware Player pid=2600
version=12.5.7 build=build-5813279 option=Release
2017-08-03T11:00:23.971+02:00| vmx| I125: The process is 64-bit.
2017-08-03T11:00:23.971+02:00| vmx| I125: Host codepage=windows-1250
encoding=windows-1250
2017-08-03T11:00:23.971+02:00| vmx| I125: Host is Windows 10, 64-bit
(Build 15063)
2017-08-03T11:00:23.929+02:00| vmx| I125: VTHREAD initialize main thread
0 "vmx" host id 10020
2017-08-03T11:00:23.933+02:00| vmx| I125: LOCALE windows-1250 -> NULL
User=41a System=41a
2017-08-03T11:00:23.933+02:00| vmx| I125: Msg_SetLocaleEx:
HostLocale=windows-1250 UserLocale=NULL
2017-08-03T11:00:23.934+02:00| vmx| I125: FILE: FileCreateDirectoryRetry:
Non-retriable error encountered (C:\ProgramData\VMware): Cannot create a
file when that file already exists (183)
2017-08-03T11:00:23.934+02:00| vmx| I125: FILE: FileCreateDirectoryRetry:
Non-retriable error encountered (C:\ProgramData\VMware\VMware
Workstation): Cannot create a file when that file already exists (183)
2017-08-03T11:00:23.934+02:00| vmx| I125: FILE: FileCreateDirectoryRetry:
Non-retriable error encountered (C:\ProgramData\VMware): Cannot create a
file when that file already exists (183)
2017-08-03T11:00:23.934+02:00| vmx| I125: FILE: FileCreateDirectoryRetry:
```

Figure 4-16 *vmware.log file*

NOTE
Player keeps up to six rotations of the *vmware.log* file: *vmware.log*, *vmware-0.log*, *vmware-1.log*, etc.

Log in automatically to a Windows virtual machine

Player includes a neat feature called **Autologin** that enables to you log in automatically to a Windows virtual machine. This feature can be particularly useful if you are using a VM for testing purposes and need to restart the guest operating system frequently.

The prerequisites for the Autologin feature are:

- the guest operating system of the VM needs to be Windows 2000 or later.
- the account you would like to use to log in automatically must be a local user account.
- VMware Tools needs to be installed.

Here are the steps to enable this feature:

1. Power on the VM.

2. Select the VM from the library and go to Player > Manage > Virtual Machine Settings.

3. Under the Options tab, select Autologin and click **Enable**:

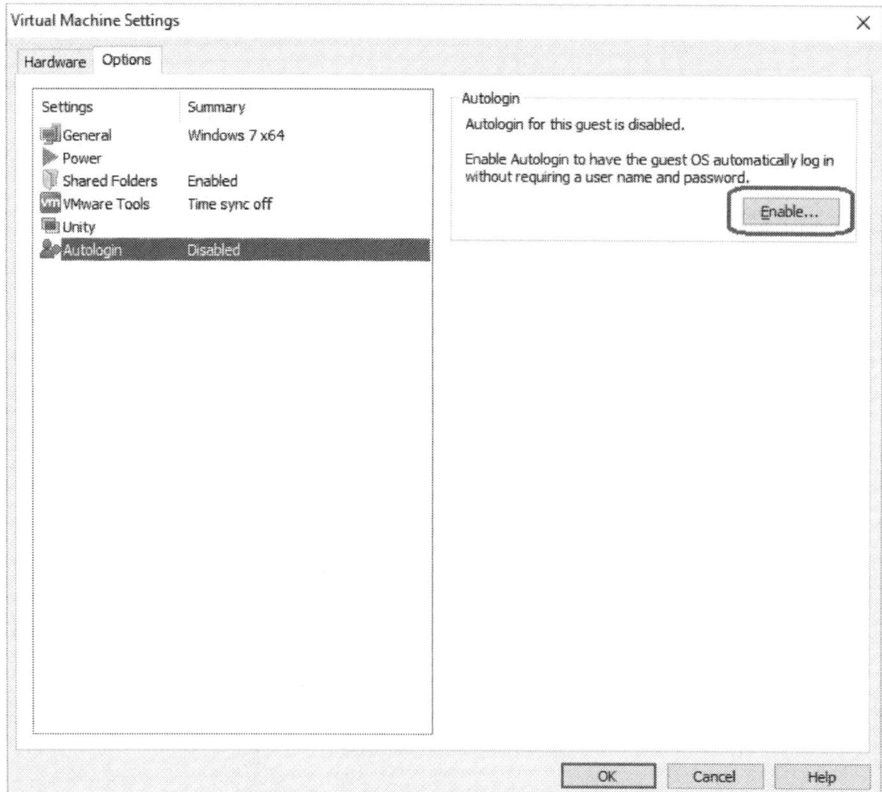

Figure 4-17 *Enabling Autologin*

4. Enter the user credentials:

Figure 4-18 *Enter user credentials used for Autologin*

5. Restart the virtual machine to test whether the user will automatically be logged in.

NOTE
The user used for autologin needs to be a local user account. Domain users are not supported.

Summary

In this chapter you've learned how to change basic properties of a virtual machine - its name, working directory location, and the amount of RAM allocated to it. You've learned about UUID and how to configure a VM to always keep the same UUID. We've then discussed how you can use log files to find out more about your VM's operations and how to use the Autologin feature to log in automatically to a Windows virtual machine.

In the next chapter we will start adding virtual devices to our VMs. We will also talk a little bit about the virtual disks and how to manage them.

This page intentionally left blank

This page intentionally left blank

This page intentionally left blank

Chapter 5 - Working with devices and disks

IN THIS CHAPTER

Adding devices to virtual machines

Learning about virtual disks

Expanding, compacting, and defragmenting virtual disks

Enabling the Enhanced virtual keyboard feature

In this chapter I will show you how to add various devices to virtual machines, such as virtual CD-ROMs, floppy drives, parallel and serial ports, and disks. You will learn how you can compact and defragment virtual disks and how to add more space to a disk when you need it. Lastly, I will explain the Enhanced virtual keyboard feature that offers better handling of international keyboards and keyboards with extra keys.

Add a CD-ROM drive

It is possible to add one or more DVD or CD-ROM drives to a virtual machine in Player. Drives can be connected to physical CD-ROM drives or ISO images.

You can configure the virtual DVD or CD drive as either IDE or SCSI, regardless of the type of the physical drive you will connect it to. For example, if the host computer has an IDE DVD or CDROM drive, you can set up the virtual machine's drive as either SCSI or IDE and connect it to the host's drive.

Here are the steps to add a DVD or CD-ROM drive to a virtual machine in Player:

1. Select Player > Manage > Virtual Machine Settings.

2. On the Hardware tab, click Add:

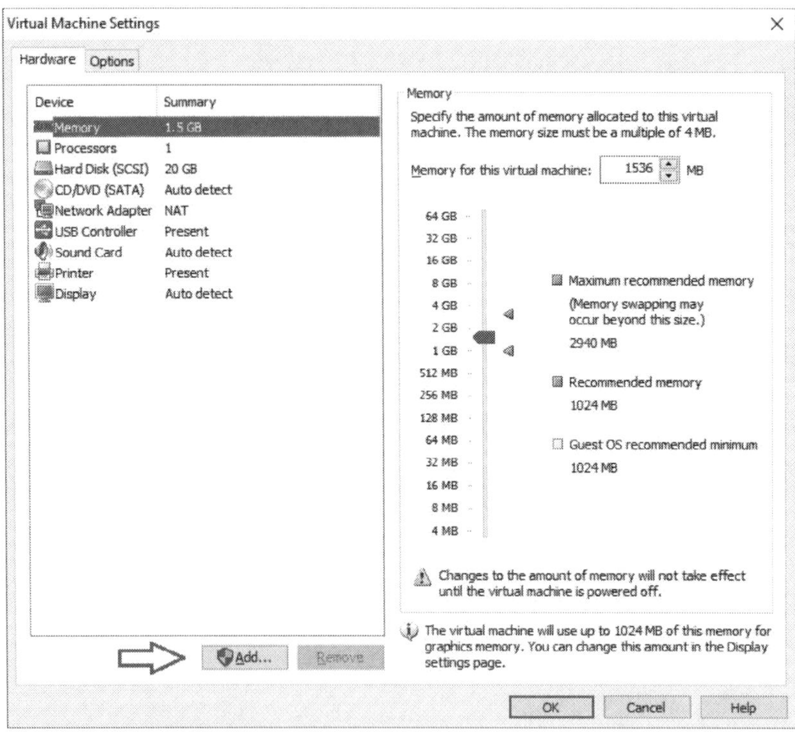

Figure 5-1 *Adding new hardware*

3. The Add Hardware wizard opens. Select CD/DVD Drive as the hardware type:

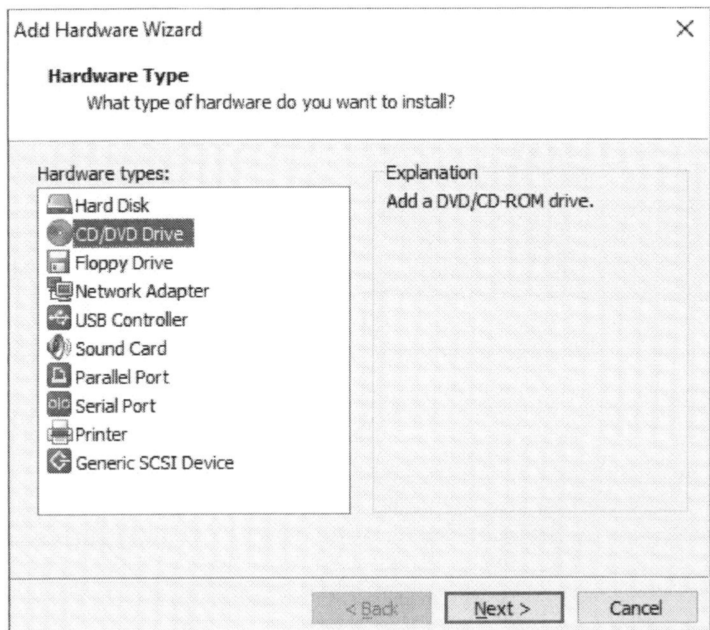

Figure 5-2 *Adding CD/DVD drive*

4. Select whether you want to connect the drive to a physical drive or an ISO image file:

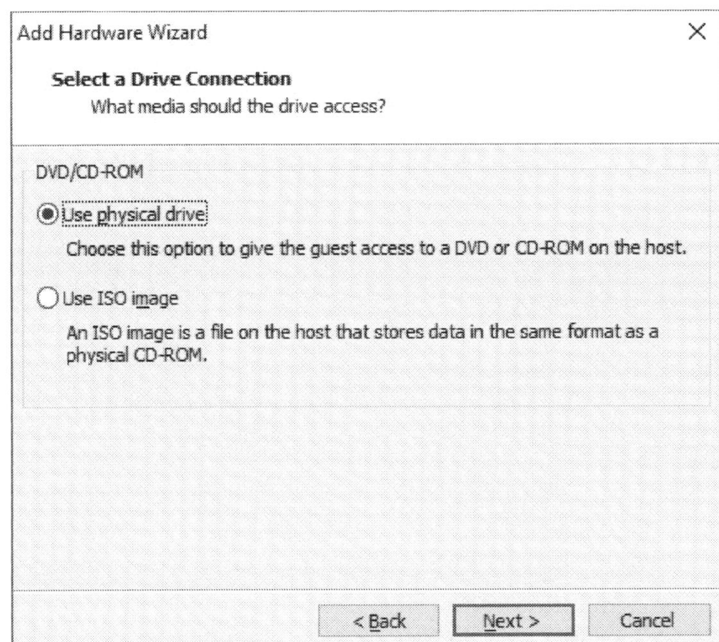

Figure 5-3 *Choose the drive connection*

5a. If you've selected the **Use physical drive** option in the previous step, you will need to select a specific drive, or select the **Auto detect** option to allow Player to auto-detect the drive to use. To connect the drive to the virtual machine when the virtual machine is powered on, check the **Connect at power on** option:

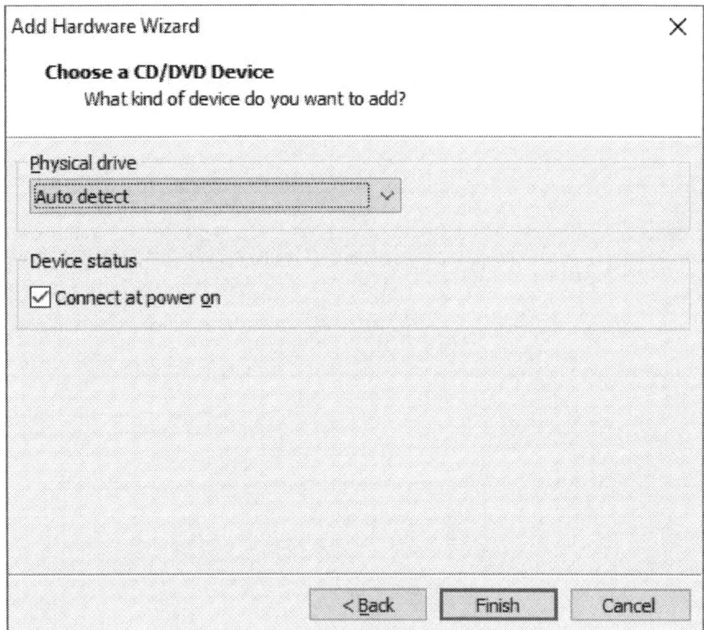

Figure 5-4 *Physical drive options*

5b. If you've selected the **Use ISO image** option in the previous step, you will need browse to the location of the ISO image file. This option is usually used when installing an operating system in a virtual machine:

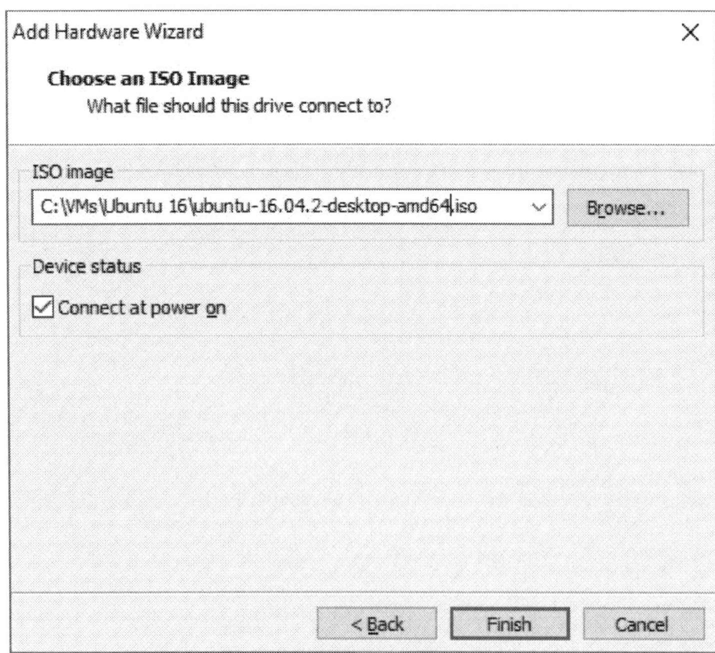

Figure 5-5 *Specifying ISO file location*

6. Click Finish to add the drive to the virtual machine.

The drive should appear in the guest operating system:

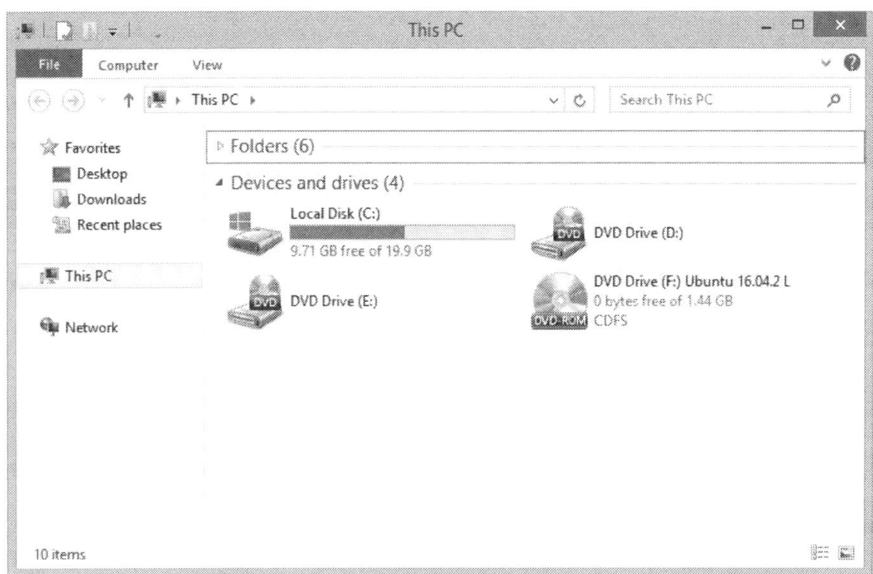

Figure 5-6 *DVD drive should be listed under Devices and drives*

NOTE
You cannot play DVD movies in a VM, unless you install a DVD player application that does not require video overlay support in the video card.

Configure Legacy Emulation Mode

In some cases, the physical DVD or CD drive you've added to your VM may not work correctly when the guest operating system is communicating directly with the drive. Also, certain drives and their drivers do not work correctly in raw mode. However, there is an option you can use to work around these problems - **Legacy Emulation Mode**.

The legacy emulation mode for a DVD or CD drive connected to your virtual machine helps avoid direct communication problems between a guest operating system and a DVD/CDROM drive. When this mode is turned on, you can read from data discs in the DVD/CD drive, but some other functions are not available (e.g. recording CDs, reading multisession CDs, and performing digital audio extraction).

Here is how you can configure Legacy Emulation Mode if you've encountered problems using your DVD-ROM or CD-ROM drive in a virtual machine:

1. Power off the virtual machine.

2. Select Player > Manage > Virtual Machine Settings.

3. Select the CD/DVD drive and click Advanced:

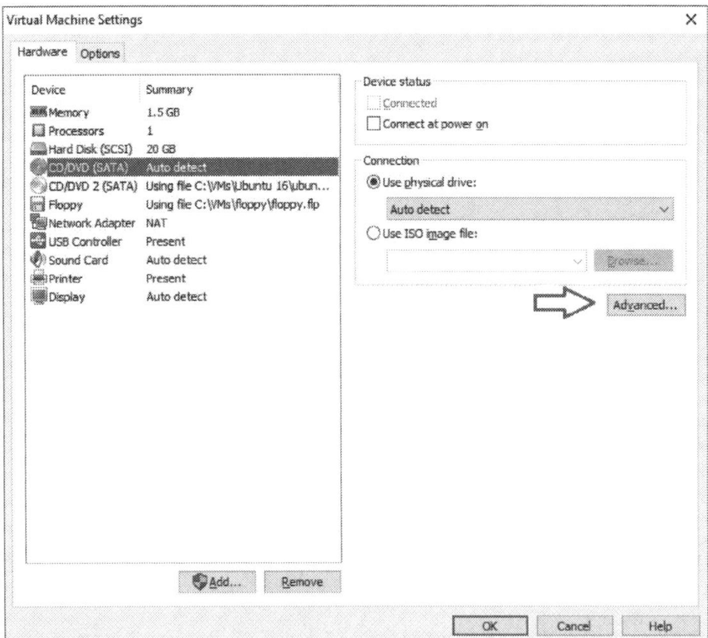

Figure 5-7 *Entering CD/DVD-ROM advanced settings*

4. Check the **Legacy emulation** checkbox and click OK:

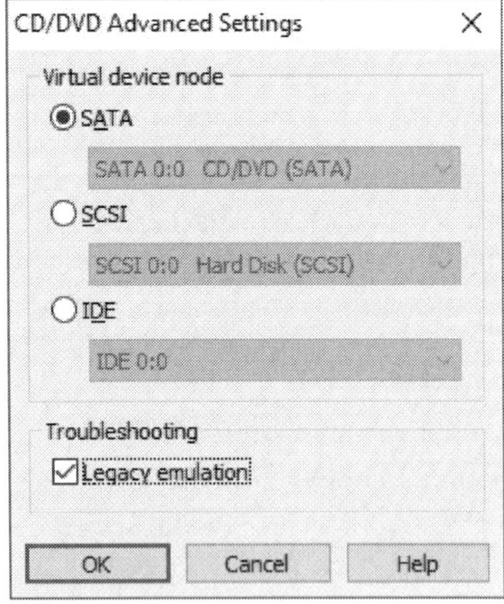

Figure 5-8 *Enable Legacy emulation*

NOTE

If you run more than one virtual machine with their CD-ROM drives in Legacy Emulation Mode at the same time, you must start the virtual machines with their CD-ROM drives disconnected. This prevents multiple virtual machines from being connected to the CD-ROM drive at the same time.

Add a floppy drive

It is possible to add up to two floppy drives to a virtual machine in Player. A virtual floppy drive can be configured to connect to a physical floppy drive, an existing floppy image file, or a blank floppy image file.

Here is how you can add a floppy drive to a virtual machine:

1. Power off the virtual machine. A floppy drive can't be added while the VM is powered on.

2. Select the virtual machine from the Library and go to Player > Manage > Virtual Machine Settings.

3. On the Hardware tab, click Add.

4. The Add Hardware wizard opens. Select **Floppy Drive** as the hardware type:

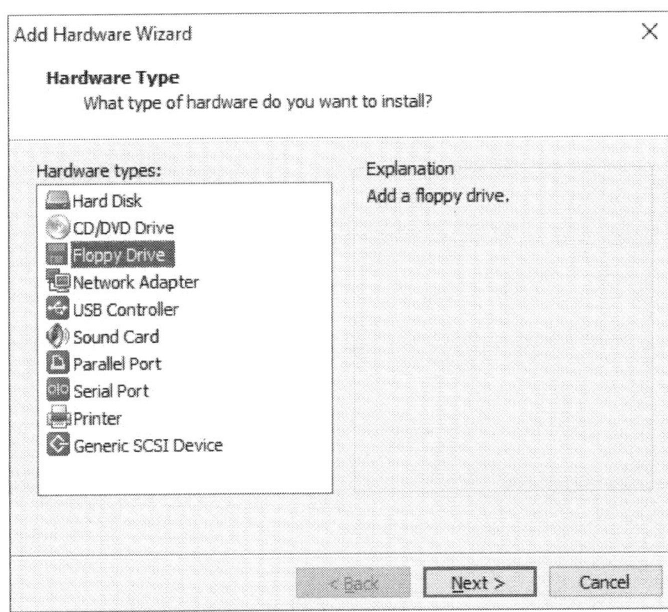

Figure 5-9 *Adding a floppy drive*

5. Select the floppy media type. Three options are available:

- **Use a physical floppy drive** - the virtual machine uses a physical floppy drive on the host computer.
- **Use a floppy image** - the drive connects to an existing floppy image file (.flp).
- **Create a blank floppy image** - the drive connects to a blank floppy image file (.flp).

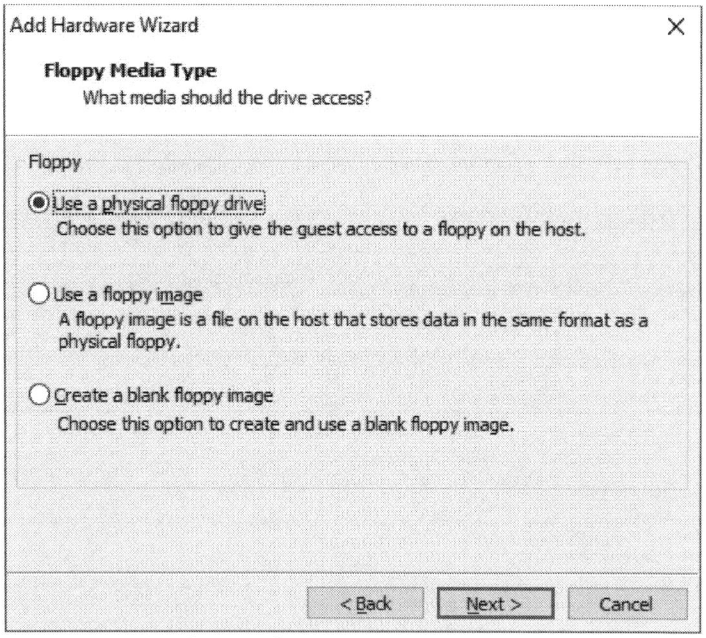

Add Hardware Wizard

Floppy Media Type
What media should the drive access?

Floppy

(•) Use a physical floppy drive
Choose this option to give the guest access to a floppy on the host.

( ) Use a floppy image
A floppy image is a file on the host that stores data in the same format as a physical floppy.

( ) Create a blank floppy image
Choose this option to create and use a blank floppy image.

< Back | Next > | Cancel

Figure 5-10 *Floppy drive options*

5a. If you've selected the **Use a physical floppy drive** option in the previous step, you need to select the specific floppy drive or select the **Auto detect** option to allow Player to auto-detect the drive to use. To connect the drive to the virtual machine when the virtual machine is powered on, check the **Connect at power on** option:

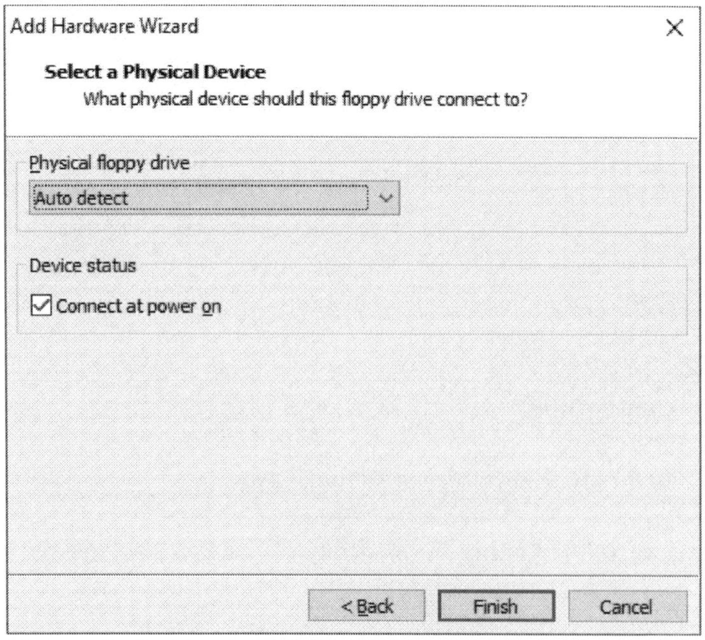

Add Hardware Wizard

Select a Physical Device
What physical device should this floppy drive connect to?

Physical floppy drive
Auto detect

Device status
[x] Connect at power on

< Back | Finish | Cancel

Figure 5-11 *Physical floppy drive options*

5b. If you've selected the **Use a floppy image** or **Create a blank floppy image** option in the previous step, you will need browse to the location of the floppy image file on the host system (or specify where the blank image will be stored, in case you've selected the latter option):

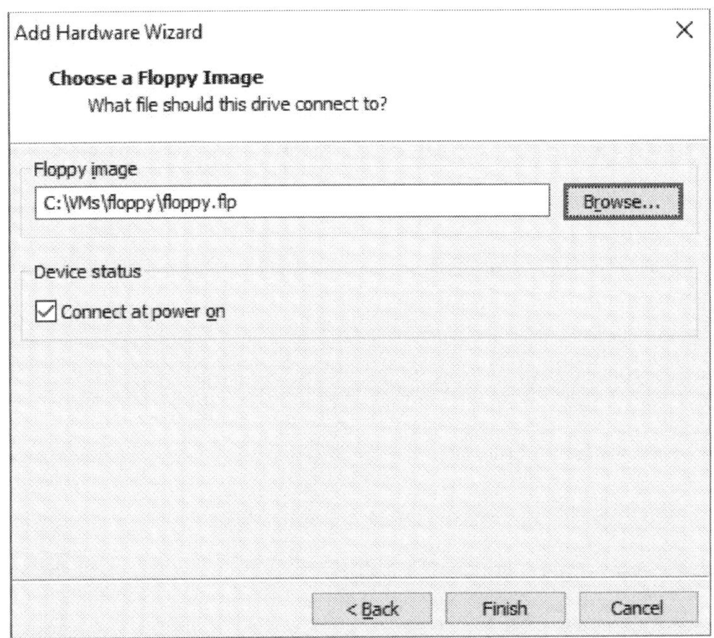

Figure 5-12 *Specifying image file location*

6. Click Finish to add the drive to the virtual machine.

The drive should appear in the guest operating system after you power on the VM:

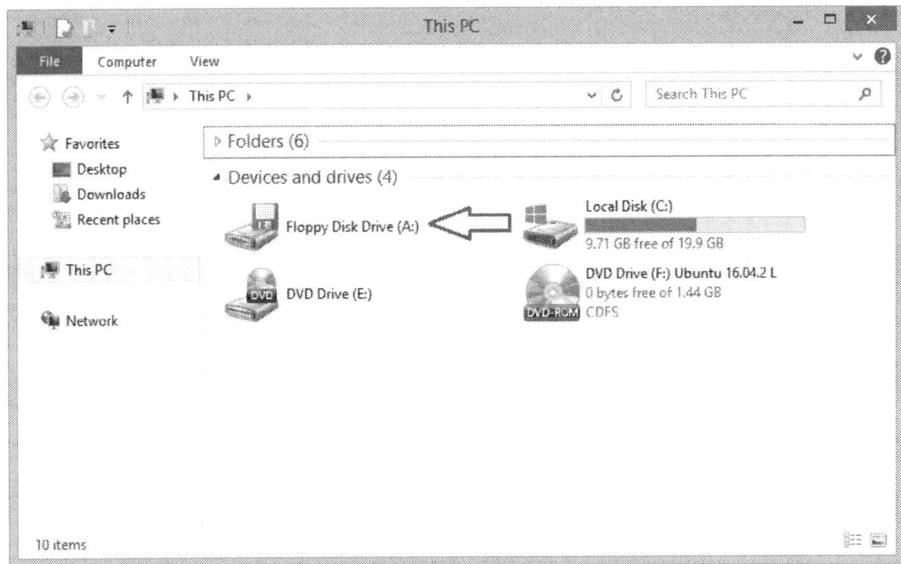

Figure 5-13 *Floppy drive listed under Devices and drives*

Configure a USB Controller

In order to use USB devices, a virtual machine must have a USB controller configured. The USB controller in VMware Workstation Player supports the following USB device types:

- **USB 1.1 UHCI (Universal Host Controller Interface)** - supported for all virtual machine hardware versions.
- **USB 2.0 EHCI (Enhanced Host Controller Interface)** - supported if the virtual machine hardware is compatible with Workstation 6 and later virtual machines.
- **USB 3.0 xHCI (Extensible Host Controller Interface)** - available for Linux guests running a kernel version 2.6.35 or later and for Windows 8 guests or later. The virtual machine hardware must be compatible with Workstation 8 or later virtual machines. All USB device types are supported, including USB 1.1, 2.0, and 3.0 devices.

In order to use USB devices inside a virtual machine, the host operating system must support USB. You do not need to install device drivers for USB devices in the host operating system to use those devices in the virtual machine.

NOTE
USB human interface devices (such as the keyboard and mouse) do not appear in the **Removable Devices** menu and are not available to connect to the virtual machine by default. To connect such devices to the virtual machine, you need to enable the **Show all USB input devices** option, as explained in the **Connect USB HIDs to a virtual machine** lesson in one of the previous sections.

Add a USB controller

A virtual machine must have a USB controller in order to use USB devices and smart card readers. A USB controller is added by default when a virtual machine is created. You can't add more than one USB controller per VM.

If you remove a USB controller that was added by default, you can add it back later. Here are the steps:

1. Power off the virtual machine.

2. Select the virtual machine from the library and go to Player > Manage > Virtual Machine Settings.

3. On the Hardware tab, click Add.

4. The Add Hardware wizard opens. Select USB Controller as the hardware type:

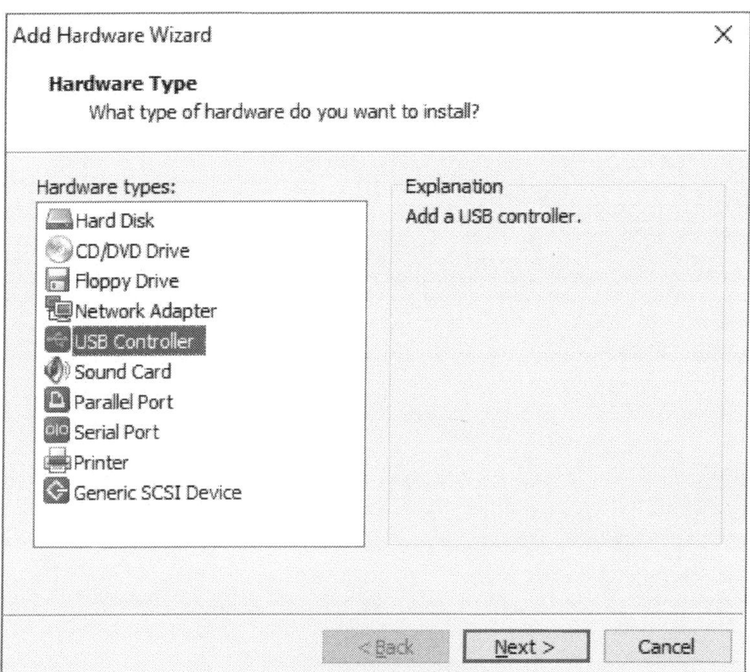

Figure 5-14 *Adding an USB controller*

5. You need to configure the following options:

- **USB compatibility** - the USB version (1.1, 2.0, or 3.0).
- **Automatically connect new USB devices to this virtual machine when it has focus** - when enabled, new USB devices will be connected to the virtual machine when the virtual machine window has focus. If this option is disabled, new USB devices will be connected only to the host system, even when the focus is in the VM.
- **Show all USB input devices** - by default, USB human interface devices (HIDs), such as the keyboard and mouse, do not appear in the **Removable Devices** menu and are not available to connect to the virtual machine. To connect such devices to the virtual machine, this options needs to be checked.
- **Share Bluetooth devices with the virtual machine** - enables support for Bluetooth devices.

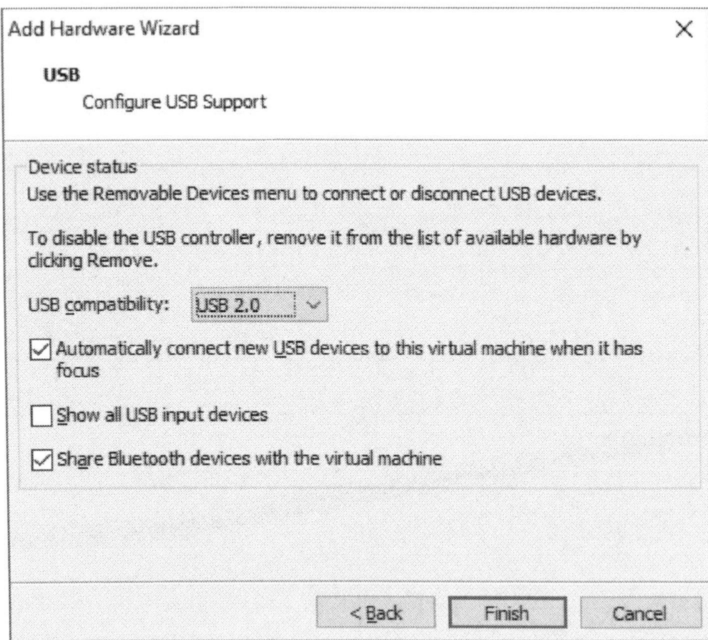

Figure 5-15 *USB controller options*

6. Click Finish to finish adding the USB controller.

Enable isochronous USB devices

Isochronous USB devices, such as modems, speakers and webcams, require timing coordination in order to work correctly. You need to enable support for isochronous USB devices to be able to use them in a virtual machine in VMware Workstation Player. Note that the guest operating system must support USB 2.0 and USB 3.0 in order to use this feature.

Here are the steps to enable support for isochronous USB devices in VMware Workstation Player:

1. Select the virtual machine from the library and go to Player > Manage > Virtual Machine Settings.

2. Select USB Controller on the Hardware tab. Selecting USB 2.0 or 3.0 enables support for isochronous USB devices, so from the **USB compatibility** list, select one of the following options:

- **USB 2.0** - available if the virtual machine hardware is compatible with Workstation 6 or later virtual machines.
- **USB 3.0** - available for Linux guests running a kernel version 2.6.35 or later and for Windows 8 or later guests. The virtual machine hardware must be compatible with Workstation 8 or later virtual machines.

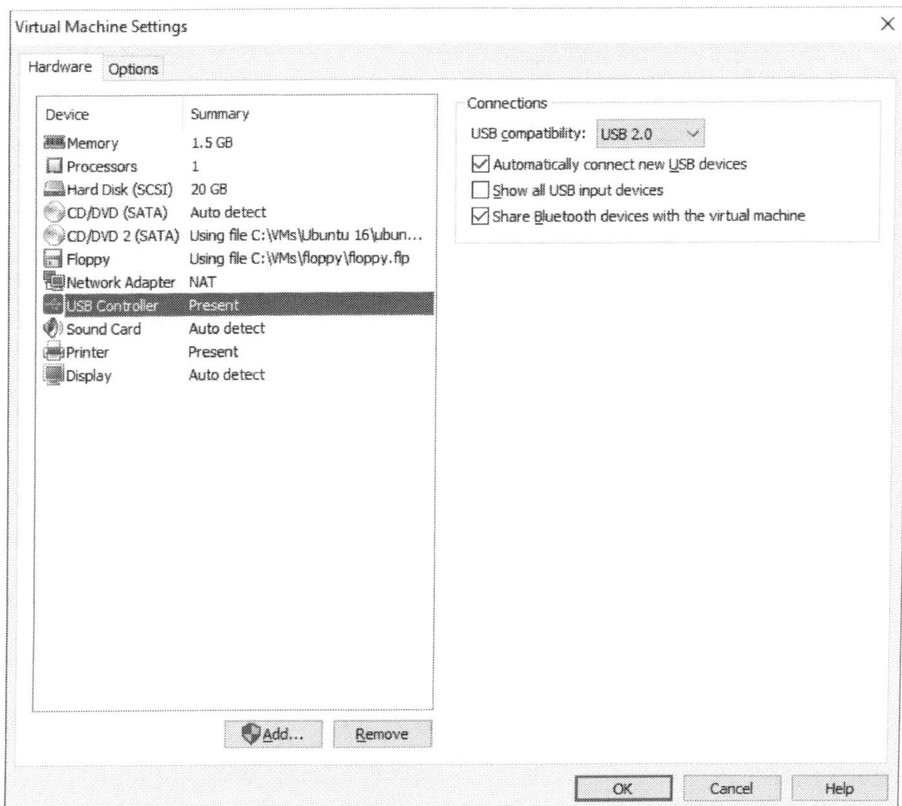

Figure 5-16 *Enabling support for isochronous USB devices*

What is a virtual disk?

A **virtual disk** is a file (or a set of files) stored on the host system that appears as a physical disk drive to the guest operating system. Virtual hard disk files store information such as the operating system, program files, and data files. They have a *.vmdk* extension.

The New Virtual Machine wizard creates a virtual machine with a single disk drive. You can add more disk drives to a virtual machine, remove disk drives from a virtual machine, and change the existing disk drives' settings. By default, the actual files that the virtual hard disk uses start small and grow to their maximum size as needed, but they can also be configured so that all of the disk space is allocated when the virtual disk is created.

A key advantage of virtual hard disks is their portability. Because they are stored as files on the host filesystem, you can move them easily to a new location on the same computer or to a different computer.

In the picture below you can see virtual disk files of my Windows 8.1 virtual machine on the host filesystem:

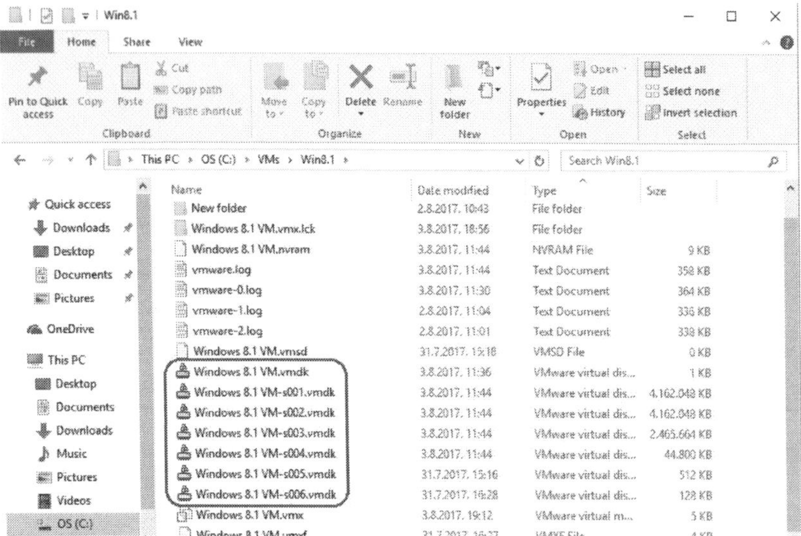

Figure 5-17 *Virtual disk files on the host OS*

Virtual hard disks overview

Virtual hard disk files store information such as the operating system, program files, and actual data. They are named *<VM-NAME>.vmdk* (for example, *Windows 8.1 VM.vmdk* for the virtual machine named *Windows 8.1 VM*). Virtual hard disks can be configured as either IDE or SATA disks for the guest operating system. If the guest operating system has a driver for the LSI Logic or BusLogic SCSI adapter, a virtual disk can also be configured as a SCSI disk.

The files that make up virtual hard disks can be stored on IDE, SATA, or SCSI hard disks, or any other type of fast-access storage media. The size of virtual disks can be up to 8TB. Each virtual hard disk can be stored in one or more files, depending on the size of the virtual hard disk and the host operating system.

You can also configure a virtual hard disk to use a set of files limited to 2GB per file, which can be useful if you plan to move the virtual hard disk to an older file system that does not support files larger than 2GB.

Add a new virtual hard disk

You can add up to 4 IDE devices, up to 60 SCSI devices, and up to 120 SATA devices to a virtual machine in VMware Workstation Player. Here is how you can add a new virtual hard disk to your virtual machine:

1. Select the virtual machine from the library and go to Player > Manage > Virtual Machine Settings.

2. Click Add on the Hardware tab.

3. The New Hardware wizard opens. Select **Hard Disk** as the hardware type:

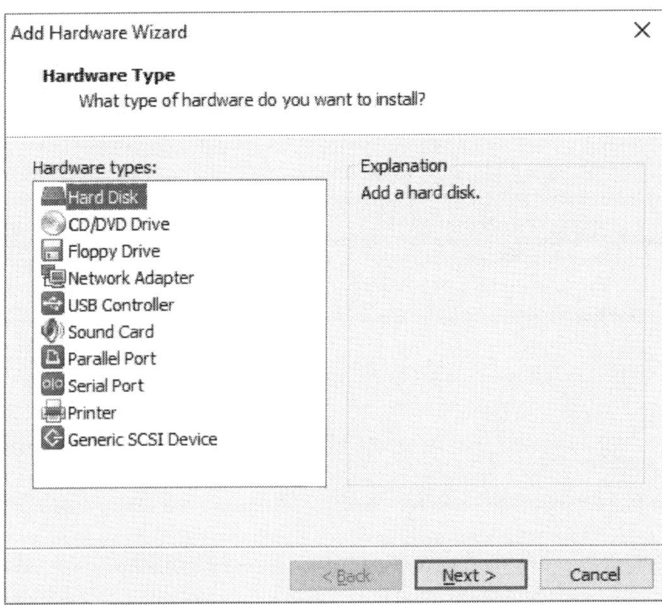

Figure 5-18 *Adding a new virtual HDD*

4. Select the disk type. Three options are available:

- **IDE** - creates an IDE disk. You can add up to four IDE devices to a virtual machine.
- **SCSI** - creates a SCSI disk. You can add up to 60 SCSI devices to a virtual machine. It is recommended that you use this option.
- **SATA** - create a SATA disk. You can add up to 120 SATA devices: four controllers and 30 devices per controller.

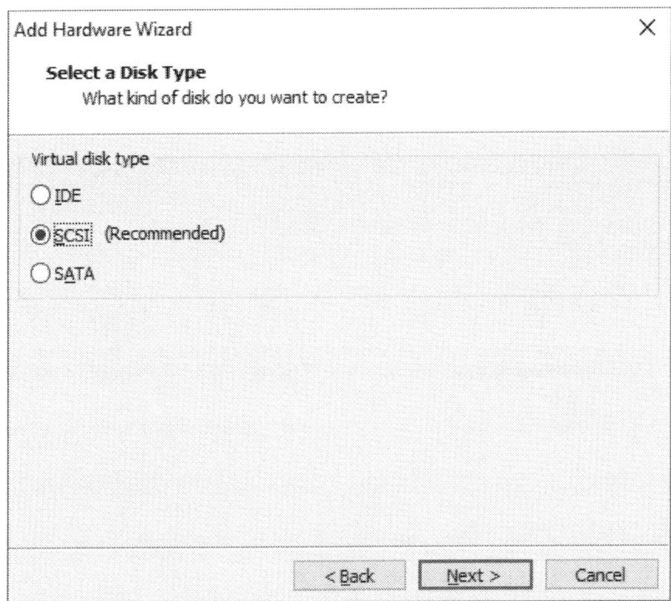

Figure 5-19 *Choose the disk type*

5. Select the **Create a new virtual disk** option:

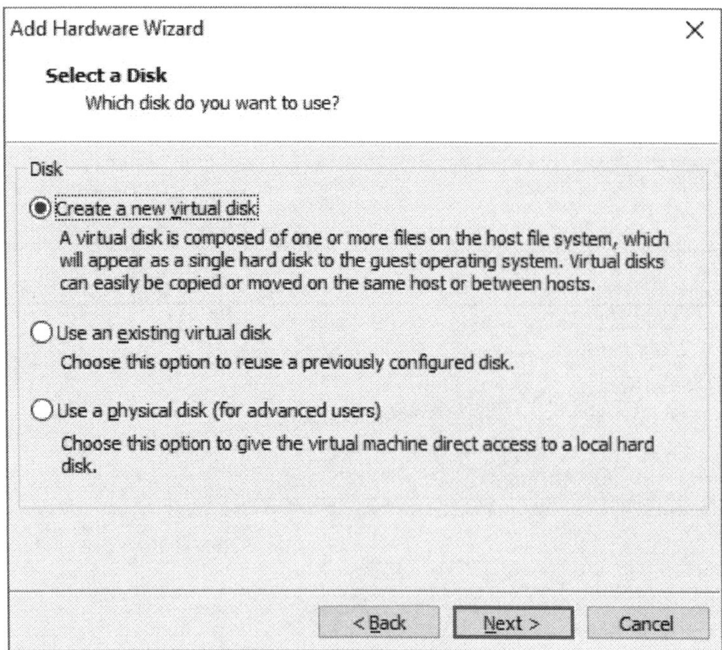

Figure 5-20 *Create new virtual HDD*

6. Set the virtual disk size and choose how to allocate the disk space. You can choose between the following options:

- **Allocate all disk space now** - this option enhances performance, but requires all of the physical disk space to be available immediately. Use this option if you will frequently transfer large amounts of data to the guest virtual machine.
- **Store virtual disk as a single file** - select this option if the virtual disk will be stored on a file system that doesn't have a file size limitation.
- **Split virtual disk into multiple files** - select this option if the virtual disk will be stored on a file system that has a file size limitation and does not support files larger than 2 GB (such as older version of FAT or ext file systems):

Figure 5-21 *Specifying disk size and allocation type*

7. Select the filename and location and click Finish to add the new virtual hard disk:

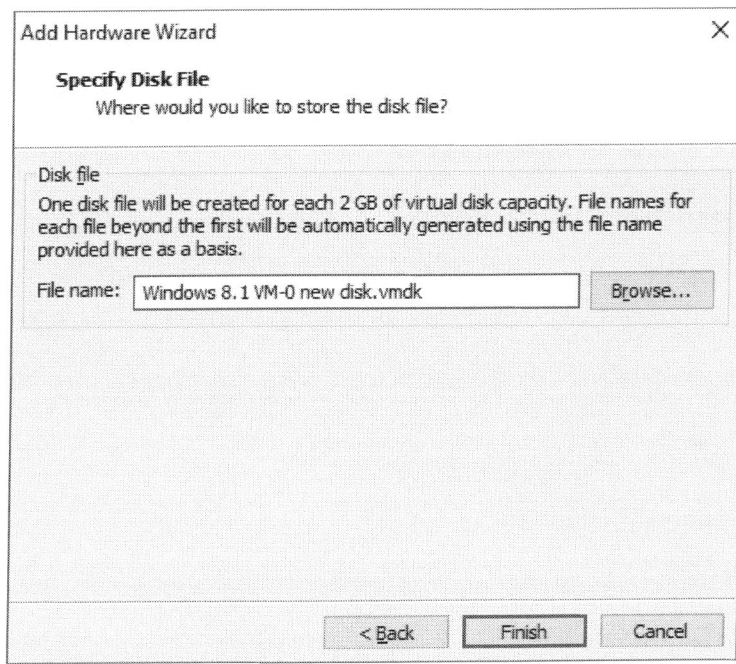

Figure 5-22 *Specifying where to store the disk*

The guest operating system should see the new virtual hard disk as a new blank disk. You will need to format the disk before using it, just like you would do if you've added a physical disk:

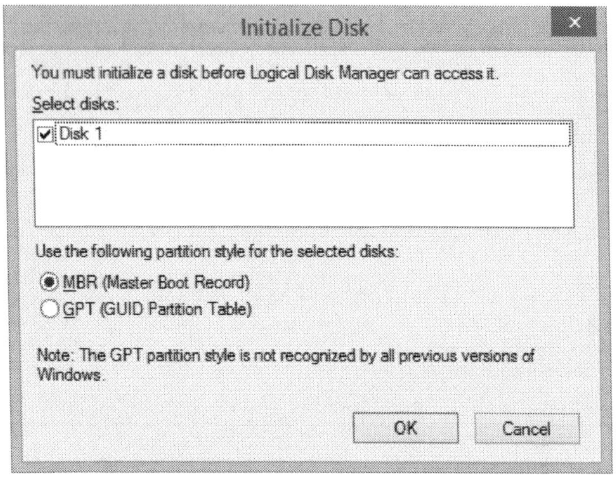

Figure 5-23 *Initializing the disk in Windows*

Add an existing virtual hard disk

You can add an existing virtual hard disk to a virtual machine in Player. Here are the steps:

1. Select the virtual machine from the library and go to Player > Manage > Virtual Machine Settings.

2. Click Add on the Hardware tab.

3. The New Hardware wizard opens. Select Hard Disk as the hardware type.

4. Select the disk type:

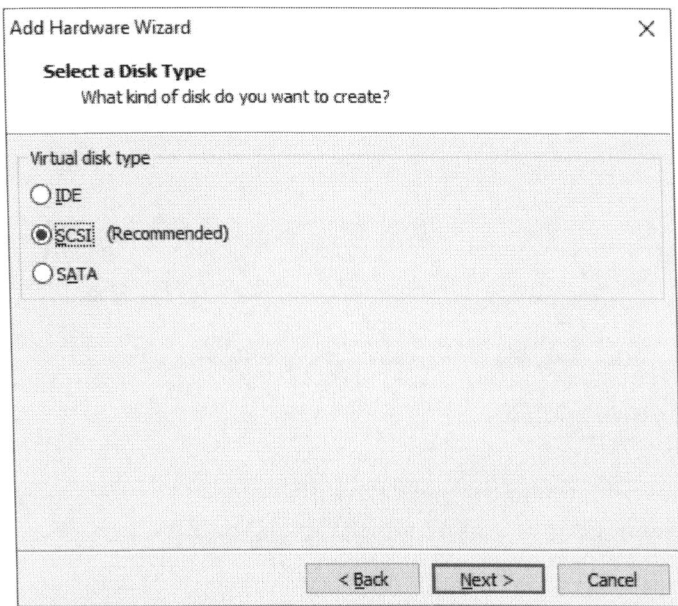

Figure 5-24 *Selecting the disk type*

5. Select the **Use an existing virtual disk** option:

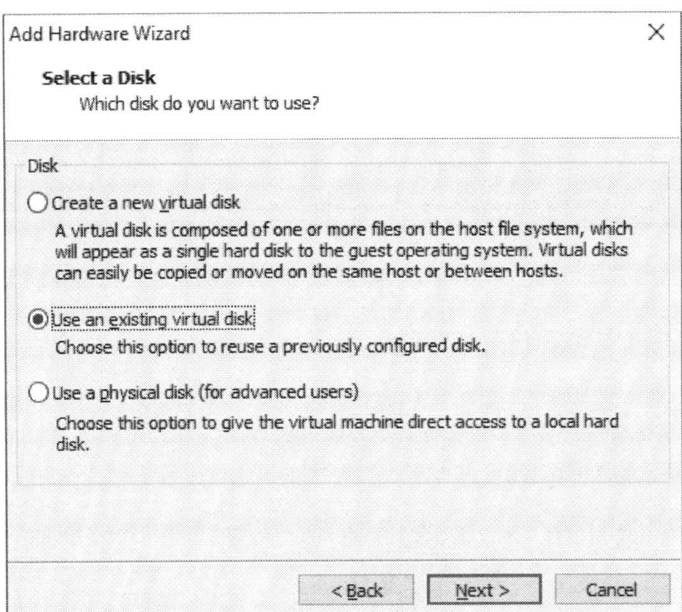

Figure 5-25 *Use an existing disk*

6. Browse to the disk file and click Finish:

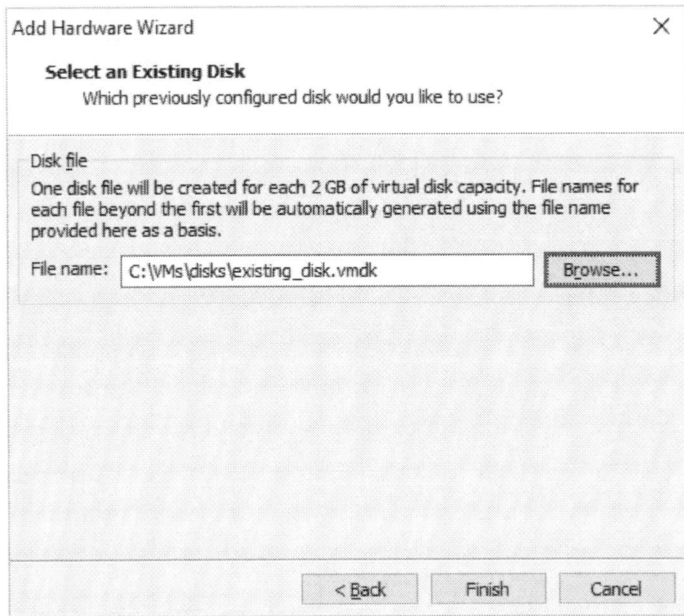

Figure 5-26 *Finish adding the existing disk*

7. If the disk is formatted in the way the guest OS understands it, the disk should be mounted automatically and you should be able to access its contents immediately:

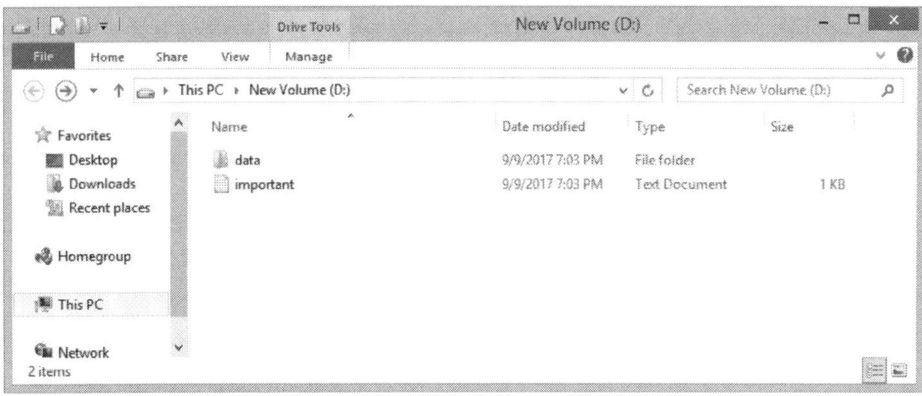

Figure 5-27 *The disk contents*

Virtual machine files

Each VM consists of several types of files that are stored on the host operating system. Here is a list and a brief description of the files that make up a virtual machine:

- **Configuration file (<VM name>.vmx)** - the primary configuration file that stores the settings of a virtual machine.
- **BIOS file (<VM name>.nvram)** - a file that contains the virtual machine's BIOS.
- **Log files (vmware.log or <VM name>.log)** - a virtual machine log file.
- **Paging file (<VM name>.vmem)** - the virtual machine paging file.
- **Disk file (<VM name>.vmdk)** - the virtual disk file that stores the contents of the virtual machine hard disk.
- **Snapshot data file (<VM name>.vmsd)** - a file that stores information and metadata about snapshots (note that snapshots are supported by VMware Workstation Pro).
- **Snapshot state file (<VM name>.vmsn)** - a file that stores the running state of a virtual machine at the time you take the snapshot.
- **Suspend state file (<VM name>.vmss)** - a file that stores the state of a suspended virtual machine.

Here is a list of files that make up my Ubuntu 16 virtual machine:

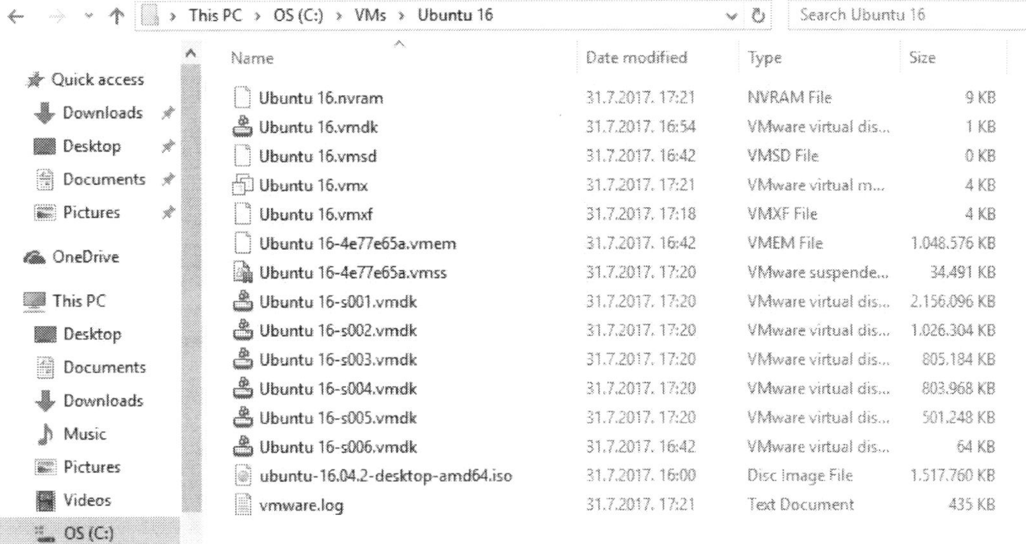

Figure 5-28 *Files that make up my Ubuntu 16 VM*

Some of the files that make up a virtual machine can be opened and edited in a text editor. For example, here is the *Ubuntu 16.vmx* file opened in Notepad:

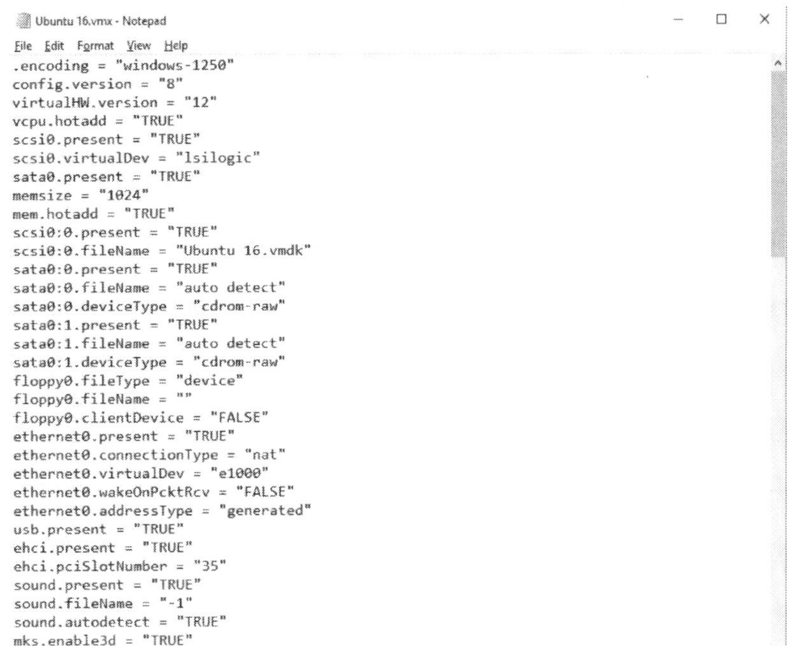


```
.encoding = "windows-1250"
config.version = "8"
virtualHW.version = "12"
vcpu.hotadd = "TRUE"
scsi0.present = "TRUE"
scsi0.virtualDev = "lsilogic"
sata0.present = "TRUE"
memsize = "1024"
mem.hotadd = "TRUE"
scsi0:0.present = "TRUE"
scsi0:0.fileName = "Ubuntu 16.vmdk"
sata0:0.present = "TRUE"
sata0:0.fileName = "auto detect"
sata0:0.deviceType = "cdrom-raw"
sata0:1.present = "TRUE"
sata0:1.fileName = "auto detect"
sata0:1.deviceType = "cdrom-raw"
floppy0.fileType = "device"
floppy0.fileName = ""
floppy0.clientDevice = "FALSE"
ethernet0.present = "TRUE"
ethernet0.connectionType = "nat"
ethernet0.virtualDev = "e1000"
ethernet0.wakeOnPcktRcv = "FALSE"
ethernet0.addressType = "generated"
usb.present = "TRUE"
ehci.present = "TRUE"
ehci.pciSlotNumber = "35"
sound.present = "TRUE"
sound.fileName = "-1"
sound.autodetect = "TRUE"
mks.enable3d = "TRUE"
```

Figure 5-29 *Example VM configuration file*

Compact a virtual hard disk

You can compact a virtual hard disk in order to reclaim unused space. If a disk has empty space, this process reduces the amount of space the virtual hard disk occupies on the host system drive.

The prerequisites:

- the virtual disk should not be mapped or mounted.
- disk space must not be preallocated for the virtual hard disk.

Here is how you would compact a virtual hard disk:

1. Power off the virtual machine.

2. Select the virtual machine from the library and go to Player > Manage > Virtual Machine Settings.

3. On the Hardware tab, select the virtual hard disk you would like to compact and click **Compact**:

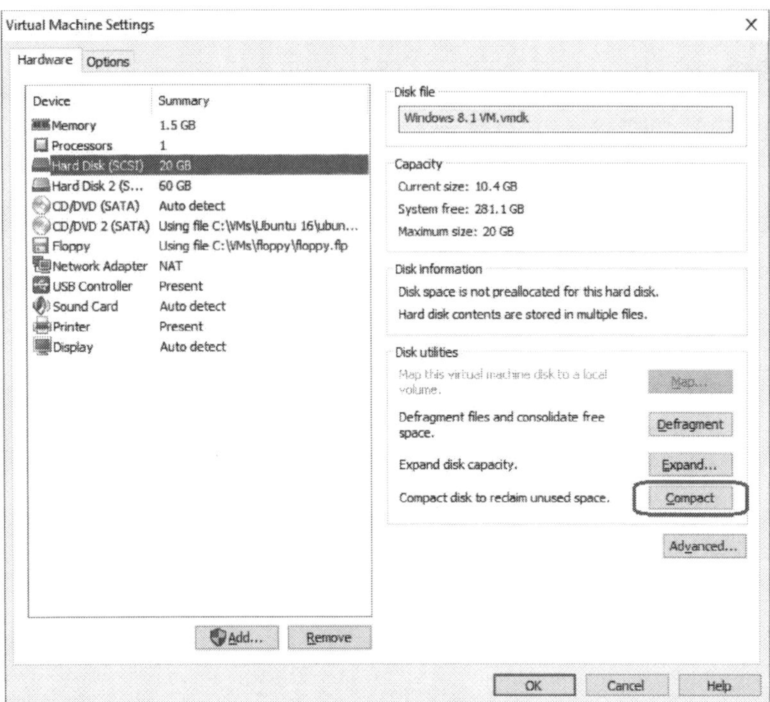

Figure 5-30 *Compacting the virtual disk*

4. The compact process should start:

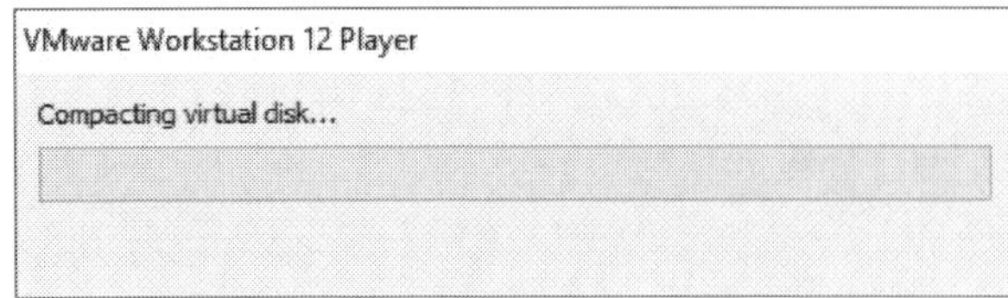

Figure 5-31 *Compacting in progress*

4. The process lasts for a couple of minutes, depending on the size of the disk and the speed of your computer. When the process completes, click OK.

5. Note that in my case the disk size was reduced by almost 2 GB (from 10.4 GB to 8.6 GB):

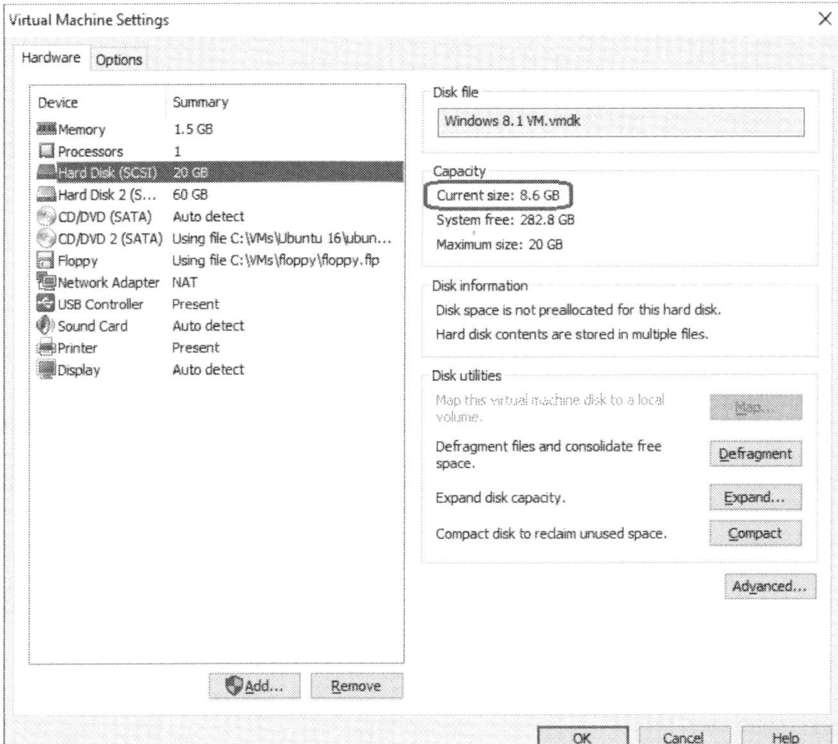

Figure 5-32 *Reduced virtual disk size after the compact operation*

Expand a virtual hard disk

You can expand a virtual hard disk in order to get more storage space. After you expand a virtual disk, you need to use a disk management software in order to increase the size of an existing partition on the virtual hard disk to match the expanded size. The software you will use depends on the type of the guest operating system installed in the virtual machine. For Windows guests, you can use a built-in utility called **Disk Management**. For Linux guests, use tools such as **fdisk** or **parted**.

The prerequisites:

- the virtual disk must not be mapped or mounted.
- the virtual machine should not have snapshots.
- the virtual machine should not be a linked clone or the parent of a linked clone.

Let's say that I want to expand a disk in my Windows 8.1 VM. Right now, the disk has 60 GB of allocated space:

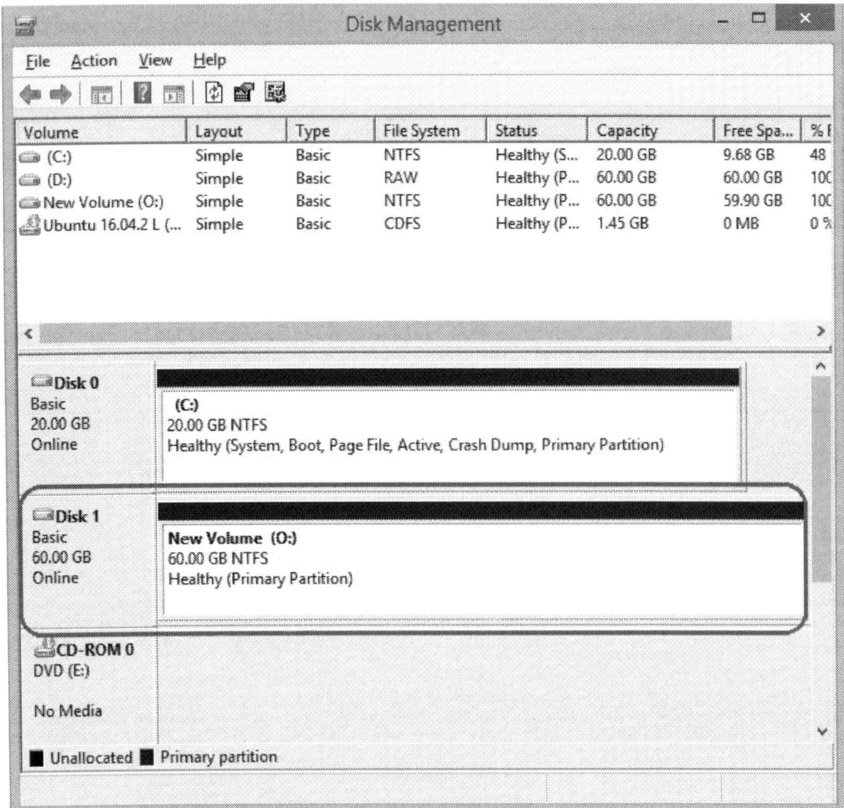

Figure 5-33 *Disk size before expanding*

Here are the steps to expand a virtual hard disk:

1. Power off the virtual machine.

2. Select the virtual machine from the library and go to Player > Manage > Virtual Machine Settings.

3. Select the virtual hard disk to expand and click **Expand**:

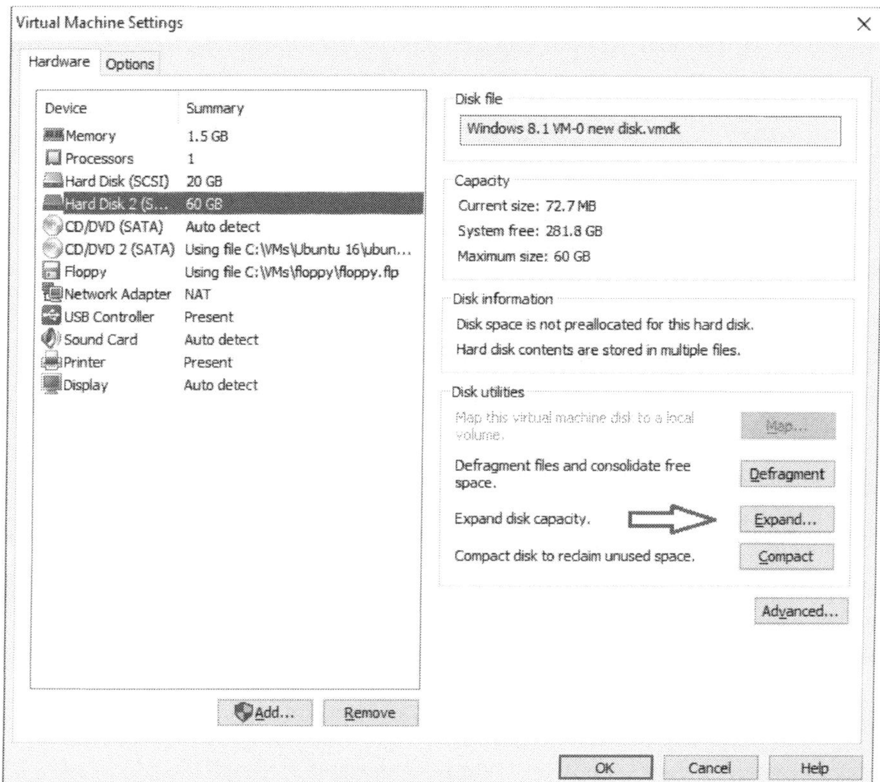

Figure 5-34 *Expanding a virtual HDD*

4. Set the new maximum size for the virtual hard disk. The size can be between 0.001GB and 2TB.

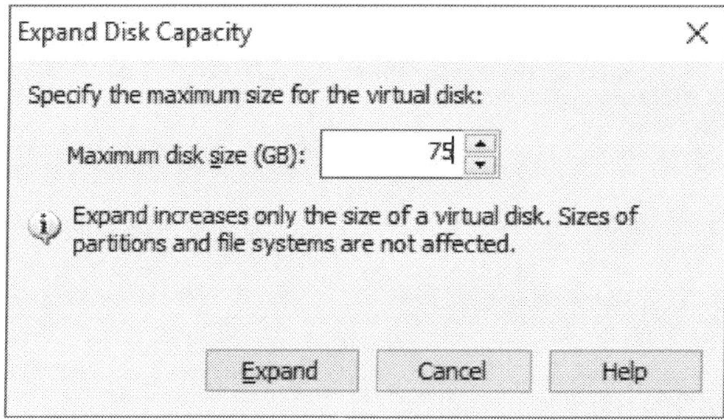

Figure 5-35 *Choosing the new disk size*

5. Click OK when the expand process completes.

6. Now, power on the VM. You will need to use a disk management utility in the guest operating system in order to increase the disk partition size to match the expanded virtual disk size. Since I'm using Windows, I will need to enter the **Disk Management** utility and prepare the disk for usage there:

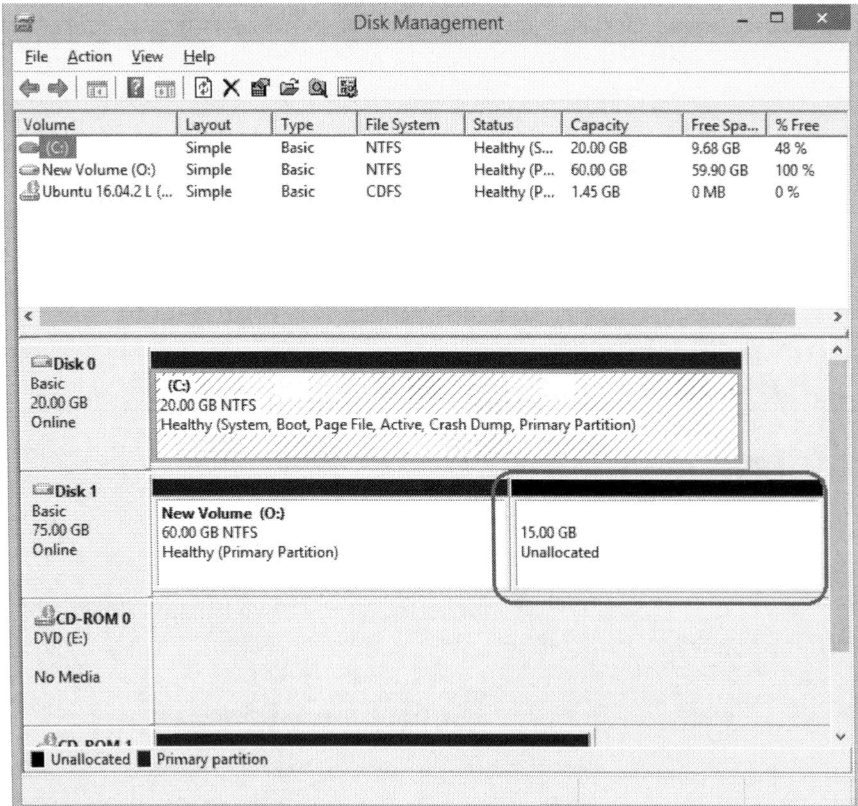

Figure 5-36 *Allocating new disk space in Windows*

Defragment a virtual hard disk

Just like physical disk drives, virtual hard disks can become fragmented. You use the Player's defragmentation tool to defragment a virtual hard disk. Defragmentation rearranges files, programs, and unused space on the virtual hard disk in order to improve the disk's performance.

Here are the prerequisites:

- the virtual disk must not be mapped or mounted.
- adequate free working space must be available on the host system. There must be free space equal to the size of the virtual disk file.

Here is how you can defragment a virtual hard disk:

1. Power off the virtual machine.

2. Select the virtual machine from the library and go to Player > Manage > Virtual Machine Settings.

3. Select the virtual hard disk you would like to defragment and click **Defragment**:

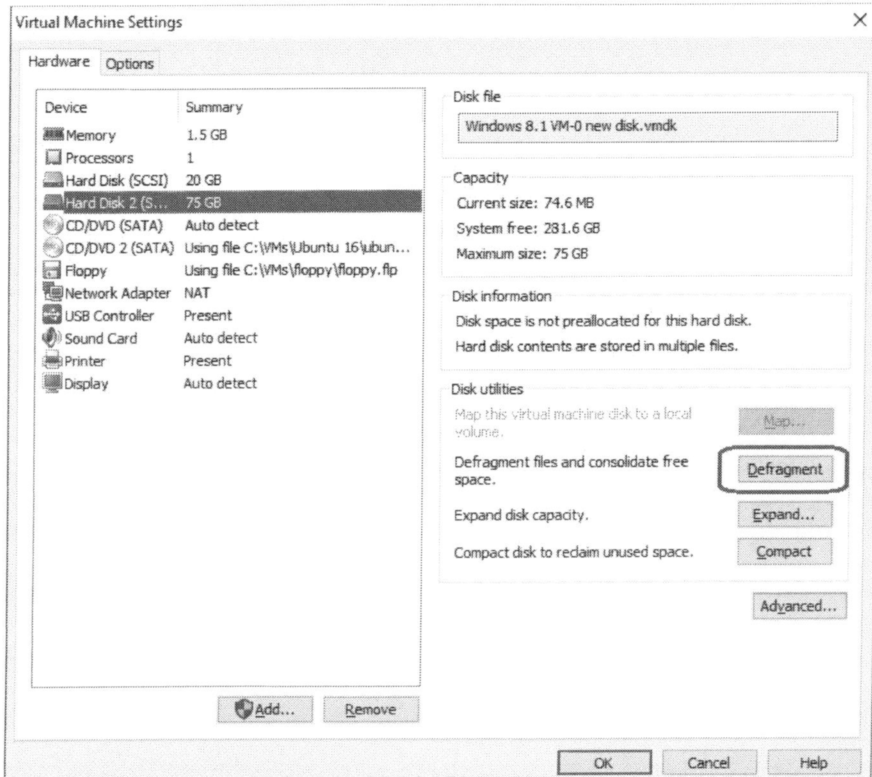

Figure 5-37 *Defragmenting a virtual HDD*

4. Click OK when the process is completed.

Remove a virtual hard disk

Removing a virtual hard disk disconnects it from a virtual machine in Player. Virtual disk files are not removed from the host system. After a virtual hard disk has been removed from a virtual machine, it can be mapped or mounted to the host system or added to another virtual machine, as explained in the lesson **Add an existing virtual hard disks**.

Here is how you would remove a virtual hard disk:

1. Select the virtual machine from the library and go to Player > Manage > Virtual Machine Settings.

2. Select the virtual hard disk you would like to remove and click **Remove**:

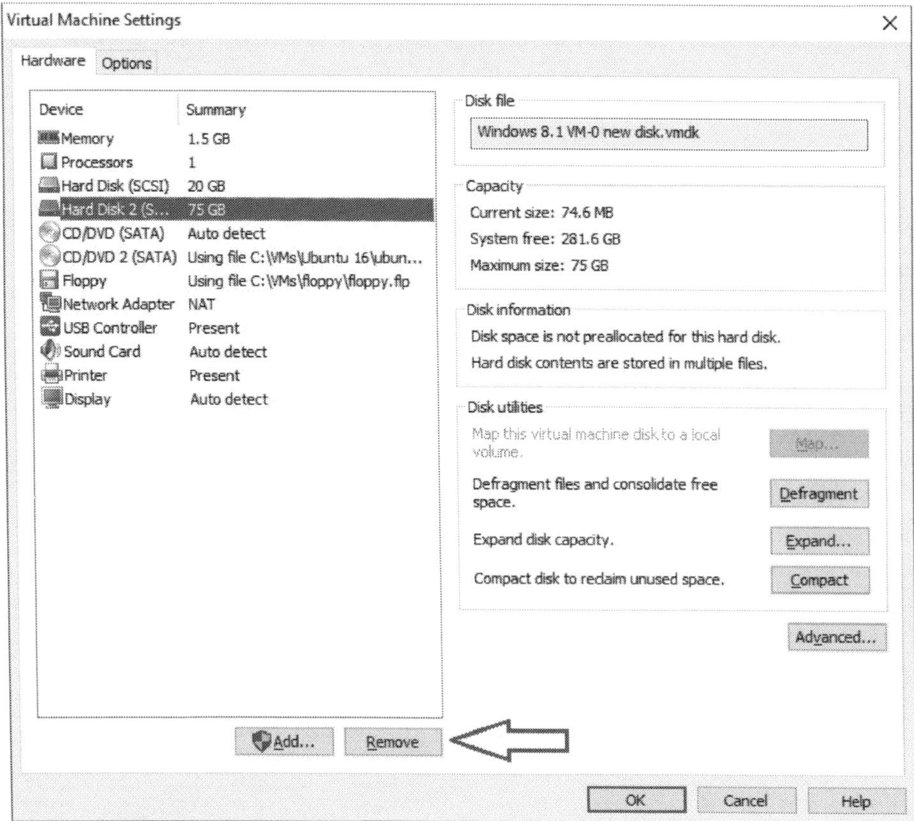

Figure 5-38 *Remove a virtual HDD*

The disk should be removed from the VM. As mentioned, removing the disk doesn't delete the virtual disk files from the host system:

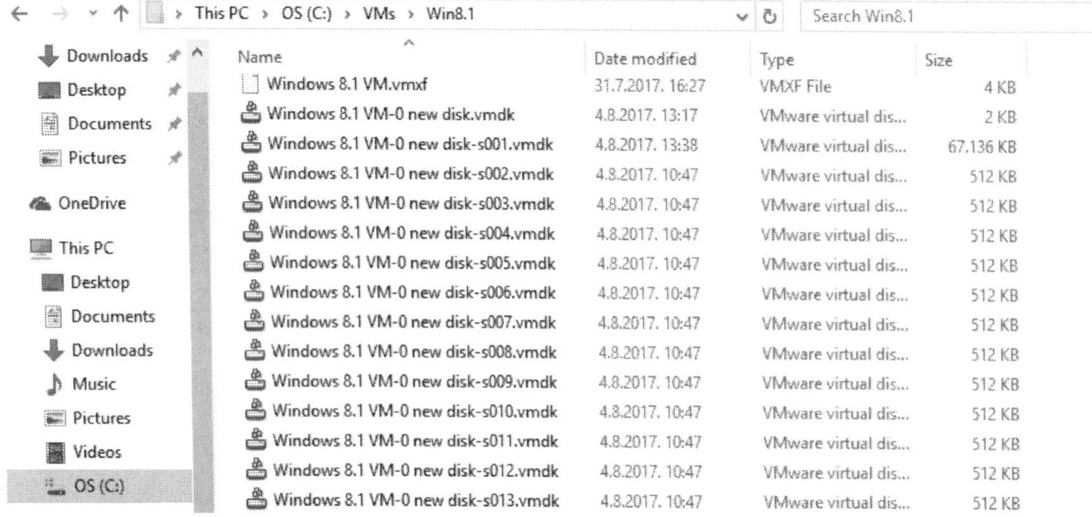

Figure 5-39 *Removing a virtual HDD doesn't remove the files*

Add a virtual parallel port

A virtual machine in VMware Workstation Player can use up to three bidirectional parallel (LPT) ports. Virtual parallel ports can be configured to send output to parallel ports or to files on the host system.

NOTE
Although rarely used today, parallel ports can still be found on some older printers or scanners. Most modern computers do not even provide a parallel port anymore.

Here is how you can add a virtual parallel port to a virtual machine:

1. Power off the virtual machine.

2. Select the virtual machine from the library and go to Player > Manage > Virtual Machine Settings.

3. Click Add on the Hardware tab.

4. Select Parallel port as the hardware type:

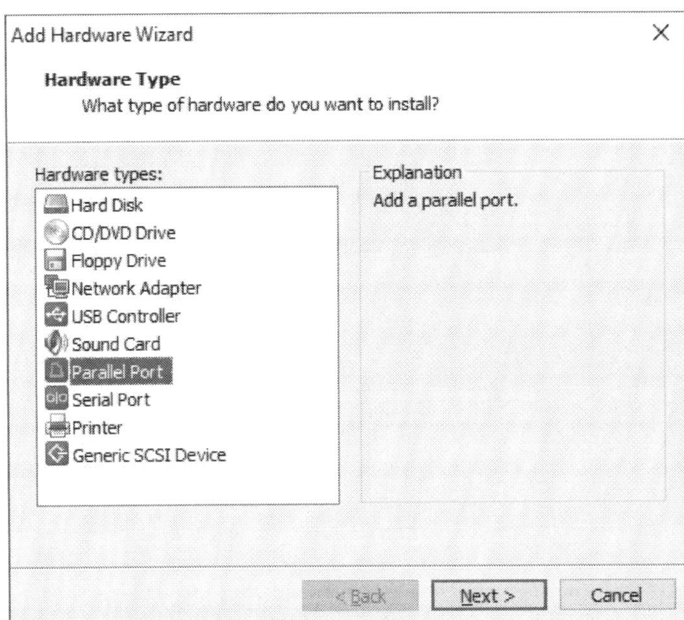

Figure 5-40 *Adding a parallel port*

5. Select where the virtual parallel port will send output. Two options are available:

- **Use physical parallel port on the host** - send output to the parallel port on the host system.
- **Output to file** - send output from the virtual parallel port to a file on the host system.

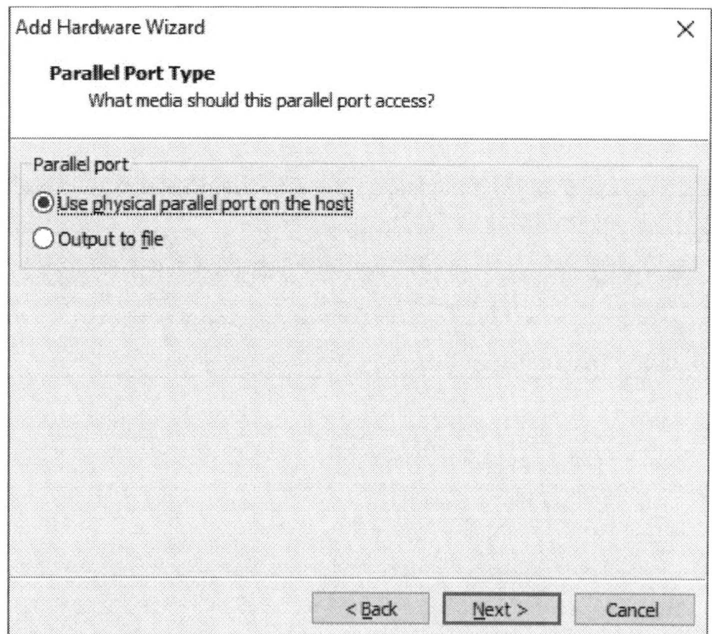

Figure 5-41 *Select where the virtual parallel port will send output*

5a. If you've selected the **Use physical parallel port on the host** option in the previous step, you need to select the physical parallel port or select the **Auto detect** option to allow Player to autodetect the port to use. To connect the virtual parallel port to the virtual machine when the virtual machine is powered on, check the **Connect at power on** option:

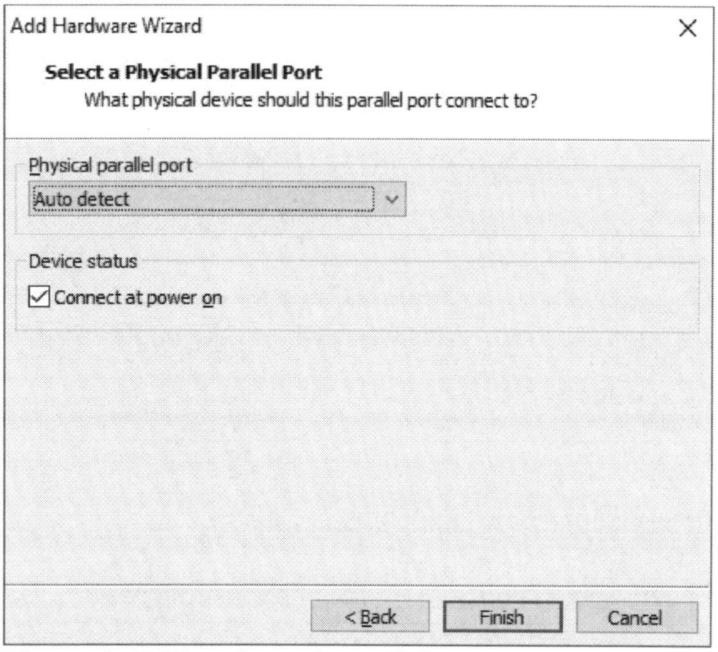

Figure 5-42 *Use physical parallel port on the host*

5b. If you've selected the **Output to file** option, you will need to select the output file:

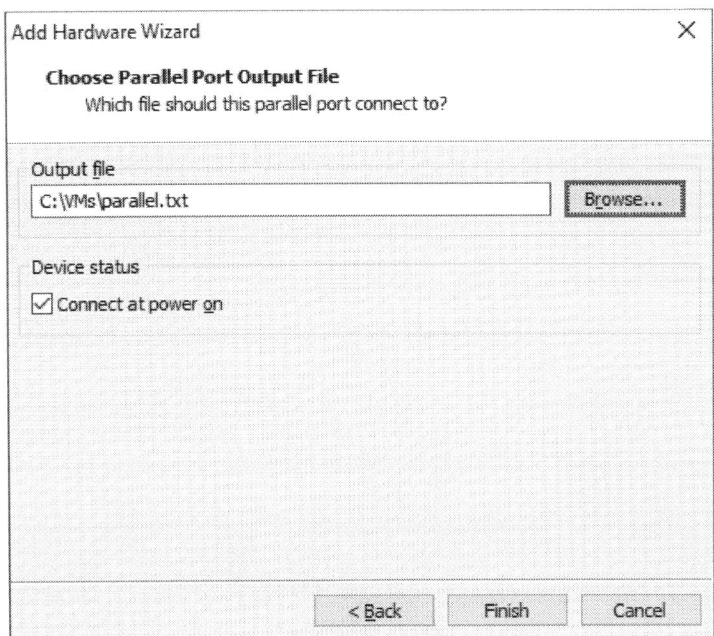

Figure 5-43 *Select the output file*

6. Click Finish to finish adding the virtual parallel port.

Add a virtual serial port

To make devices such as modems and printers accessible to the virtual machine, you must add a virtual serial port. A virtual machine in VMware Workstation Player can use up to four serial (COM) ports. They can be configured to send output to physical serial ports, files, or named pipes.

Here is how you can add a virtual serial port to a virtual machine:

1. Power off the virtual machine.

2. Select the virtual machine from the library and go to Player > Manage > Virtual Machine Settings.

3. Click Add on the Hardware tab.

4. Select Serial port as the hardware type:

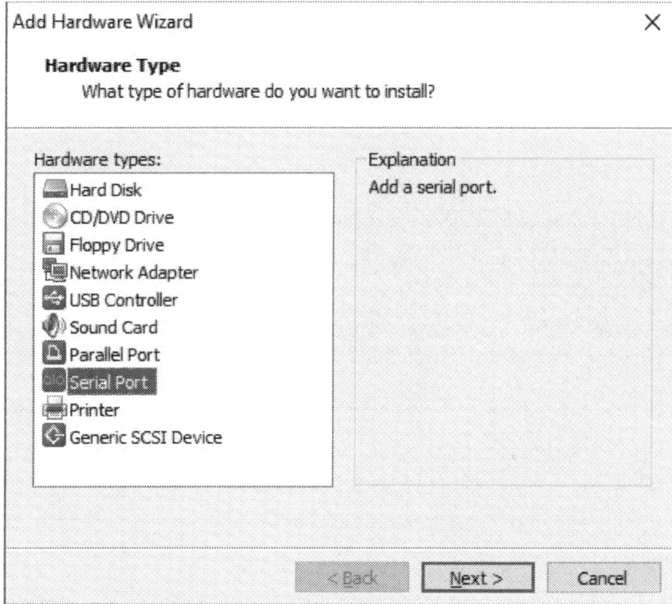

Figure 5-44 *Adding a serial port*

5. Select where the virtual serial port will send output. Three options are available:

- **Use physical serial port on the host** - send output to a physical serial port on the host system. Of course, your host needs to be equipped with such port.
- **Output to file** - send output to a file on the host system.
- **Output to named pipe** - set up a direct connection between two virtual machines, or between a virtual machine and an application on the host system.

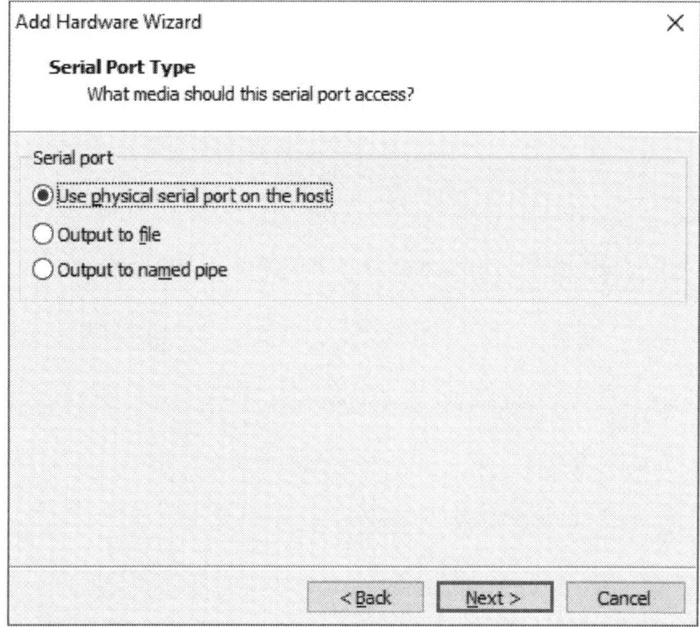

Figure 5-45 *Select the port type*

5a. If you've selected the **Use physical serial port on the host** option in the previous step, you will need to select the physical serial port or select the **Auto detect** option to allow Player to auto-detect the port to use. To connect the virtual serial port to the virtual machine when the virtual machine is powered on, check the **Connect at power on** option:

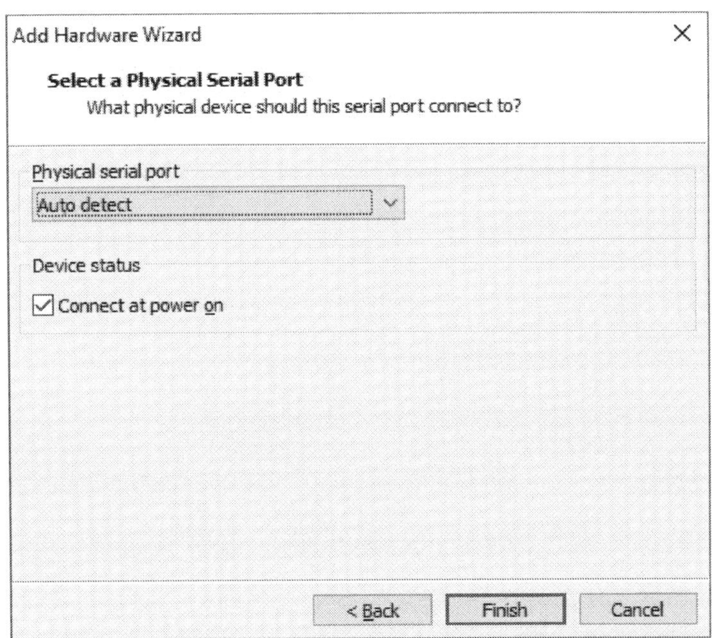

Figure 5-46 *Use physical serial port on the host*

5b. If you've selected the **Output to file** option, you will need to select the output file:

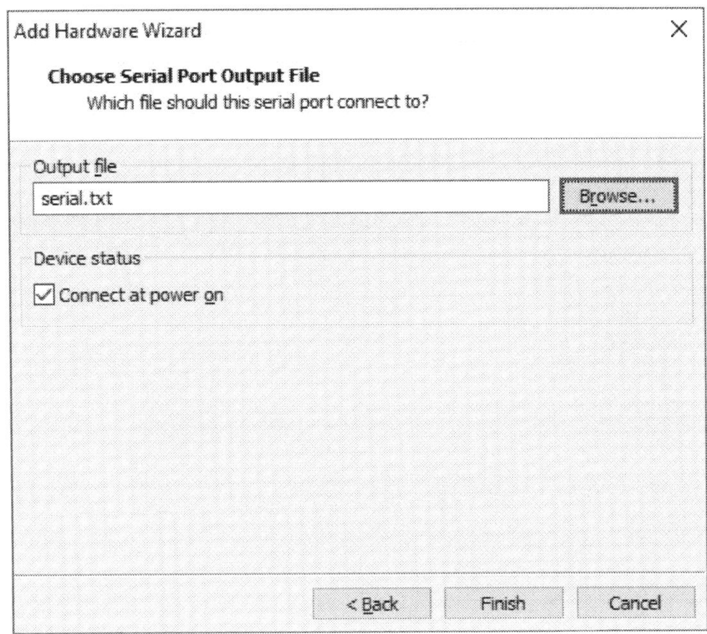

Figure 5-47 *Select the output file*

5c. If you've selected the **Output to named pipe** option, you will need to configure the named pipe. The configuration depends on the operating system version.

6. Click Finish to add the virtual serial port.

Add a generic SCSI device

The guest operating system can have direct access to SCSI devices connected to the host system, such as scanners or tape drives. A virtual machine can use the generic SCSI driver to run any SCSI device supported by the guest operating system.

You must add a generic SCSI device to the virtual machine to map virtual SCSI devices on the virtual machine to physical generic SCSI devices on the host system. Up to 60 generic SCSI devices can be added to a virtual machine.

Here is how you can add a generic SCSI device to a virtual machine in VMware Workstation Player:

1a. If you are using Windows host system, run Player as a user who has administrative access.

1b. If you are using Linux host system, log in as a user who has read and write permissions for the SCSI device.

2. Select the virtual machine from the library and go to Player > Manage > Virtual Machine Settings.

3. Click Add on the Hardware tab.

4. Select **Generic SCSI Device** as the hardware type:

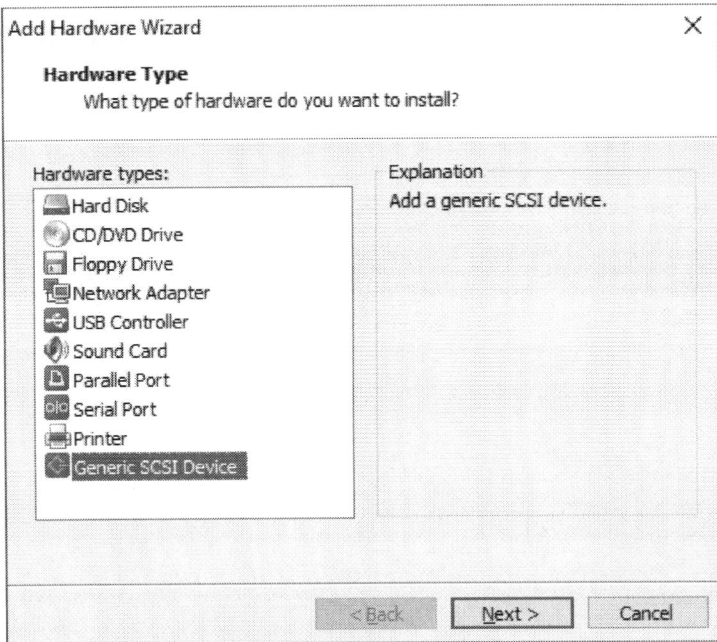

Figure 5-48 *Add generic SCSI device*

5. Select the physical SCSI device to map to the virtual SCSI device. To connect the SCSI device to the virtual machine when the virtual machine is powered on, check the **Connect at power on** option.

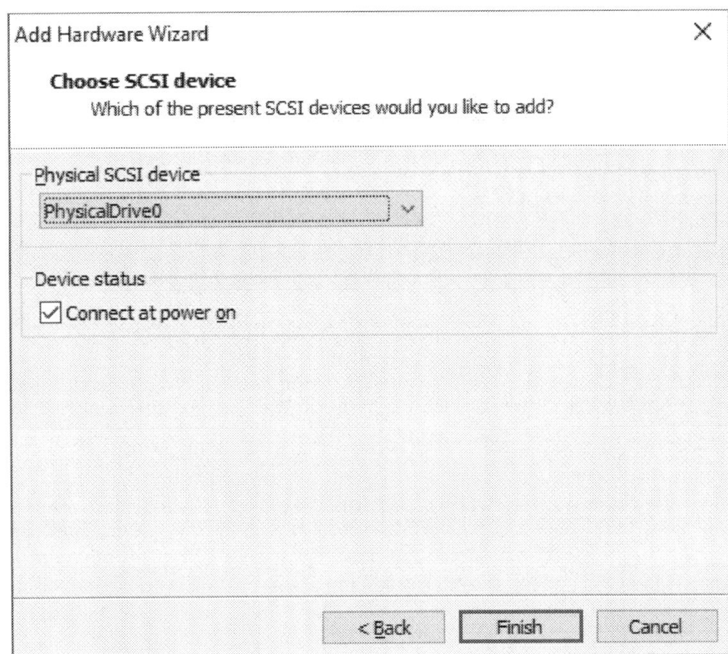

Figure 5-49 *Select the physical SCSI device to map to the virtual SCSI device*

6. Click Finish to add the device.

Virtual SMP (Symmetric Multi-Processing)

Virtual SMP (Symmetric Multi-Processing) enables a single virtual machine in VMware Workstation Player to use two or more processors simultaneously. This feature increases the processing capacity of a virtual machine and is usually used when you run resource intensive applications (e.g. databases or CRM applications) in a VM.

You can assign processors and cores per processor to a virtual machine on a host system that has at least two logical processors. The following hosts are considered to have two logical processors:

- multiprocessor hosts with two or more physical CPUs.
- single-processor hosts with a multicore CPU.
- single-processor hosts with hyperthreading enabled.

Here is how you can configure the four-way virtual symmetric multiprocessing (SMP) for an existing virtual machine:

1. Select the VM from the library and go to Player > Manage > Virtual Machine Settings.

2. On the Hardware tab, select Processors. On the right side, change the **Number of processor cores** setting to 4 and click OK:

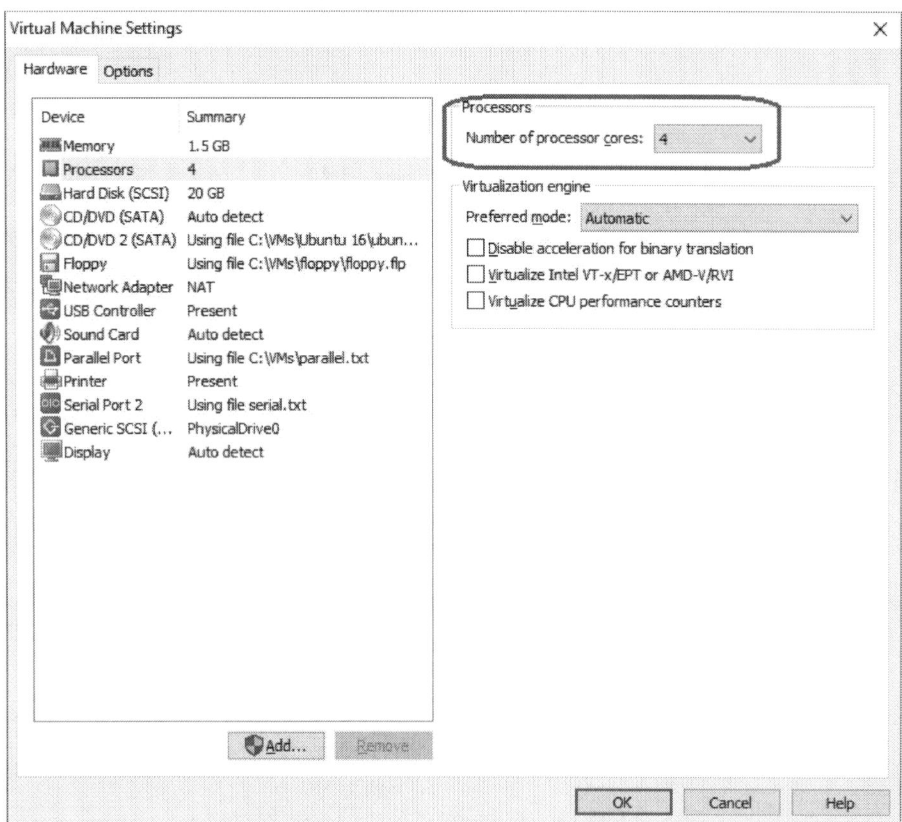

Figure 5-50 *Changing the number of CPU cores*

Enhanced virtual keyboard feature

The **Enhanced virtual keyboard feature** is useful if you have a non-US keyboard, since it offers better handling of international keyboards and keyboards with extra keys. This feature also improves security because it processes raw keyboard input as soon as possible and bypasses Windows keystroke processing and any malware that is not already at a lower layer. Note that this features is available only on Windows host systems.

You can choose to install the Enhanced virtual keyboard driver during the Player installation. If you didn't install it then, here are the steps to do it at a later stage:

1. Log in to your computer as an administrator.

2. Go to the Programs and Features menu in Control Panel. Find VMware Player under the list of the installed programs, and select Change:

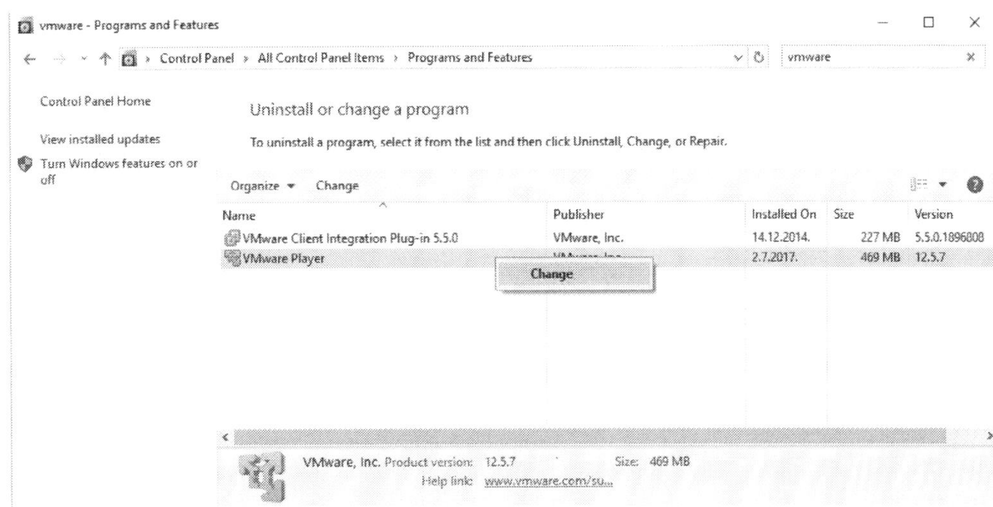

Figure 5-51 *Change Player features*

3. Click Next in the Welcome window. Choose Change on the next screen:

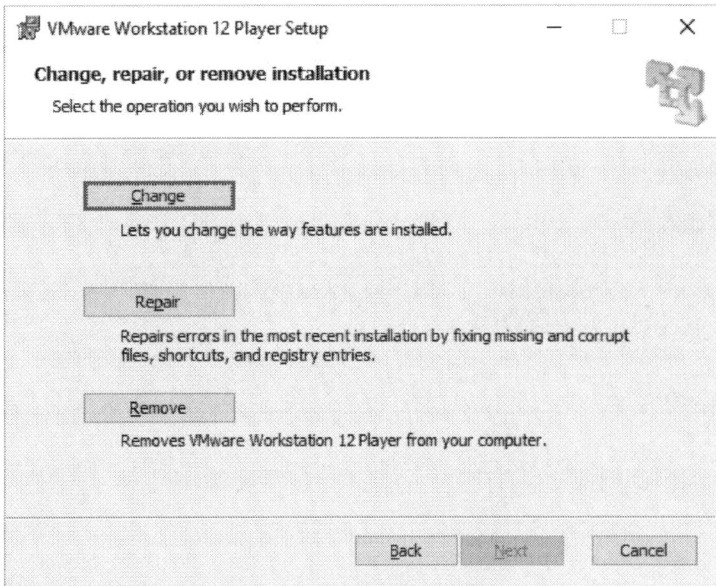

Figure 5-52 *Change Player installation*

4. Check the **Enhanced Keyboard Driver** checkbox to install the feature:

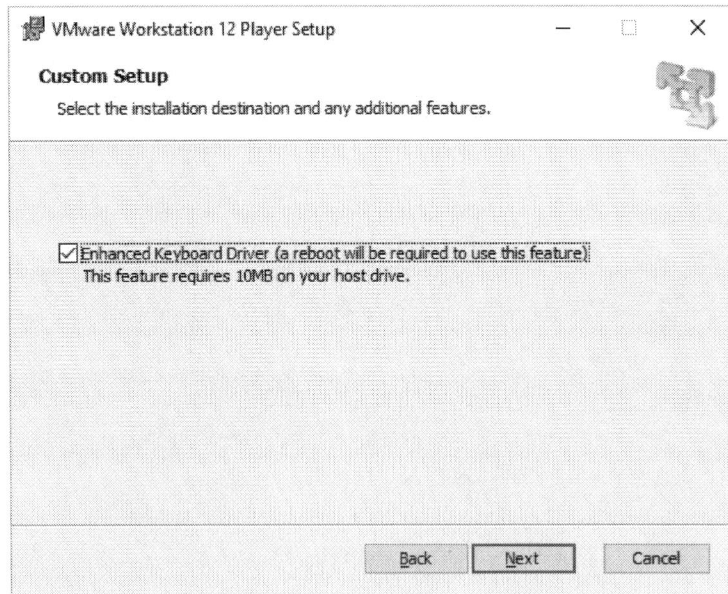

Figure 5-53 *Install Enhanced Keyboard Driver*

5. Once the installation finishes, restart your computer.

Once you've installed the Enhanced virtual keyboard driver, you can modify some of the options. Here are the steps:

1. Power off the virtual machine.

2. Select the virtual machine from the library and go to Player > Manage > Virtual Machine Settings.

3. Go to the Options tab and select General. From the **Enhanced virtual keyboard** drop-down menu, select one of these three options:

- **Off** - do not use the Enhanced virtual keyboard feature.
- **Use if available (recommended)** - use the Enhanced virtual keyboard feature, but only if the enhanced virtual keyboard driver is installed on the host system.
- **Required** - the virtual machine must use the Enhanced the virtual keyboard feature. If the enhanced keyboard driver is not installed on the host system, VMware Workstation Player returns an error message.

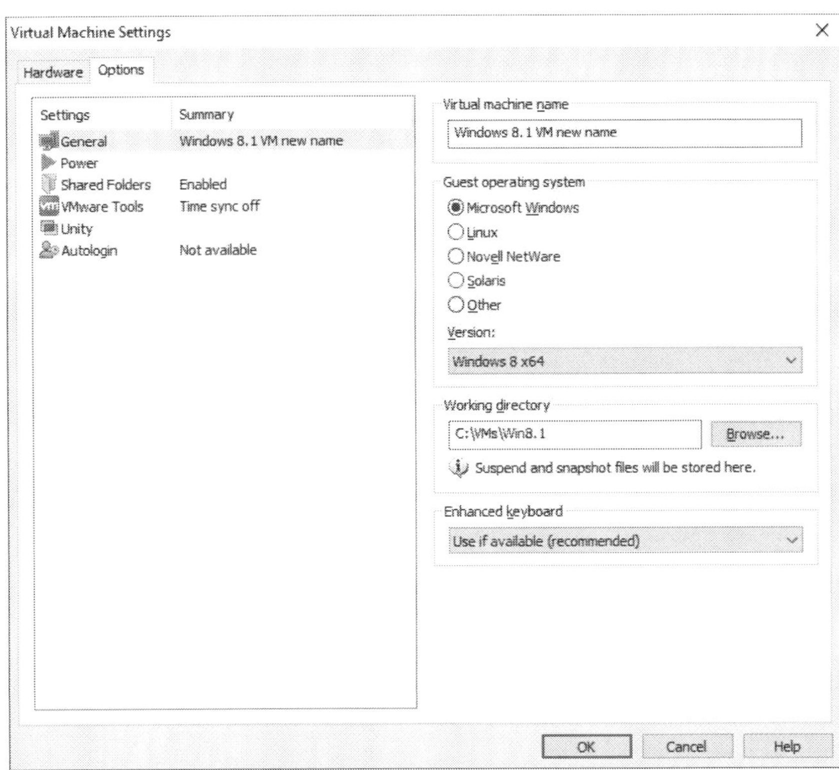

Figure 5-54 *Modify Enhanced virtual keyboard options*

4. Click OK to save the changes.

Summary

In this chapter you've learned how to add various types of devices to your VM - a floppy drive, CD/DVD-ROM drive, serial and parallel ports, and a generic SCSI device. We've mentioned virtual disks and how to perform some basic operations on them. We've then discussed how the Enhanced virtual keyboard feature offers better handling of international keyboards and keyboards with extra keys and how to enable it.

The last chapter of this book deals with different types of networking configuration available in Player - the bridged, NAT, and host-only networking.

This page intentionally left blank

This page intentionally left blank

This page intentionally left blank

This page intentionally left blank

Chapter 6 - Configuring virtual networks

IN THIS CHAPTER

Learning about different types of virtual networks

Adding virtual network adapters

Configuring bridged, NAT, and host-only networking

Limiting network bandwidth

This chapter deals with virtual networking. You will learn about different types of networking configurations available in Player (bridged, NAT, and host-only) and what are the benefits and drawbacks of each type. I will then show you how to limit the amount of network bandwidth available to the VM and how to change the MAC address of a virtual network adapter.

Virtual networking components

The virtual networking components in VMware Workstation Player are virtual switches, virtual network adapters, the virtual DHCP server, and the NAT device. Let's cover each of them in more detail.

Virtual switches

Virtual switches (also called virtual networks) connect networking components together, just like their physical counterparts. They are named VMnet0, VMnet1, VMnet2, VMnet3, etc. The following virtual switches are mapped to the specific networks by default:

- VMnet0 - Bridged
- VMnet1 - Host-only
- VMnet8 - NAT

You can create up to 20 virtual switches on a Windows host system and up to 255 virtual switches on a Linux host system. It is possible to connect an unlimited number of virtual network devices to a virtual switch on a Windows host system, but only up to 32 virtual network devices to a virtual switch on a Linux host system.

Virtual network adapters

A virtual network adapter is created when you create a VM. It appears in the guest operating system as either the **AMD PCNET PCI** or **Intel Pro/1000 MT Server** adapter. You can have up to 10 virtual network adapters for a single virtual machine. I will describe the process of adding a new virtual network adapter later in the chapter.

Virtual DHCP server

A virtual DHCP server assigns IP addresses and other network parameters to virtual machines in the host-only and NAT networking configurations.

NAT device

A NAT device passes network data between virtual machines and the external network, identifies incoming data packets intended for each VM, and sends them to the appropriate destination.

Networking configurations

Three types of networking configurations are available in VMware Workstation Player: bridged networking, NAT networking, and host-only networking. It is also possible to create custom virtual networks.

Bridged networking

A virtual machine is connected to a network using the network adapter on the host system. If the host system is on a local network, this networking configuration is often the easiest way to give your virtual machine access to it. A bridged network (**VMnet0**) is set up for you when you install Player.

NAT networking
A virtual machine does not have its own IP address on the external network. Instead, a separate private network is set up on the host system and the virtual machine gets an IP address on this private network from the virtual DHCP server. The virtual machine and the host system share a single network identity that is not visible on the external network.

A NAT network (**VMnet8**) is set up for you when you install Player. You can have only a single NAT network.

Host-Only networking
A network that is completely contained within the host computer is created. This networking configuration provides a network connection between the virtual machine and the host system by using a virtual network adapter that is visible on the host operating system.

A host-only network (**VMnet1**) is set up when you install Player.

Add a virtual network adapter

Up to 10 virtual network adapters can be added to a virtual machine in VMware Workstation Player. Here are the steps to add a new virtual network adapter to a VM:

1. Select the VM from the library and go to Player > Manage > Virtual Machine Settings.

2. Click Add on the Hardware tab.

3. Select **Network Adapter** as the hardware type:

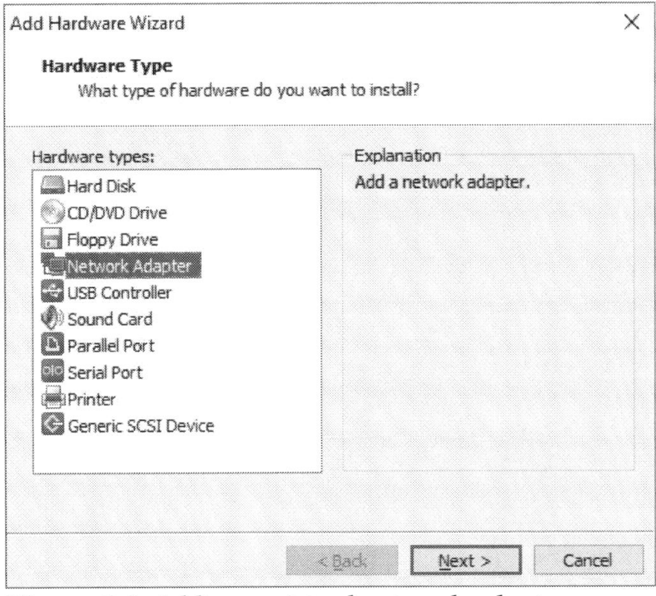

Figure 6-1 *Adding a virtual network adapter*

4. Select the network adapter type. Three options are available:

- **Bridged: Connected directly to the physical network** - the virtual machine is connected to the network by using the network adapter on the host system.
- **NAT: Used to share the host's IP address** - the virtual machine does not have its own IP address on the external network. Instead, a separate private network is set up on the host system and the virtual machine gets an IP address on this private network from the virtual DHCP server. The virtual machine and the host system share a single network identity that is not visible on the external network.
- **Host-only: A private network shared with the host** - a network that is completely contained within the host computer.

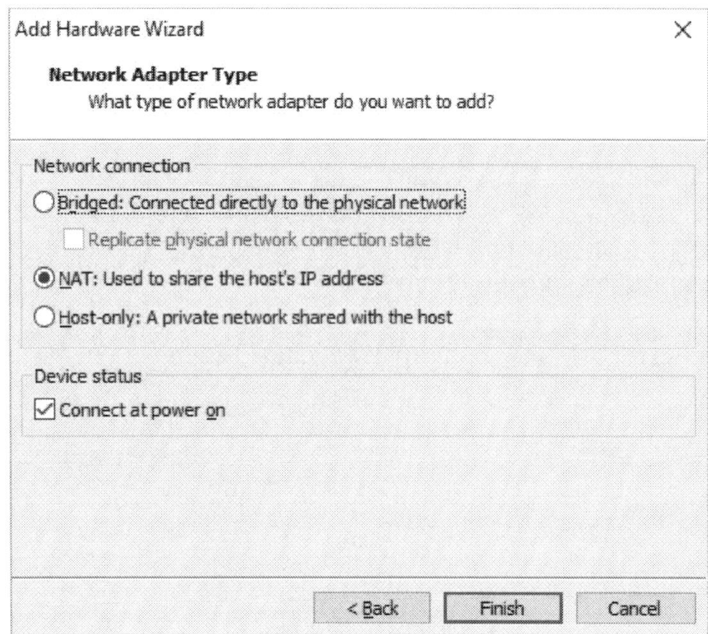

Figure 6-2 *Choosing the network type*

5. Click Finish to finish adding the virtual network adapter.

I've added a new virtual network adapter to my Windows 8.1 virtual machine. So now I have two network adapters (the first one was added when I've created the VM):

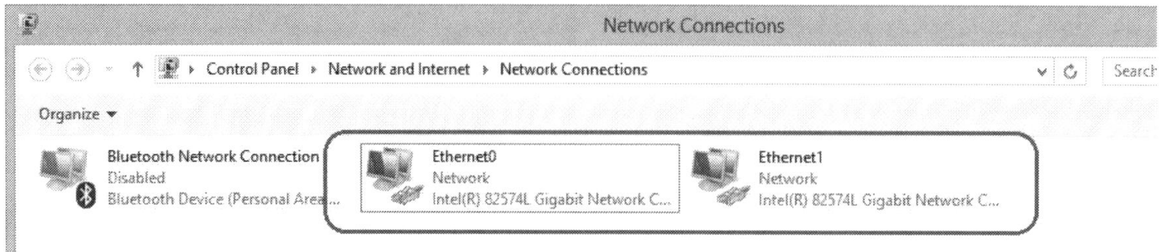

Figure 6-3 *Network adapters in a VM*

Set up bridged networking

In bridged networking, a virtual machine is connected to a network using the network adapter on the host system. This networking configuration is often the easiest way to give your virtual machine access to the network. A bridged network (**VMnet0**) is set up for you when you install Player.

In the figure below you can see an example bridged networking configuration:

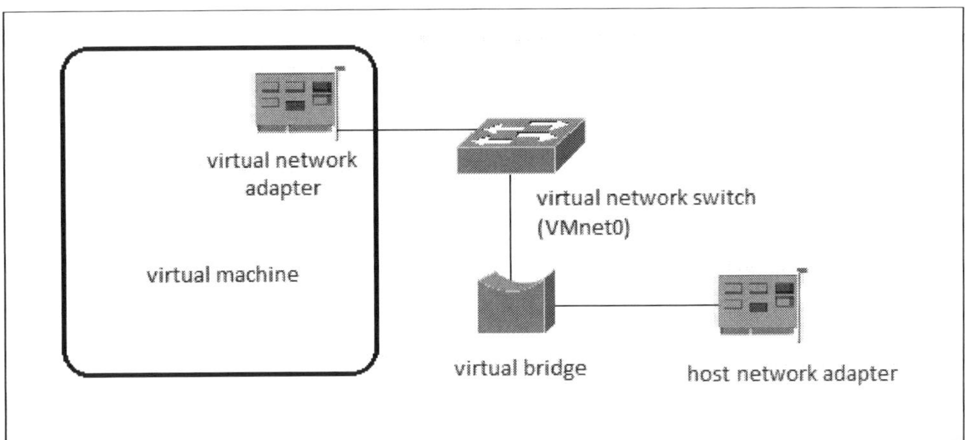

Figure 6-4 *Bridged networking*

Bridged networking works with both wired and wireless host network adapters. A virtual machine is an unique identity on the network, unrelated to the host system. It has its own IP address and can communicate with other computer on the network, as if it is a physical computer on the network. Usually, the guest operating system acquires an IP address and other network parameters from the DHCP server on the network, but you can also set the IP address and other network parameters manually in the guest operating system.

Configure bridged networking for an existing virtual machine

Here is how you can configure bridged networking for an existing virtual machine:

1. Select the virtual machine from the library and go to Player > Manage > Virtual Machine Settings.

2. On the Hardware tab, select the network adapter you would like to modify. Under Network connection, select **Bridged: Connected directly to the physical network**:

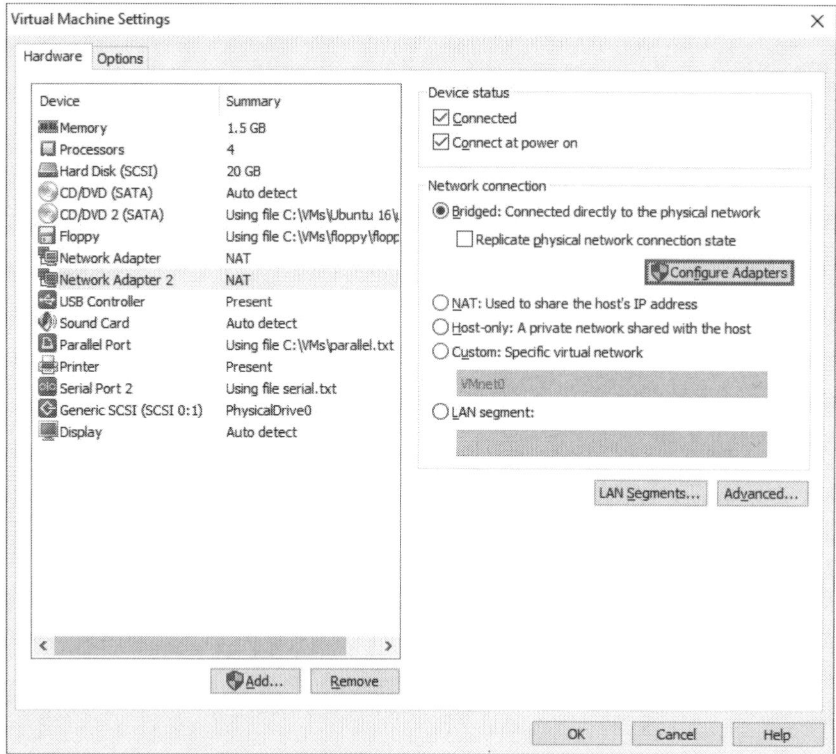

Figure 6-5 *Configuring bridged networking*

If you use the virtual machine on a laptop, check the **Replicate physical network connection state** checkbox. This option causes the IP address to be renewed when you move from one wired or wireless network to another.

3. Click OK to save the changes.

I've modified the network adapter I've created in the previous lesson. The DHCP server in my local network is a router with the IP address of 192.168.5.1, which also serves as the default gateway. Since bridged networking means that a VM is an unique identity on the network, my VM will get its IP address and other network parameters from the DHCP server on my router:

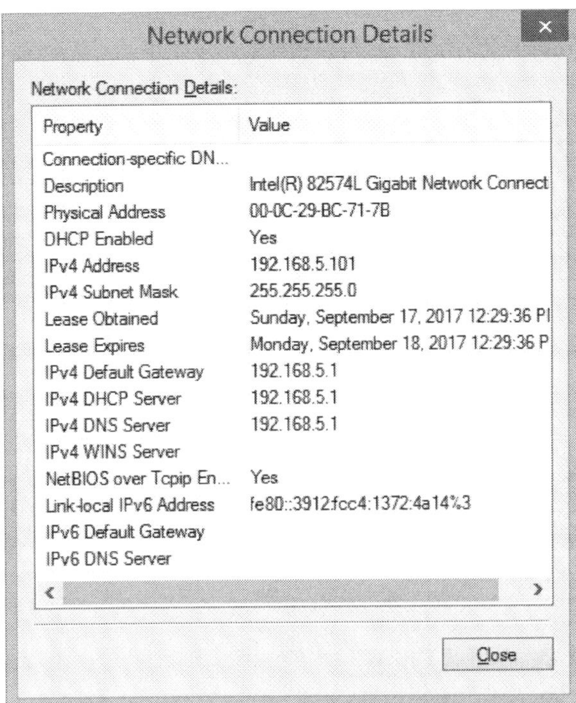

Figure 6-6 *Bridged networking IP information*

This is the DHCP table on my router, with **antun-pc** being the host OS and **Windows8-1VM** being the guest operating system running in the VM:

DHCP Table

Those devices which get their IP addresses from your DSL router are listed below.

Hostname	MAC Address	IP Address	Expires In
tuna-pc	94:de:80:b0:1b:2b	192.168.5.100	0 seconds
Windows8-1VM	00:0c:29:bc:71:7b	192.168.5.101	23 hours, 58 minutes, 22 seconds

Figure 6-7 *DHCP table on my router*

Other hosts on the network will see the VM as a unique entity on the network. The logical view of my bridged network looks like this:

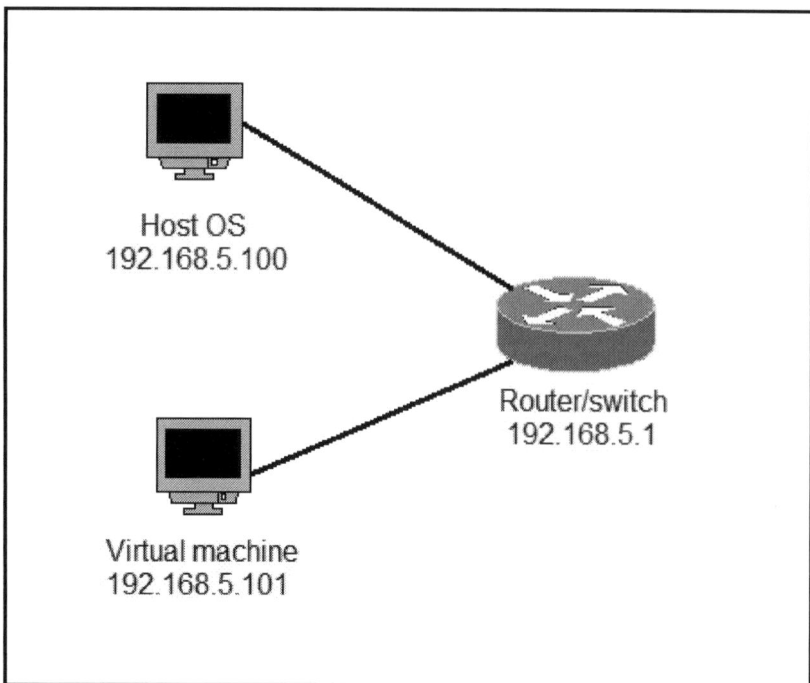

Figure 6-8 *Logical view of my bridged network*

Set up NAT networking

In NAT (Network Address Translation) networking, a virtual machine does not have its own IP address on the external network. Instead, a separate private network is set up on the host system and the virtual machine gets its IP address on this private network from the virtual DHCP server. A VM configured for NAT networking uses a different IP address from a different IP subnet to the one in use on the physical network.

The virtual machine and the host system share a single network identity that is not visible on the external network. When the virtual machine sends a request to access a network resource, it appears to the network resource as if the request is coming from the host system. Virtual machines can reach the outside network and can communicate with other hosts on the LAN.

In the figure below you can see an example NAT configuration:

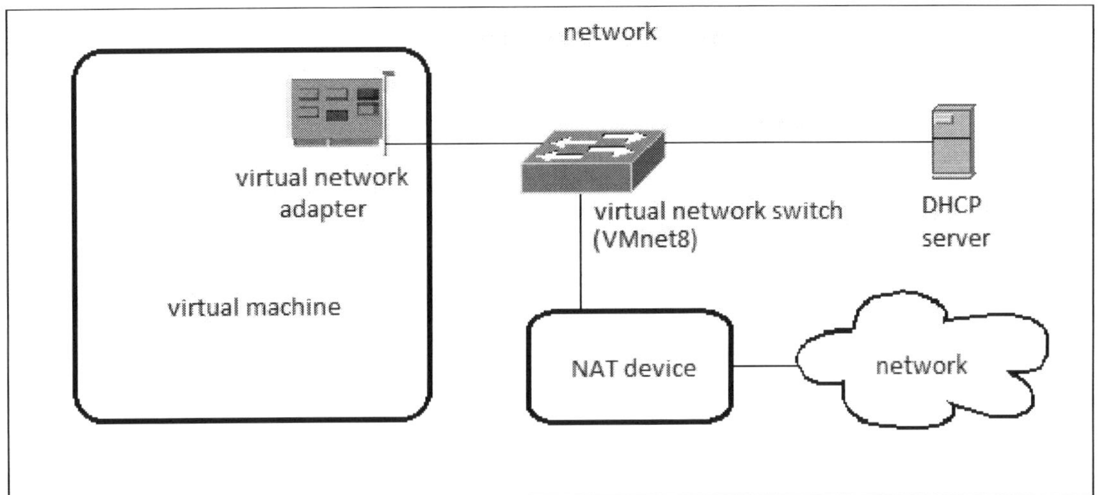

Figure 6-9 *NAT networking*

A NAT network **(VMnet8)** is set up for you when you install Player. The host system has a virtual network adapter on the NAT network that enables the host system and virtual machines to communicate. The NAT device passes network data between virtual machines and the external network, identifies incoming data packets intended for each virtual machine, and sends them to the appropriate destination.

Configure NAT networking for an existing virtual machine

Here is how you can configure NAT networking for an existing virtual machine in Player:

1. Select the virtual machine from the library and go to Player > Manage > Virtual Machine Settings.

2. On the Hardware tab, select the network adapter you would like to modify. Under Network connection, select **NAT: Used to share the host's IP address**:

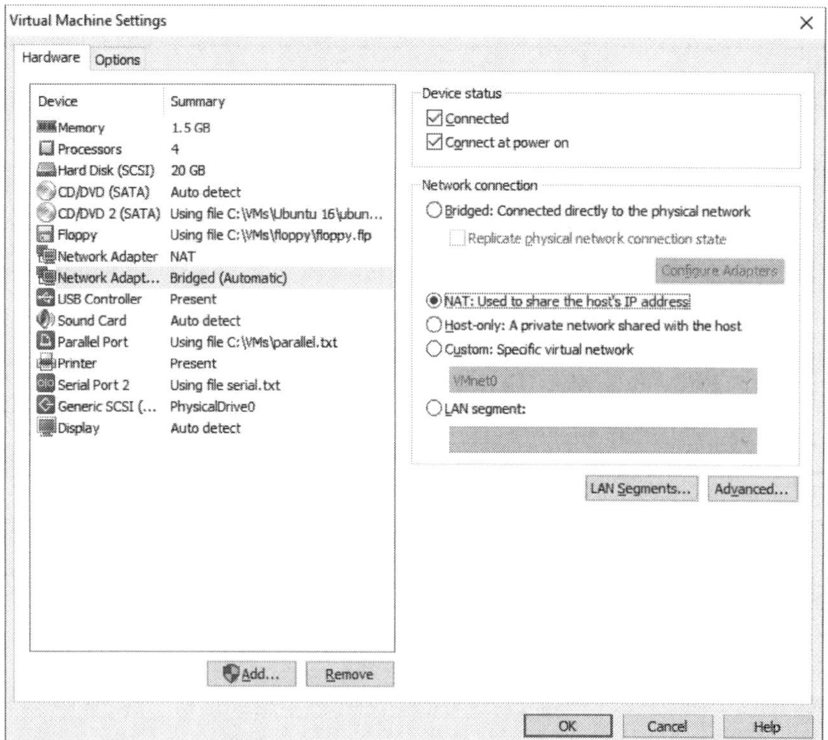

Figure 6-10 *Configuring NAT networking*

3. Click OK to save the changes.

If I change the network adapter type in my **Windows 8.1 VM** back to NAT, the IP address and other paramters of the adapter will change. Notice that the network adapter no longer gets its DHCP information from the DHCP server on the local network - the virtual DHCP server provides all the parameters instead:

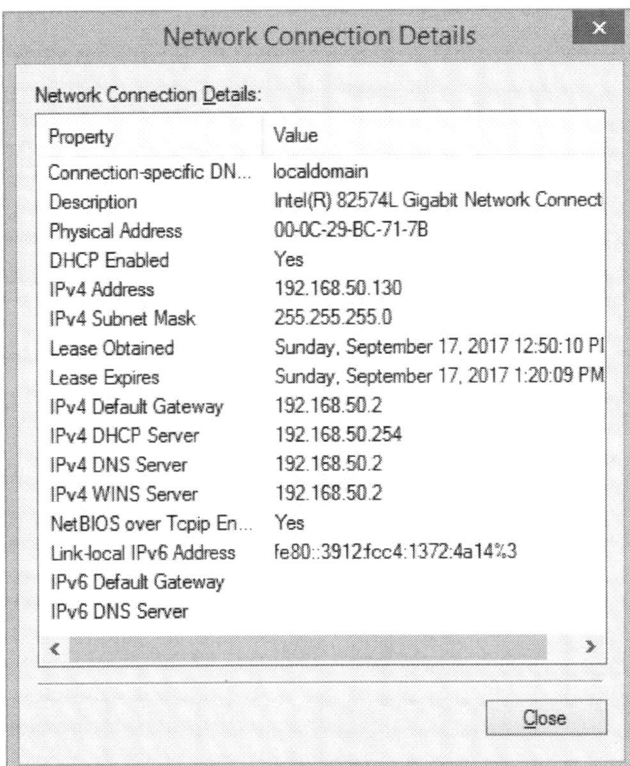

Figure 6-11 *NAT networking IP information*

Set up host-only networking

In host-only networking, a network completely contained within the host computer is created. This networking configuration provides a network connection between the virtual machine and the host system by using a virtual network adapter that is visible on the host operating system. The virtual DHCP server provides IP addresses on the host-only network. This type of networking is usually used for testing purposes (e.g. running malware in a VM without worrying that the malware will reach other hosts on your local network or the Internet).

In the figure below you can see an example host-only networking configuration:

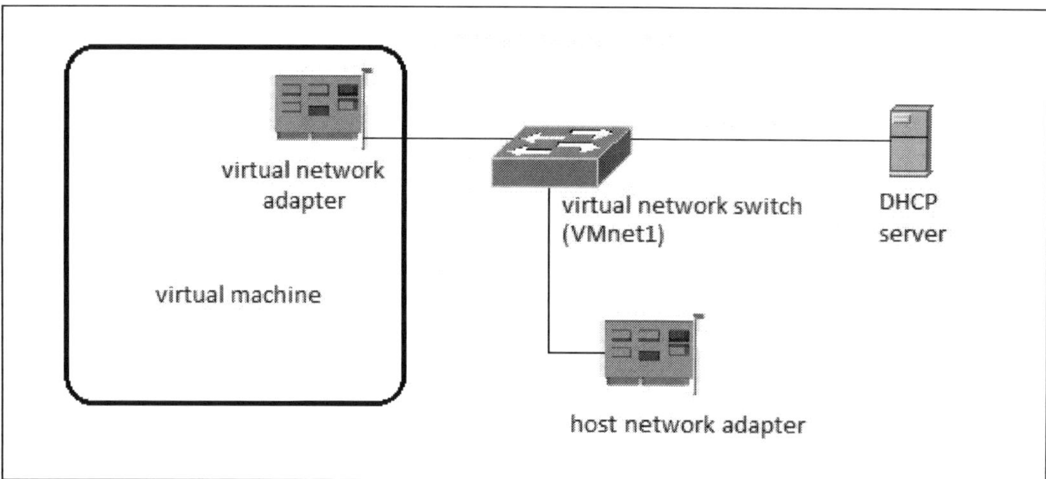

Figure 6-12 *Host-only networking*

A host-only network (**VMnet1**) is set up for you when you install Player. In the default configuration, a virtual machine is isolated and cannot connect to the Internet or reach other hosts on the LAN.

Here is how you can configure host-only networking for an existing virtual machine:

1. Select the virtual machine from the library and go to Player > Manage > Virtual Machine Settings.

2. On the Hardware tab, select Network Adapter. Under Network connection, select **Host-only: A private network shared with the host**:

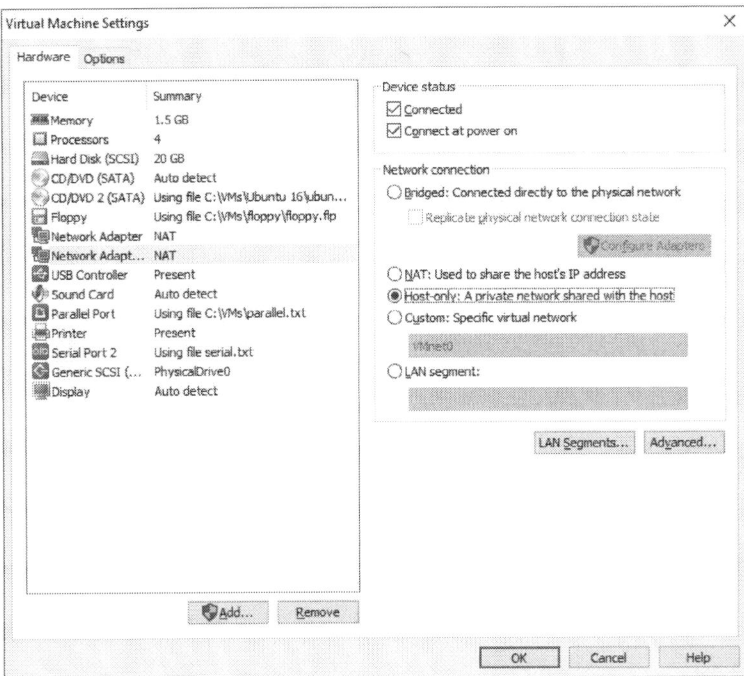

Figure 6-13 *Configuring host-only networking*

(Optional) You can also connect the adapter to a custom host-only network. Under Network connection, select **Custom: Specific virtual network** and select the custom host-only network:

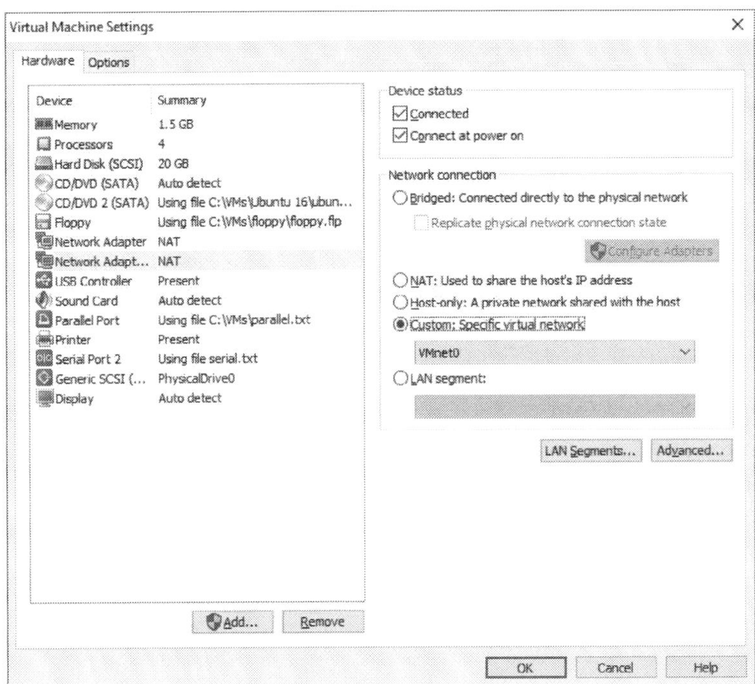

Figure 6-14 *Custom networking configuration*

3. Click OK to save the changes.

If I change the network adapter type in my **Windows 8.1** virtual machine to host-only, the network adapter will get the IP address from the virtual DHCP server and the VM will not be able to access the Internet. Notice the lack of the default gateway:

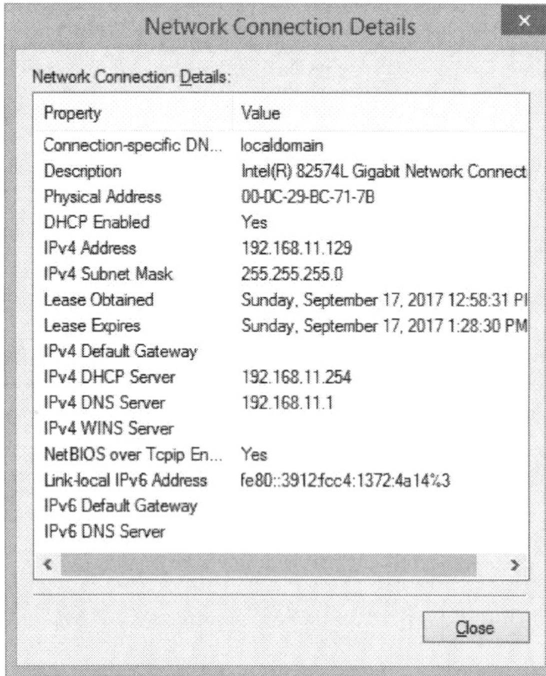

Figure 6-15 *Host-only networking IP information*

NOTE
To configure host-only networking for a new virtual machine, select the **Customize Hardware** option during the New Virtual Machine wizard.

Limit network bandwidth for a VM

You can limit the network bandwidth available to a VM. This feature can come in handy when you are downloading a large software package in the VM that is slowing down your Internet connection, and you want to continue browsing the Internet on your host computer. Another use of this feature would be to test how applications you are developing react to a limited network bandwidth.

It is possible to limit both the upload and download speed. Here is how you can do that:

1. Go to Player > Manage Virtual Machine Settings. Select the network adapter for which you want to limit the bandwidth and click the **Advanced** button:

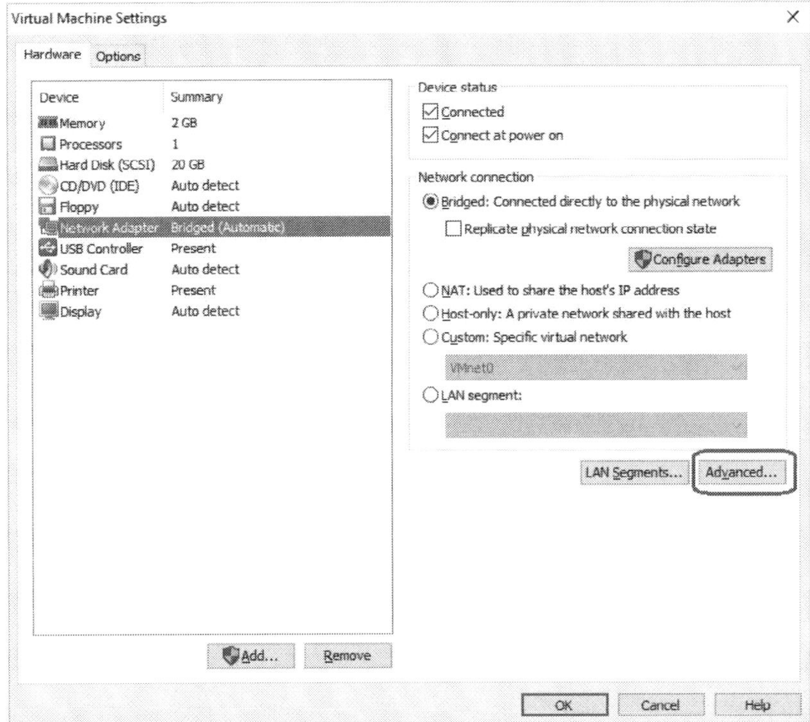

Figure 6-16 *Advanced network configuration*

3. You can limit both the upload and download speed. Under the **Bandwidth** drop down menu, choose one of the network connection types listed or enter the value manually in the **Kbps** field. I will limit my VM to 1 Mbps of the incoming data transfer rate:

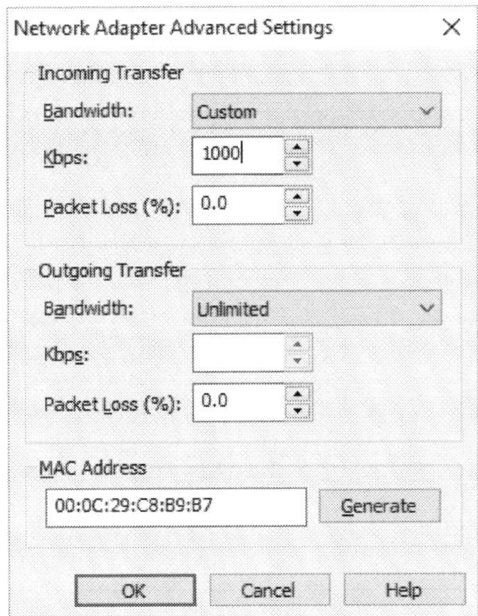

Figure 6-17 *Limit incoming bandwidth*

I can test whether the download speed of my VM has been limited to 1 Mbps by using websites such as *fast.com*:

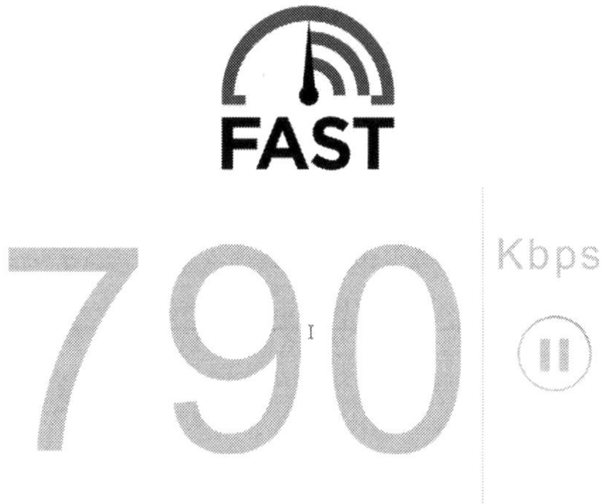

Figure 6-18 *The VM has limited network bandwidth*

Configure packet loss percentage

Under the Advanced setting of a virtual network adapter, there are also **Packet Loss** fields for incoming and outgoing transfers. These fields allow you to specify the packet loss percentage. For example, if you are developing an application and would like to test how it works in networks in which 50% of packets are dropped, entering 50 in these fields will allow you to simulate such conditions:

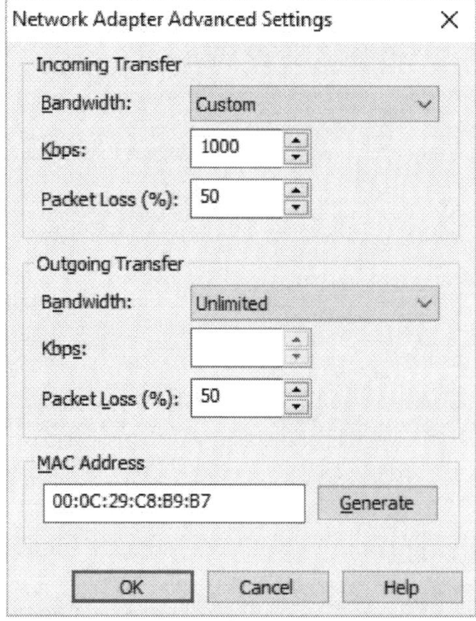

Figure 6-19 *Configuring the packet loss percentage*

Now if I try to ping a public IP address, many packets will be dropped:

```
C:\>ping 8.8.8.8 -n 10

Pinging 8.8.8.8 with 32 bytes of data:
Reply from 8.8.8.8: bytes=32 time=78ms TTL=128
Reply from 8.8.8.8: bytes=32 time=77ms TTL=128
Request timed out.
Request timed out.
Request timed out.
Reply from 8.8.8.8: bytes=32 time=76ms TTL=128
Request timed out.
Request timed out.
Request timed out.
Request timed out.

Ping statistics for 8.8.8.8:
    Packets: Sent = 10, Received = 3, Lost = 7 (70% loss),
Approximate round trip times in milli-seconds:
    Minimum = 76ms, Maximum = 78ms, Average = 77ms
```

Change VM's MAC address

A MAC address is a 48-bit address that is used for communication between two hosts in an Ethernet environment. The address is written in the form of 12 hexadecimal digits, with the first six hexadecimal characters representing the vendor. That is why VM's addresses usually start with 00:50:56 or 00:0C:29 - these identifiers are assigned to VMware.

Player automatically assigns each of its virtual network adapters an Ethernet MAC address. You can use the **Advanced** settings under the virtual network adapter menu to change the adapter's MAC address.

Here are the steps to change to assign a new MAC address to the network adapter:

1. Make sure that the VM is not in the suspended state. The VM can either be powered on or powered off.

2. Go to Player > Manage Virtual Machine Settings. Select the network adapter for which you want to change the MAC address and click the **Advanced** button.

3. Click on the Generate button to let Player determine the new MAC address of enter the address manually:

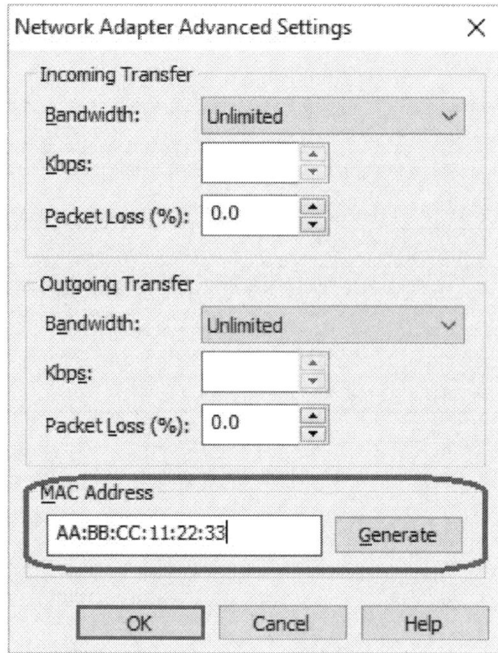

Figure 6-20 *Changing the MAC address*

4. Power off the VM and then power it back on. You can verify that the MAC address has indeed been changed by running the *ipconfig/all* command (of course, this command works only if you are running Windows as your guest OS):

```
C:\Users>ipconfig/all
...
Ethernet adapter Local Area Connection:

   Connection-specific DNS Suffix  . :
   Description . . . . . . . . . . . : Intel(R) PRO/1000 MT Network Connection
   Physical Address. . . . . . . . . : AA-BB-CC-11-22-33
   DHCP Enabled. . . . . . . . . . . : Yes
   Autoconfiguration Enabled . . . . : Yes
   Link-local IPv6 Address . . . . . : fe80::3105:21ee:e3d0:d5de%11(Preferred)
   IPv4 Address. . . . . . . . . . . : 192.168.5.105(Preferred)
   Subnet Mask . . . . . . . . . . . : 255.255.255.0
   Lease Obtained. . . . . . . . . . : Wednesday, September 06, 2017 9:52:24 PM
   Lease Expires . . . . . . . . . . : Thursday, September 07, 2017 9:52:23 PM
...
```

NOTE
Many routers offer an option to reserve certain IP addresses to device with specific MAC addresses. You can test whether the reservation will work by changing the MAC address of your virtual network adapter to a reserved address and verifying that the router will provide the valid IP address.

Summary

In the last chapter of this book we've talked about different types of virtual networking. You've learned about bridged, NAT, and host-only networking and differences between them. I showed you how to add and configure a new virtual network adapter. We've also learned how to limit network bandwidth available to a VM and how to change the virtual network adapter's MAC address.

This page intentionally left blank

This page intentionally left blank

This page intentionally left blank

Afterword

Congratulations! You've learned the basics of VMware Workstation Player. From here, you can go in a number of different directions. You can try out other free desktop virtualization applications (such as Oracle VM VirtualBox) or you can continue with some more advanced VMware products, such as VMware Workstation Pro or even start with server virtualization technology such as VMware vSphere.

I hope you have learned what you wanted when reading this book. If you encounter any problems or have a question regard the topic feel free to contact me at *info@it-courses.org*. I will try respond to your email within 3 business days. Thank you!

This page intentionally left blank

Appendix A - VMware Workstation Player use cases

At the beginning of the book I've mentioned some scenarios in which you would use VMware Workstation Player. In this appendix I will describe two of those scenarios in more detail.

Run virtual appliances

Virtual appliances are prebuilt and preconfigured virtual machine images that can be deployed on VMware Workstation Player. These appliances are usually packaged in the OVA (Open Virtualization) format or come as a zip file containing a virtual disk file (*.vmdk*) and a *.vmx* configuration file.

A virtual appliance usually contains a complete software stack needed to run a particular product. For example, consider the situation in which you need a virtual machine with WordPress installed in it. Without virtual appliances, you would have to go through the following scenario:

1. Find and download an ISO file containing the operating system that WordPress will be installed on.

2. Install and configure the OS in VMware Workstation Player.

3. Install a local server and database that WordPress will use.

4. Download and install WordPress.

5. Configure WordPress to use the installed web server and database.

With virtual appliances, you can download an image that already contains the server, database, and WordPress installed and have a fully functional WordPress installation in a matter of minutes.

One of the largest free open source libraries of virtual appliances is **The Turnkey Linux Virtual Appliance Library** (*https://www.turnkeylinux.org/*). This library contains hundreds of Debian-based VM images, available for free download. One of such appliances contains the whole WordPress installation, and can be downloaded from here: *https://www.turnkeylinux.org/wordpress*

Appliances are usually available in different formats. Since we are going to install the appliance in VMware Workstation Player, we will download the appliance as the zip file that contains the virtual disk and configuration file. So click on the VMDK link to start the installation:

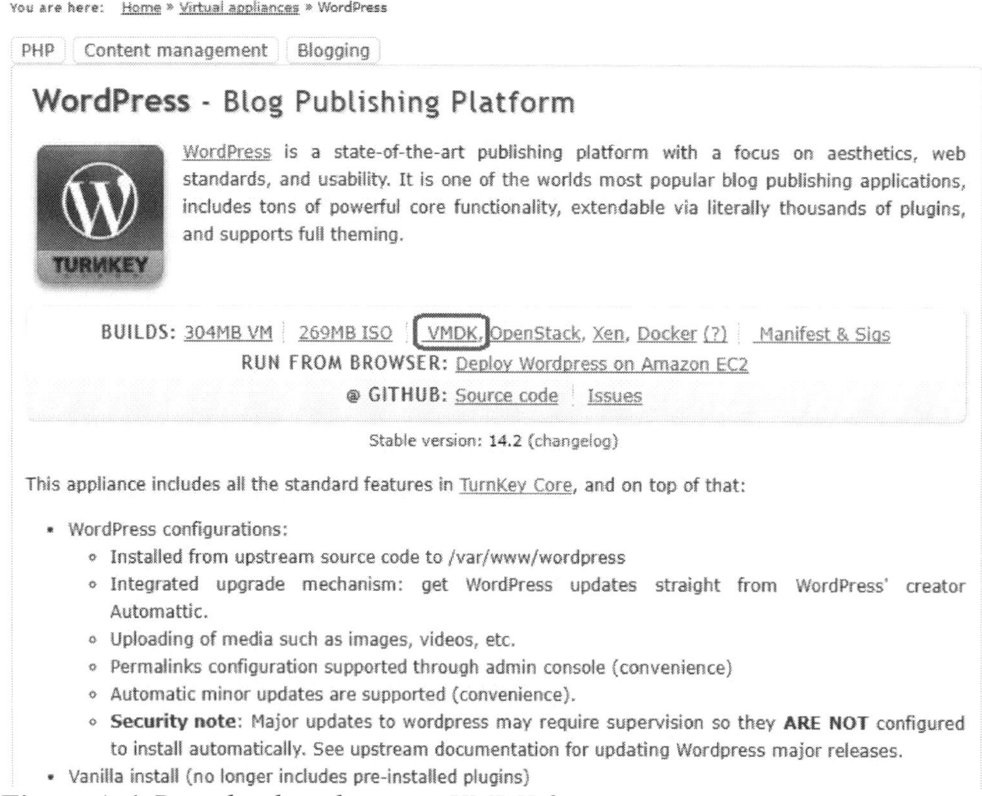

Figure A-1 *Download appliance in VMDK format*

After the download finished, extract the zip file:

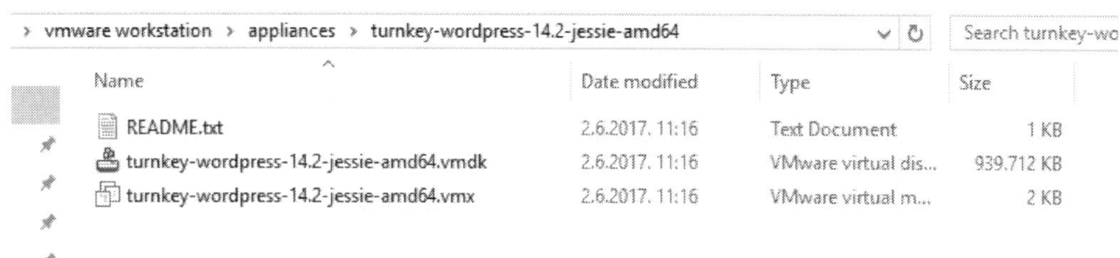

Figure A-2 *Extracted appliance zip file*

Next, open VMware Workstation Player and select Player > File > Open. Browse to the location of the extracted *.vmx* file and click Open:

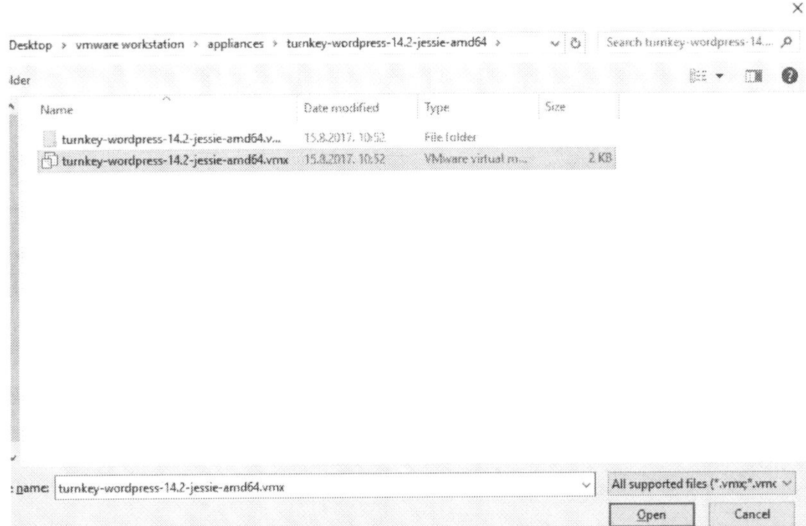

Figure A-3 *Open virtual appliance*

The VM should appear in the library. Click **Play virtual machine** to start it:

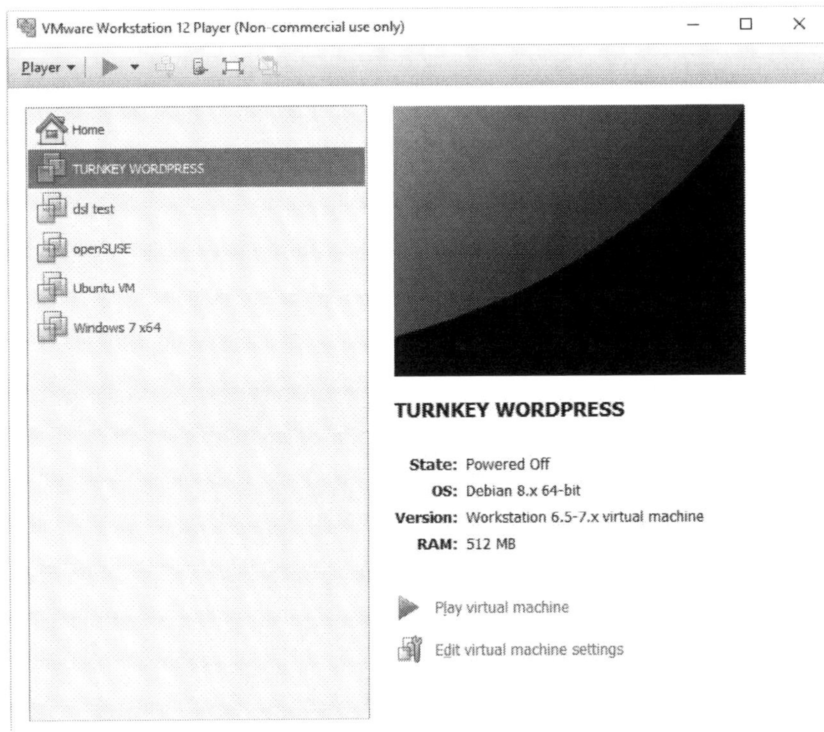

Figure A-4 *Start virtual appliance*

After you start the appliance, you will be asked a series of questions (the root password, the WordPress admin password...). Answer these questions and the configuration should finish without your further intervention.

After all configuration finishes, the VM will boot into the **TurnKey Configuration Console** with information about your WordPress installation:

Figure A-5 *TurnKey Configuration Console*

To access WordPress, simply point your browser to the IP address specified in the console:

Figure A-6 *Accessing WordPress installed in the appliance*

NOTE
VMware has an online marketplace where you can browse and download virtual appliances and plugins for various VMware products. You can check it out at the following link:
https://marketplace.vmware.com/vsx/

Install and try Linux

Let's say that you've been using Windows all your life, and finally decided to give Linux a try. Two options for installing Linux are usually available:

- install Linux alongside Windows. First you install Windows, and then create a new partition on your hard drive and install Linux on it. This process is known as dual-booting.
- install Linux on an older machine that you don't use anymore.

Instead of dual-booting or installing Linux on an older machine, you could simply install Linux inside a virtual machine and try it out. The whole process should last less than an hour, depending on the speed of your computer and your internet connection.

Linux has many different distributions, and sometimes it is difficult to pick a right one for a beginner. I recommend installing Ubuntu, simply because it is one of the most popular Linux distribution and a lot of guides and how-tos are available online for it. Here are the steps to install Ubuntu in a virtual machine in VMware Player:

1. Download the Ubuntu .iso file on the following link:

https://www.ubuntu.com/download/desktop

2. Once the file has been downloaded, run Player and go to Player > File > New Virtual Machine.

3. Browse to the location of the .iso file. You will notice that Player has recognized the operating system included in the image and will use the Easy Install feature for installation:

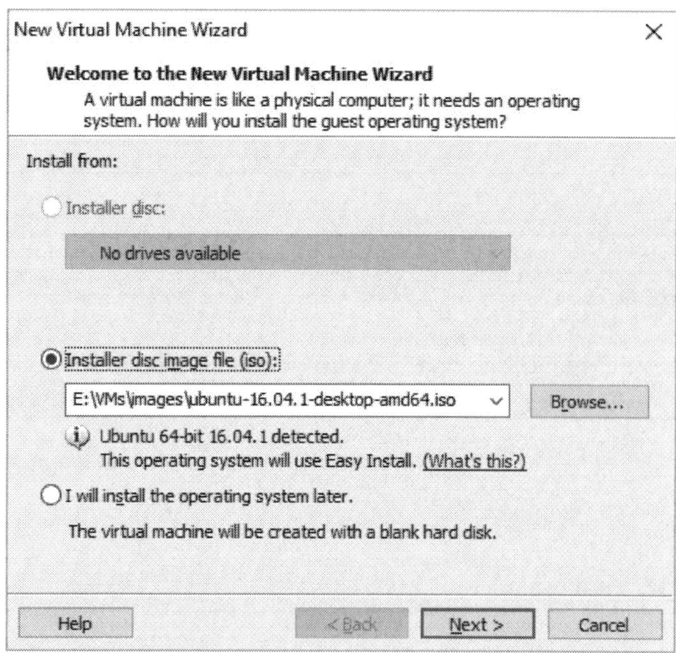

Figure A-7 *Installing Ubuntu from an image file*

4. Enter the Easy Install information - the full name, username and password:

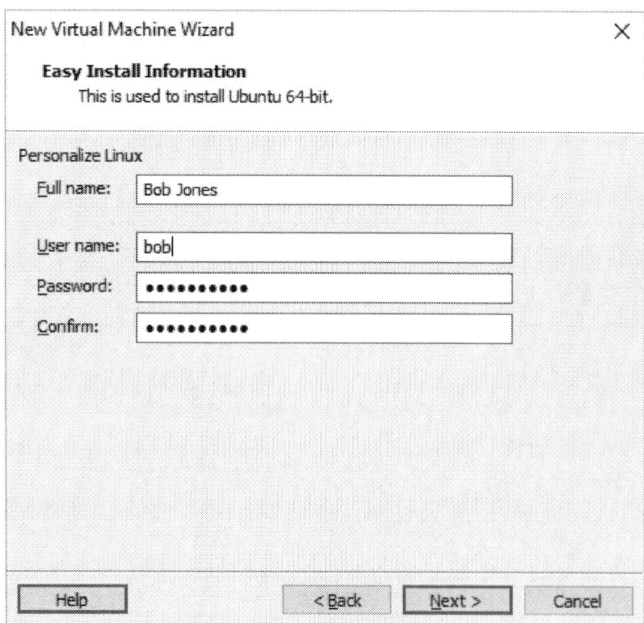

Figure A-8 *Easy Install information*

5. Enter the VM name and the location on the host system where it will be stored:

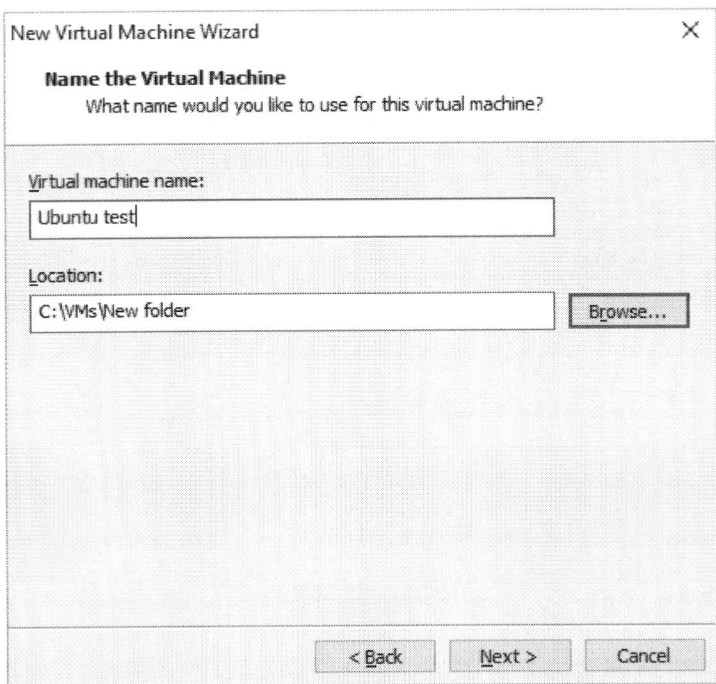

Figure A-9 *Choosing the VM name and location*

6. Choose the virtual disk size and whether to split the disk into multiple files or not:

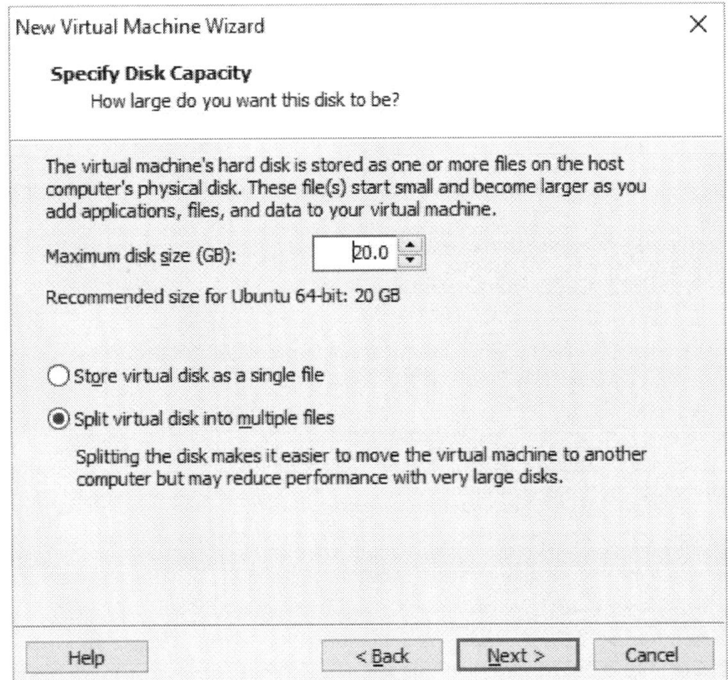

Figure A-10 *Virtual disk options*

7. Click Finish to start creating the VM. Leave the checkbox on to power the VM after it has been created:

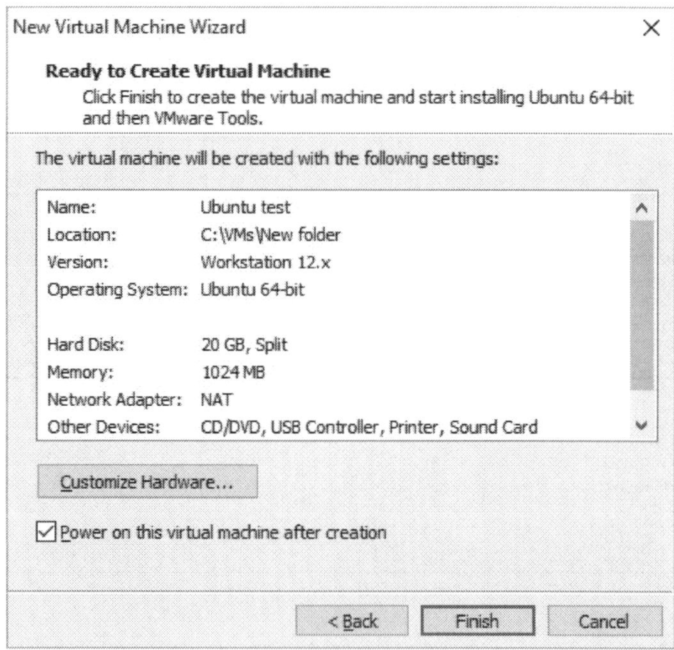

Figure A-11 *Create Ubuntu VM*

8. The Ubuntu installation should start automatically. Since you've provided the Easy Install information, the process should finish without your intervention.

9. Once the process finishes, you should get the login screen. Log in using the credentials you've defined:

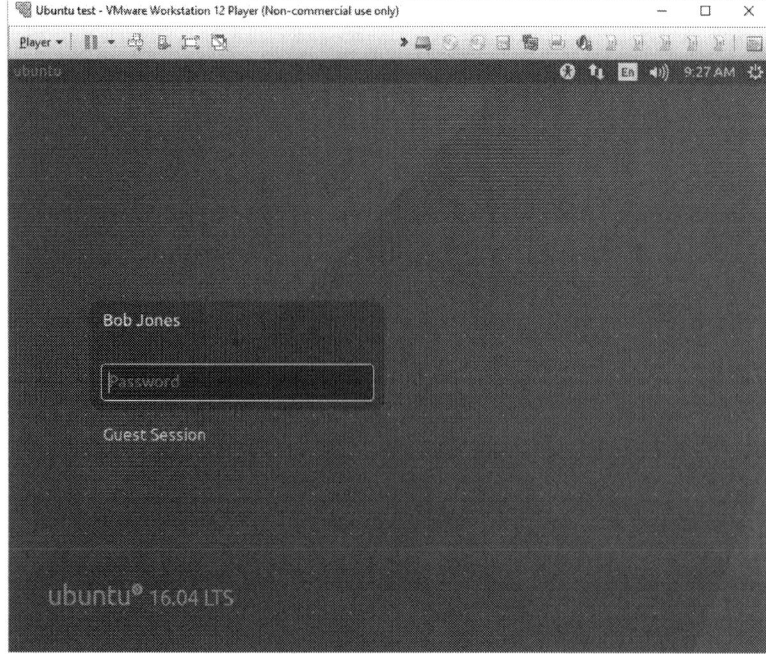

Figure A-12 *Log in to Ubuntu*

10. And that's it, your Ubuntu system should be ready for you to start experimenting:

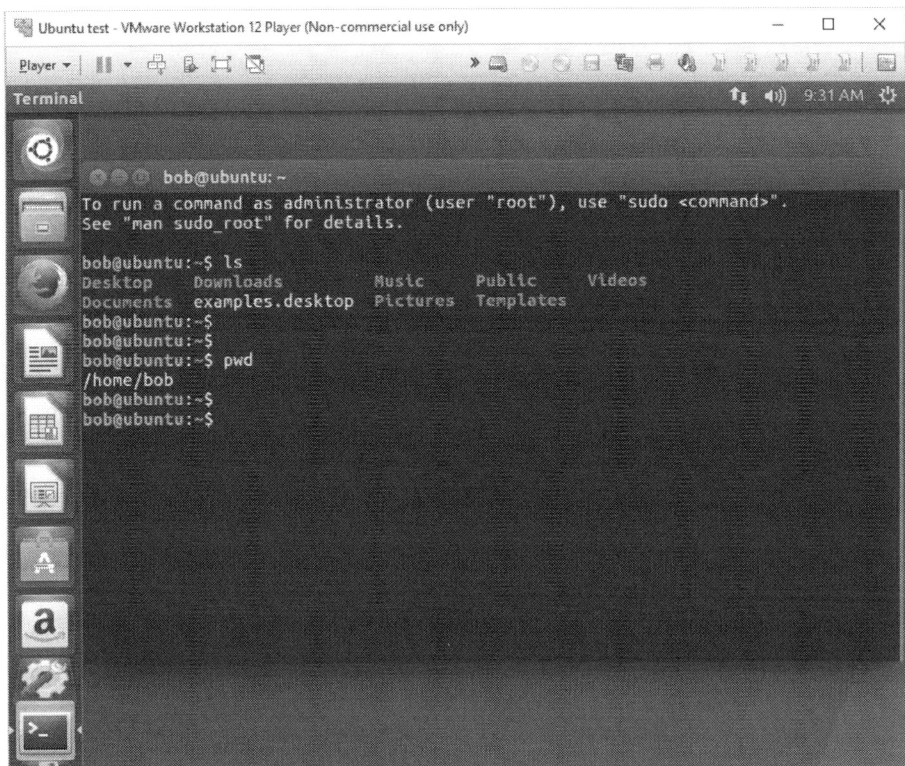

Figure A-13 *Start experimenting with Linux*

NOTE
There are tons of Linux tutorials available online. You can check out my Linux tutorial here: *http://geek-university.com/course/free-linux-course/*

This page intentionally left blank

Appendix B - VMware Workstation Player Preferences Menu

You can use the **Preferences** menu to change various global configuration settings for Player. This menu can be accessed by selecting Player > File > Preferences:

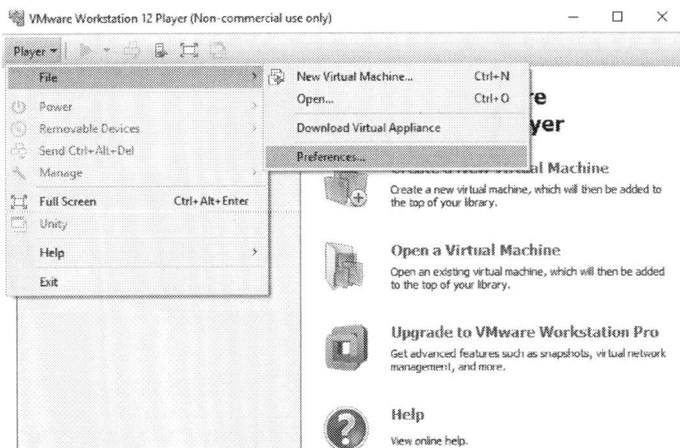

Figure B-1 *Accessing the Preferences menu*

This opens up the Preferences window:

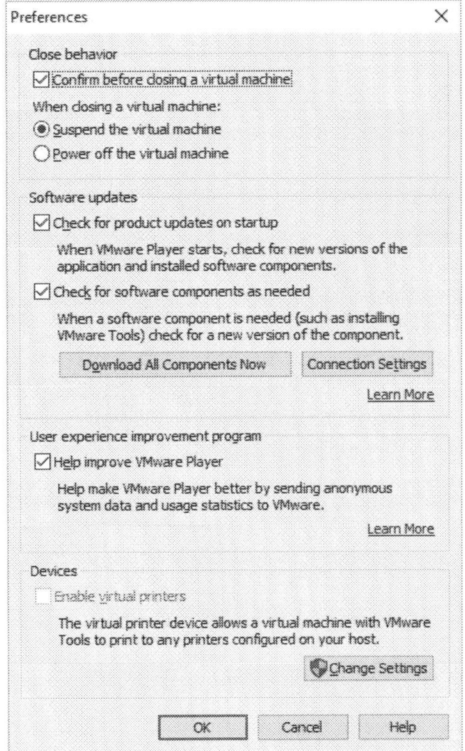

Figure B-2 *Preferences window*

The following settings can be modified:

- **Confirm before closing a virtual machine** - if enabled, you will be prompted for a confirmation before a VM is closed.
- **When closing a virtual machine** - specifies what happens when you close a VM. The first option (Suspend the virtual machine) will suspend the VM, and the second option (Power off the virtual machine) will power off the VM when you close it.
- **Software updates** - you can specify whether Player will check for newer versions of the application and installed components when you start it. You can also specify whether Player will check for a new version of a component (such as VMware Tools) when it is required.
- **Download All Components Now** - downloads all of the available software components to the host system. This option is useful is if you are planning to use a VM at a later time when you do not have Internet access.
- **Connection Settings** - if you use a proxy server to connect to the Internet, you can configure its settings here.
- **Help improve VMware Player** - check this box if you would like to send system data and usage statistics to VMware.
- **Enable virtual printer** - check this box if you would like to enable the virtual printer. The virtual printer allows you to print from a VM to any printer connected to the host computer without having to install additional drivers in the virtual machine.

This page intentionally left blank

This page intentionally left blank

Appendix C - Enabling VT-x

In order to run VMware Workstation Player, your Intel CPU needs to have the Intel's technology for virtualization (VT-x) enabled. This technology is usually enabled by default, but some laptop vendors are known to disable it by default. If VT-x is disabled, you can turn it on in BIOS.

Here are the steps:

1. Reboot the computer and open the system's BIOS menu. This is usually done by pressing the delete key, the F1 key, or some other key, depending on your motherboard.

2. Open the **Processor** submenu. It is usually found under the Chipset, Advanced CPU Configuration, Northbridge, or BIOS Features menu.

3. Find and enable **Intel Virtualization Technology**:

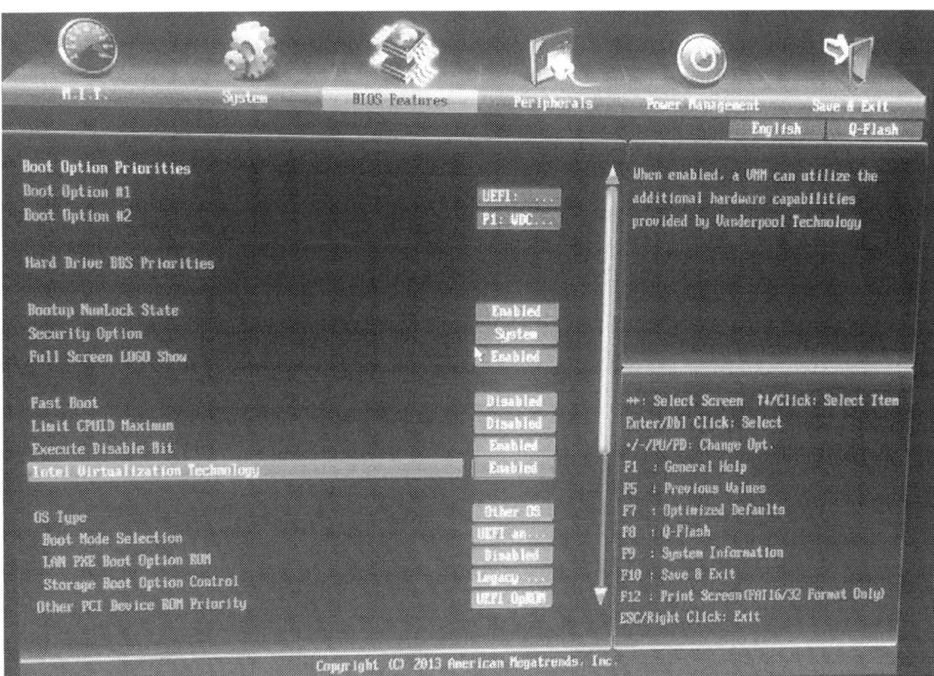

Figure C-1 *Enabling VT-x*

4. Select Save & Exit.

This page intentionally left blank

Appendix D - Finding out the UUID of a virtual machine

The UUID is a 128-bit integer, written in hexadecimal. To find out the UUID your VM uses, download the FirmwareTablesView program from NirSoft:

http://www.nirsoft.net/utils/firmware_tables_view.html

Extract the downloaded zip file and run the FirmwareTablesView.exe file. Under the Firmware Provider column, find SMBIOS and select it. In the lower part of the screen you should see the UUID your VM uses:

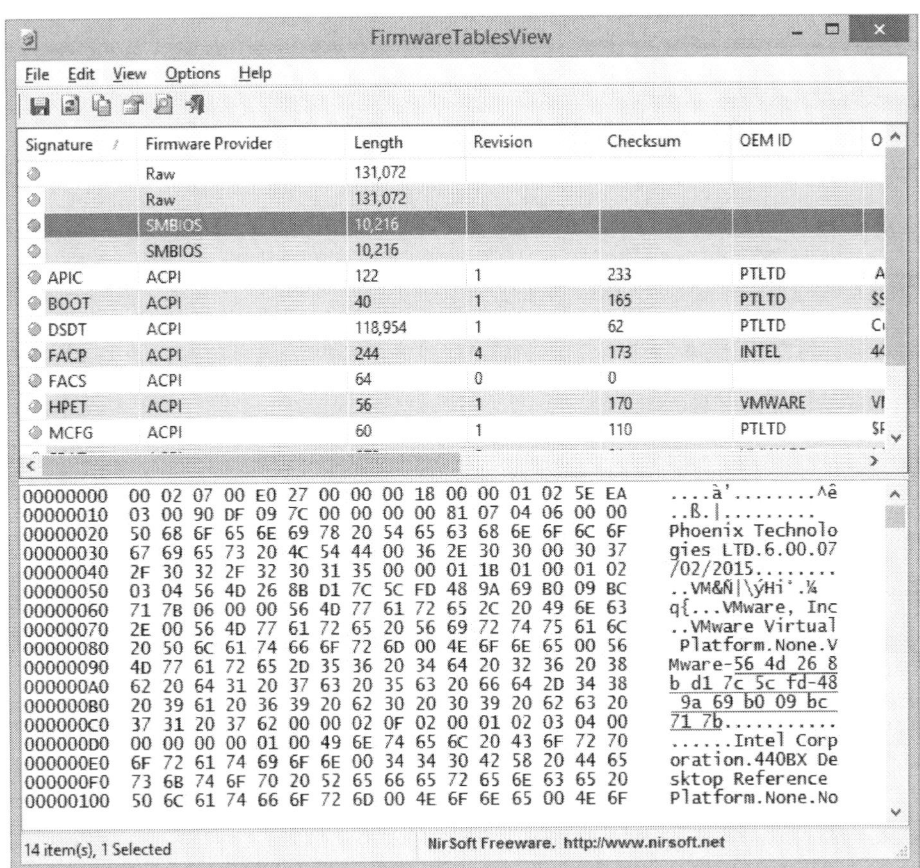

D-1 *Finding out VM UID*

An UUID consists of 32 hexadecimal characters. As shown in the picture, my VM has the UUID of **56 4d 26 8b d1 7c 5c fd-48 9a 69 b0 09 bc 71 7b**.

This page intentionally left blank

Glossary

Autologin - a feature in Player that enables to you log in automatically to a Windows virtual machine.

bridged networking - a networking configuration in which a virtual machine is connected to a network by using the network adapter on the host system. A virtual machine is an unique identity on the network, unrelated to the host system. It has its own IP address and can communicate with other computers on the network, as if it is a physical computer on the network.

Compact - an option in Player that enable you to compact a virtual hard disk in order to reclaim unused space.

Copy and Paste - a feature in Player that enables you to easily cut, copy, and paste text and files between applications running on the host system and applications running in a virtual machine.

Damn Small Linux - a Linux distribution used in this book, notable for its small size (only 50MB).

Defragment - an option in Player that enables you to defragment a virtual hard disk in order to improve performance.

Drag-and-Drop - a feature in Player that enables you to easily move files between the host system and virtual machines.

Easy Install feature - a feature in Player for automating the guest operating system installation.

Enhanced virtual keyboard - a feature in Player that offers better handling of international (non-US) keyboards and keyboards with extra keys.

Expand - an option in Player that enable you to expand a virtual hard disk to get more storage space.

guest operating system - the OS installed in a virtual machine.

host-only networking - a networking configuration in which a network completely contained within the host computer is created. This networking configuration provides a network connection between the virtual machine and the host system by using a virtual network adapter that is visible on the host operating system.

host operating system - the physical machine on which you install Player.

hypervisor - a software component that enables virtual machines to interact with installed hardware.

Intel VT-x - Intel's technology for virtualization that needs to be enabled in BIOS in order to run VMware Workstation Player.

ISO image - a single file that replicates the contents of an optical disc. ISO files are used to distribute large programs over the Internet, including operating systems such as Microsoft Windows or Linux.

Isochronous USB devices - USB devices such as modems, speakers and webcams, that require timing coordination in order to work correctly.

Legacy Emulation Mode - the setting in Player that enables you to work around direct communication problems between a guest operating system and a DVD/CDROM drive.

Message Log - the log that each VM includes. It contains various warning information, such as driver and display errors.

NAT device - a virtual device that passes network data between virtual machines and the external network, identifies incoming data packets intended for each virtual machine, and sends them to the appropriate destination.

NAT networking - a networking configuration in which a VM does not have its own IP address on the external network. Instead, a separate private network is set up on the host system and a virtual machine gets its IP address on this private network from the virtual DHCP server. The virtual machine and the host system share a single network identity that is not visible on the external network.

Perl - a cross-platform programming language. Required in order to install VMware Tools in Linux.

Shared folders - a feature in Player that enables you to share files between the virtual machines and the host system.

Suspend - a feature in Player that enables you to save the current state of a virtual machine and recover it at the later stage.

type 1 hypervisor - a hypervisor that runs directly on the host's hardware to control the hardware and manage guest operating systems.

type 2 hypervisor - a hypervisor that runs on a conventional operating system, just like any other computer program. VMware Workstation Player is an example of a type 2 hypervisor.

USB HIDs (human interface devices) - a device class for human interface devices such as keyboards, mice, and game controllers. By default, these devices do not appear in the Removable Devices menu in a virtual machine.

Unity Mode - a feature in Player that enables you to display applications from virtual machines directly on the host system desktop.

Universal Unique Identifier (UUID) - a unique identifier for a VM that ensures that the virtual machine is properly identified.

virtual appliances - prebuilt and preconfigured virtual machine images that can be deployed on VMware Workstation Player. They are usually packaged in the OVA (Open Virtualization Format) format or come as a zip file containing a virtual disk file (.vmdk) and a .vmx configuration file.

virtual DHCP server - a virtual device that assigns IP addresses to virtual machines in the host-only and NAT networking configurations.

virtual disk - a file (or a set of files) on the host system that appears as a physical disk drive to the guest operating system. Virtual hard disk files store information such as the operating system, program files, and data files. They have a *.vmdk* extension.

virtual machine - a software computer that, just like a physical computer, runs an operating system and executes programs.

virtual network adapter - a network adapter for the guest OS, created during the VM creation.

Virtual SMP (Symmetric Multi-Processing) - an option in Player that enables a single virtual machine to use two or more processors simultaneously.

virtual switch - a virtual device used to connect networking components together, just like its physical counterpart.

vmware.log - the log file for a VM, stored in the VM's directory on the host system.

VMware Tools - a free set of drivers and utilities that enhances the performance of the virtual machine's guest operating system and improves management of virtual machines in VMware Workstation Player.

working directory of a VM - the directory in which the suspended state (*<VM name>.vmss*), snapshot (*<VM name>.vmsn*), virtual machine paging (*<VM name>.vmem*), and redo log files for a virtual machine are stored.

This page intentionally left blank

Printed in France by Amazon
Brétigny-sur-Orge, FR